THE LIFE AND MUSIC OF GRAHAM JACKSON

UNIVERSITY PRESS OF FLORIDA

Florida A&M University, Tallahassee
Florida Atlantic University, Boca Raton
Florida Gulf Coast University, Ft. Myers
Florida International University, Miami
Florida State University, Tallahassee
New College of Florida, Sarasota
University of Central Florida, Orlando
University of Florida, Gainesville
University of North Florida, Jacksonville
University of South Florida, Tampa
University of West Florida, Pensacola

The Life and Music of Graham Jackson

David Cason

UNIVERSITY PRESS OF FLORIDA

Gainesville/Tallahassee/Tampa/Boca Raton
Pensacola/Orlando/Miami/Jacksonville/Ft. Myers/Sarasota

Publication of this work made possible by a Sustaining the Humanities through the American Rescue Plan grant from the National Endowment for the Humanities.

Copyright 2023 by David Cason
All rights reserved
Published in the United States of America.

28 27 26 25 24 23   6 5 4 3 2 1

Library of Congress Cataloging-in-Publication Data
Names: Cason, David M., 1968- author.
Title: The life and music of Graham Jackson / David Cason.
Description: Gainesville : University Press of Florida, 2023. | Includes bibliographical references. | Contents: "We didn't have a dime . . ." — Atlanta: "This must be the promised land!" — "The ebony echo of Cab Calloway" — "Gone Mad with the wind" — "A good Chief Petty Officer" — "A Negro musician of fine character with an excellent war record" — "The familiar strains of Dixie, played by Graham Jackson" — "He is an honorable man; isn't that enough?" — Epilogue. | Summary: "This book is the first biography of Graham Jackson, a virtuosic musician whose life story displays the complexities of being a Black professional in the segregated South"— Provided by publisher.
Identifiers: LCCN 2022058905 (print) | LCCN 2022058906 (ebook) | ISBN 9780813080161 (paperback) | ISBN 9780813069777 (hardback) | ISBN 9780813070544 (pdf) | ISBN 9780813072876 (epub)
Subjects: LCSH: Jackson, Graham Washington, 1903-1983. | Accordionists—United States—Biography. | Jazz musicians—United States—Biography. | African American musicians—Georgia—Biography. | African American musicians—Southern States—Biography. | BISAC: MUSIC / Individual Composer & Musician | BIOGRAPHY & AUTOBIOGRAPHY / Music
Classification: LCC ML419.J323 C37 2023 (print) | LCC ML419.J323 (ebook) DDC 781.65092 [B]—dc23/eng/20221221
LC record available at https://lccn.loc.gov/2022058905
LC ebook record available at https://lccn.loc.gov/2022058906

The University Press of Florida is the scholarly publishing agency for the State University System of Florida, comprising Florida A&M University, Florida Atlantic University, Florida Gulf Coast University, Florida International University, Florida State University, New College of Florida, University of Central Florida, University of Florida, University of North Florida, University of South Florida, and University of West Florida.

University Press of Florida
2046 NE Waldo Road
Suite 2100
Gainesville, FL 32609
http://upress.ufl.edu

Contents

List of Figures vii

Preface ix

Acknowledgments xi

1. We Didn't Have a Dime 1
2. Atlanta: "This Must Be the Promised Land!" 6
3. The Ebony Echo of Cab Calloway 27
4. Atlanta Goes Mad with the Wind 36
5. "A Good Chief Petty Officer" 44
6. "A Negro Musician of Fine Character with an Excellent War Record" 73
7. "The Familiar Strains of Dixie, Played by Graham Jackson" 95
8. "He Is an Honorable Man. Isn't That Enough?" 107

Epilogue 127

Notes 131

Bibliography 153

Index 165

Figures

1. Graham Jackson with accordion, 1942 Rose Bowl dinner 52
2. Graham Jackson with Navy officer 56
3. Graham Jackson at a 1944 bond drive dinner 61
4. Graham Jackson performing for Franklin Roosevelt and Bette Davis in October 1944 67
5. FDR's hearse passing Georgia Hall 71
6. Graham Jackson with Secretary of the Treasury Henry Morgenthau Jr. 74
7. Graham Jackson in uniform with actor Paul Muni 75
8. Graham Jackson's home at 60 Whitehouse Drive 76
9. Coca-Cola ad with accordion player Graham Jackson 77
10. Graham Jackson with Strom Thurmond and Herman Talmadge 83
11. Graham Jackson performing on Ed Sullivan's *Toast of the Town* 85
12. Graham Jackson with Dave Garroway 86
13. Graham Jackson with Eleanor Roosevelt 87
14. Graham Jackson and his choir 93
15. John F. Kennedy at the Little White House in Warm Springs 97
16. Graham Jackson reaching to shake hands with Lyndon Johnson 99
17. Johnny Reb's Dixieland Restaurant 103
18. Graham Jackson performing for Governor Lester Maddox 115
19. Graham Jackson with members of the State Board of Corrections and Governor Jimmy Carter 122

viii · Figures

20. Graham Jackson accepting proclamation as Official Musician of the State of Georgia 123

21. Autographed photo of Graham Jackson with President Jimmy Carter and First Lady Roselyn Carter 124

22. Graham Jackson with sons, Gerald and Graham Jr. 125

23. Graham Jackson performing on WSB radio 128

24. Graham Jackson performing on piano and organ 130

Preface

9:06 a.m. April 13, 1945, Warm Springs, Georgia.

The crowd dispersed slowly from the train station. The soldiers loaded solemnly onto trucks for the ride back to Fort Benning. The disbelief was obvious on the somber faces of the patients at the Warm Springs Institute. He was really and truly gone. So often, the healing waters of the springs did their work. So often, the old vigor was generated by the bucolic peace of his simple, white home. The old timers believed the miracle, just as FDR did.

Graham Jackson's tearful rendition of "Going Home" finished its echoes from the entrance of Georgia Hall on the grounds of the institute. Chief Petty Officer Jackson, a talented musician and longtime friend of Roosevelt, often traveled from his home in Atlanta to perform for the president. Unbeknown to Jackson, a chance photo by *Life Magazine* photographer Ed Clark seared an image on the collective memory of a grieving nation. Jackson's tearful countenance reflected the anguish of the nation as it mourned its fallen leader.

If this story seems familiar, it is because it is a part of the mythology of FDR's final chapter. Graham Jackson is a set piece in that story. His name and image appear in countless publications as the ultimate symbol of the nation's grief and anguish. If one searches online for "Black accordion player," Jackson will appear. Some texts refer to his naval uniform; some that did not dig deep enough erroneously call him a Coast Guardsman. These portrayals of Jackson are one-dimensional at best. Digging deeper shows a very talented, complex individual. This individual was born and came to manhood during the nadir of Jim Crow. He was orphaned and raised by an aunt, yet he still completed high school and attended college.

Jackson used his natural talents, savvy, and showmanship to make a name for himself as a jazz artist, a swing artist, and a spiritual artist. He was one of the first African Americans to perform on radio. He cultivated connections with dozens of wealthy White patrons. He was one of the first African Americans to appear in ads for Coca-Cola. He was one of the first African Americans to join the Navy in World War II and hold the rank of chief petty officer. But much more importantly, he was a gifted music teacher who spent five decades training young artists. As a smart entertainer, Jackson used that image to cement himself as FDR's favorite entertainer, and he built a home in Atlanta in the style of that simple, white cottage. He performed for six presidents in his lifetime. He was a musical icon in Atlanta and the Official Musician of the State of Georgia. In his classic history of Atlanta, author Harold H. Martin describes the scene: "Atlantans, however, remember equally vividly another picture, not of FDR but his friend and favorite minstrel, Graham Jackson of Atlanta. It shows Jackson, tears streaming down his face, playing 'Going Home' on his accordion as Roosevelt's train left Warm Springs en route to Washington by way of Atlanta."[1]

His story is much more than the story of a musician who made it big. His story is much more than the story of an African American who surmounted huge obstacles to be successful. His son Graham Jr. describes his father as a strict but loving father who instilled in him and his brother the importance of hard work, and always stressed that they were to carry themselves with an air of professionalism. Jackson lived a life that tells an amazing story: An American story of overcoming adversity and using one's natural abilities to the fullest.

Acknowledgments

This story started with an amazing signature. I was fortunate to have the opportunity to work as a volunteer for a decade at the Roosevelts' Little White House State Historic Site in Warm Springs, Georgia. This wonderful relationship started because of a good friend, Robert Prater. He served for many years as the mayor of Warm Springs and as a Franklin Roosevelt impersonator at the Little White House. Bob's invitation to join the Friends of the Little White House opened up incredible opportunities for me and many of my students who interned there as well. As a member of this group, I was blessed to be able to help raise funding for major projects. It was during this time that site manager Robin Glass introduced me to the archival holdings of the site. It was a dream come true to gaze on the original blueprints for this small cabin and touch objects once used by Roosevelt. Robin gave me unlimited access to the files and ephemera housed there. It was in these folders that I stumbled upon Graham Jackson's signature.

Jackson's story is a huge part of the story of Warm Springs and the Little White House. As guests travel from the museum to the home, the last room they encounter contains the unfinished portrait of Roosevelt and next to that the iconic photo of Jackson. The musician was a fixture at each anniversary remembrance of FDR's death for thirty years. In those old folders were autographed photos of Jackson given to various members of the Little White House staff. I was dumfounded when I noticed his bold and unique signature. Jackson regularly signed photos and album covers with an intricate musical staff on which he placed the letters of his name like they were notes. In that moment, I recall thinking that I had to know more about this larger-than-life individual!

I grew up just twenty miles west of Warm Springs. Roosevelt's life and experiences in Georgia were a part of my grandparents' lives as survivors of the Great Depression. My father regaled me with stories of his grandfather, who was a policeman in LaGrange, Georgia, and how he had shaken hands with Roosevelt on one of his visits to town. I quickly realized that Jackson's life had never been properly explored. As I began to peel back the multiple layers of his exceptional life, I was hooked. After reading hundreds of press reports on his life, I knew my mission was to tell his story. Later, when I was able to have many long conversations with his son Graham Jr., I began to see that telling Jackson's story would help fill a missing piece in the greater story of FDR, World War II, and Atlanta.

I want to also give special thanks to my wife, Amy. She stuck with me and pushed me when I needed it. Most importantly, she believed in me and tolerated my constant purchases of old books! I also want to thank my children, especially my youngest for his patience when Daddy had to work on the computer. I also appreciate the support I received from my boss, Rebecca Rozelle Stone, who not only supported my research but assisted me with research funding. Additional thanks to the staffs of the Atlanta History Center, the Auburn Avenue Research Center, Duke University Archives, Emory University Archives, and the Troup County Archives for their invaluable help and assistance.

I was fortunate to have many wonderful conversations with Graham Jackson Jr., who still lives in the famous home on Whitehouse Drive. Also, Andrew Hill, who spent many hours looking for notes from his interview with Helen Jackson almost twenty-five years ago, made this a much more complete story. Lastly and certainly not least I want to thank my father, whose love of history allowed me to explore all sorts of places in person and in my mind as a child. He gave me a spark that grew into my life's work.

1

We Didn't Have a Dime

Portsmouth, Virginia, is an old settlement in the Virginia Tidewater with indigenous populations centuries before the colonial period. As early as 1620 the site was recognized as a potential industrial shipbuilding location. The city was chartered in 1752 and named after Portsmouth, England. It is home to Norfolk Naval Shipyard and the vast harbor of Hampton Roads. As an old colonial port city, it has been a thriving and somewhat cosmopolitan hub of trade and commerce during its long history. It saw conflict during the Civil War that resulted in its capture by Confederate forces in 1861. Some months later the damaged hulk of the USS *Merrimack*, burned by retreating federal forces, was rebuilt into the ironclad CSS *Virginia*. The famous ironclad engagement between the CSS *Virginia* and the USS *Monitor* occurred in Hampton Roads harbor in 1862. The shipyard was burned a second time by retreating Confederate forces later that year. After Reconstruction and into the late nineteenth century the city served as a major economic center of shipbuilding and trade.

Graham Washington Jackson was named after his father, Graham Wilson Jackson, who was born in Greensboro, Georgia, in July 1876 and grew up in rural Greene County, Georgia. His parents, Oscar and Harriet Jackson, were formerly enslaved persons. They were married in 1867. Oscar was born in 1835 and died in 1890. Harriet Huggins was born in 1840 and died in 1910. Both are buried in Canaan Cemetery at Springfield Baptist Church in Greensboro.

While we know little about Harriet's family, we do know that Oscar was courageous enough to register to vote in 1867, taking advantage of the recently ratified Fourteenth Amendment. More importantly, the 1880 Census shows that Oscar worked as a train engineer on the Georgia Railroad, the state's oldest line. The line connected Atlanta to Augusta, Georgia, on the South Carolina state line and passed through Greensboro. This placed Oscar firmly in the Black middle class of the period, and his position as an engineer was highly unusual. Blacks were routinely hired as firemen and brakemen, two laborious and dangerous positions. Eric Arnesen reports, "The two most coveted positions in the running trades—locomotive engineers and train conductors—remained off-limits to African Americans everywhere in the United States until the late 1960s and early 1970s."[1]

Oscar Jackson's father, David, was born in Georgia around 1800 and died in 1880. Oscar's paternal grandfather was a White enslaver named Edmond Jackson, who was born in Virginia about 1786 and settled in Monroe County, Georgia. Edmond Jackson was a wealthy landowner who enslaved forty-three people and had an estate valued at $54,000 in the 1860 Census. As was tragically common, Edmond fathered David through the rape of an enslaved woman whose identity is lost to history. Given his biracial ancestry, it is no surprise that Graham Wilson Jackson is listed in the 1880 US Census as "mulatto." This now-dated and pejorative term was used in the census until 1930 to describe persons of multiracial backgrounds. Looking at the experience of others of multiracial heritage during this period, it is likely that David Jackson might have had both social and economic advantages. One of the best sources on Graham Washington Jackson's early life is an unpublished manuscript by Lillian B. Garnett, *The Inimitable Life of Graham Jackson*.[2] Garnett writes that Jackson's father worked for Excelsior Laundry in Atlanta and had a secret formula for dyeing clothes. It was his skill at dyeing that took him to Virginia, as Excelsior sent him there to start a new laundry. Apparently he moved from Greensboro to Atlanta to work for the Excelsior Laundry at 40 Wall Street. Greene County was at that time extremely rural with little employment for Blacks other than unskilled labor or sharecropping.

In his classic work *Following the Color Line*, Ray Stannard Baker argues that Black populations grew quickly in southern cities after the Civil War due to higher wages, better access to education, and a sense of security from hostile Whites.[3] Graham Wilson Jackson appears in the 1898 Portsmouth city directory with his occupation listed as "dye works." The 1900 city directory lists his business as Twin City Dyeing and Cleaning Works with a phone number. By 1903 he is listed as a laborer, and he does not appear after 1904. The 1910 Census indicates that he was a tailor who could read and write and owned his own business. No other official traces of him are found after 1913, and it is unclear when and where he died.

Graham Washington Jackson's mother, Pauline Hinton, was born in Virginia in 1878. Her father, William Hinton, was born in 1845. Her mother is not listed in the census records. As on his father's side, Graham's maternal grandparents were also formerly enslaved persons. Garnett mentions that Pauline was gifted with a beautiful singing voice. Some biographical sources have confused Pauline with "Black Patti," a well-known singer of the period from Portsmouth. Matilda Sissieretta Jones was born in 1868 and had a notable career as both a classical and popular singer.[4] Pauline and Graham Wilson Jackson married on November 8, 1899, in Portsmouth. Photos show a dapper and well-dressed Victorian couple. The groom sports a large, curled mustache and a suit and tie. The bride is dressed in a typical high-necked Victorian gown with lace and puffed shoulders. Graham Washington Jackson was born on February 22, 1903, on Canal Street in Lincolnville, one of a half-dozen Black communities in Portsmouth. His middle name came because he was born on George Washington's birthday.

Most of Jackson's early life is something of a mystery. Over the course of his long life he gave dozens of interviews. All mentions of his early life indicate extreme poverty and tribulations. Jackson's formative years coincided with the ongoing debate in the Black community between the slow path of education and training advocated by Booker T. Washington and the more radical path advocated by W.E.B. Du Bois. Jackson hewed to the more conservative Washingtonian path as he grew up. He describes himself as a musical prodigy from a very young age. He used that talent as a springboard to a high school and college education, which was relatively unusual for Black people of the period.

A constant in his early life was the church and with it, spiritual music. For all his commercial endeavors in life, spirituals and sacred music were always present. He grew up in poverty but always had access to music. His family attended Zion Baptist Church in Portsmouth. They devoted every spare minute to singing spirituals and hymns. "Wherever I was there was always an organ or piano," he told a newspaper reporter. "You practically lived for church." He added, "I was considered a musical genius because at age five I could play every hymn I heard from memory."[5] Later he described sitting in his brother's lap and playing the organ while his brother pumped the pedals.[6] Another anecdote he shared was that he took a job as a janitor at his church to earn money for music lessons. He recalled, "Times were so hard then that if I had a pot of peas and cornbread, or a plate of cabbage, I felt thankful to God. So I went out and started playing the piano for whatever money people wanted to give me. I remember the first time I played I got a dime. I thought I was on my way. Later on, I'd get quarters for my

4 · The Life and Music of Graham Jackson

playing."[7] He also cultivated relations with mentors who assisted him in taking music lessons; one such mentor was the local band leader Derrick D. Copeland. This cultivation was a skill he used his entire professional life.

He started playing a foot-powered organ as a child and reportedly did not have access to a piano until age eleven. At some point, Alma Cannon, the church organist, lent him a church key so he could practice whenever he wanted. "Boy I was thrilled," he said. "I played that organ from eight o'clock in the morning until five o'clock in the afternoon."[8]

Most accounts offer murky details as to his early home life. Often he described himself as an orphan raised by his aunt, Francis Hinton Driver. Garnett's manuscript is one of a few that address what occurred. The account is one of mystery and despair. Shortly before Jackson's birth, his father left for a hunting trip in the nearby marshes. He disappeared for three weeks. During that time, Pauline gave birth to Graham. When Graham's father did reappear, he had suffered an apparent hunting accident that resulted in the loss of an arm. This account purports that Graham Wilson Jackson had chosen not to return until after Pauline gave birth to not compromise her health. Garnett asserts, "It was too much for her nervous system. A nervous breakdown ensued. Finally, her husband had to assign her to the State Hospital in Petersburg, Virginia."[9] Central State Hospital was the only institution in the nation at that time for "Colored persons of unsound minds."[10] Her commitment papers show that she was committed on December 7, 1905, by her husband. Her symptoms progressed for two months, with bouts of melancholy, occasional violent behavior, and one attempt at suicide. Graham's father was listed in the 1910 Census as living at 304 Pearl Street, Portsmouth, and Graham was listed as living with his aunt and uncle. The brother mentioned by Graham is nowhere to be found in any of the census records, but Graham's birth certificate shows Pauline had three other living children at the time of his birth.[11]

In 1912 Pauline's sister Helen Bain decided to sell property that she inherited from their parents. Since no will was left, Helen went to the circuit court of Portsmouth to settle the estate. The settlement resulted in the appointment of a guardian ad litem to represent Pauline Jackson's interests. After taking testimony as to the state of Pauline's commitment to Central State Hospital, the court ruled that the lots would be sold and the proceeds divided among the siblings. As a result, Graham's aunt Francis Driver received $120.83 in May 1913, a tidy sum. Pauline's $120.83 was deposited in her name in the First National Bank of Portsmouth.[12] It is unclear what became of those funds when Pauline died in 1918, still institutionalized. Her death certificate indicates she died from pellagra, a niacin deficiency, likely caused in large part by her meager diet at the hospital.

Graham Jackson was a student at Chestnut Street Elementary School from 1911 to 1919. The school, founded in 1878, was the first school for Black students in Portsmouth. In 1919 Jackson attended I. C. Norcom High School, one of a handful of Portsmouth schools for African Americans. It was named after Israel Charles Norcom, a local Black community leader who had a long career as a teacher and principal. Norcom was the principal at Chestnut Street High School until his death in 1916. Shortly afterward, the high school was named in honor of Norcom. It was largely a college-preparatory high school that boasted a well-educated faculty and diverse academic clubs and activities for the students. During his high school years, Jackson continued to hone his musical skills. Jackson was honored years later as a distinguished alumnus of Norcom and composed the official "Marching Song" for the class of 1923. Jackson graduated on February 5, 1923, in a class of thirteen, ten girls and three boys. He performed "Until" by Teschmacher and a piano duet.[13]

One of the earliest musical exploits Jackson touted was his participation as a student in a piano marathon. The competition took place at Dalby Dancing School at the corner of Granby and Charlotte Streets in Portsmouth. He provided a typically colorful description of the event: "If you can picture a Sheik with a big feast spreaded out before him and a harem of fifty beautiful wives and yet the Sheik just pick up a dish and eat one grape. Well that was me." He continued, "As hours passed I began to catch cramps without warning about every hour, or say thirty to fifteen minutes, finally, all of a sudden I felt as if a million pins were sticking in me and I just fell back and I remember how the nurses and doctors were rubbing me and pulling my fingers and legs."[14] He played twenty-seven hours and thirty-two minutes and suffered cramps for the next year.

2

Atlanta

"This Must Be the Promised Land!"

Atlanta was born out of necessity and utility. The crossroads of important railroad lines, this piedmont hamlet evolved from Terminus, to Marthasville, to Atlanta in 1847. A young, upstart community, its population on the eve of the Civil War was almost ten thousand. During Reconstruction it became the new state capital. In 1900 its population was nearly ninety thousand people, more than a third of whom were Black.[1] White "redeemer" governments across the South worked to repress and disenfranchise African Americans and their growing influence during Reconstruction. After the end of Reconstruction, Black citizens lost almost all access to political rights and were returned to a condition of social and economic servitude.

New South political leaders like Henry W. Grady saw Atlanta as a model of a new industrialized South that could transcend its agrarian past and compete with the North in production. Grady, longtime editor of the Atlanta Constitution, became recognized as the spokesman for "the New South." He pushed for northern investment and diversification in agriculture as cures for the South's economic woes. He was instrumental in facilitating the growing political divide in the Georgia Democratic Party between the "Atlanta Ring," which supported industrial development, and the rural agrarian wing of the party, which pushed for the continued supremacy of King Cotton and viewed the growing political power of Atlanta as suspect.[2] One of the prime platforms to promote the New South was a series of cotton expositions held in Atlanta in the 1880s and 1890s. It was at the 1895 Cotton States and International Exposition that Booker T. Washington delivered his "Atlanta Compromise" address, which shaped race relations for the next several decades.

Washington's speech established him in the eyes of Whites as the spokesman for Blacks and helped to ease the fears of Whites with its accommodationist tone. The address was an appeal to White southerners for support for vocational education and training for Blacks. Washington stated that most Blacks did not desire social equality and that through hard work and toil they could be productive members of society without crossing social barriers that separated the races.[3] The success of the address in the eyes of Whites elevated Washington to international status. He was the first African American leader to dine in the White House and was the leading voice in Black education and White philanthropy for Black causes. Washington's mantra of hard work and vocational education would shape generations of African Americans who would focus on incremental change with little social agitation. Most in the growing Black middle class and Black elite in Atlanta would follow Washington's approach.

Later historical interpretations of Washington and his influence contrast markedly to the accepted narrative of the time. Louis R. Harlan states, "He manipulated platitudes as though they were checkers in the game of life, sometimes crowning platitude on platitude to increase their force. His aim was not intellectual clarity, but power. His genius was that of stratagem."[4]

Critics of Washington disagreed with his strategic approach as too slow and one that was guilty of selling out the civil rights of Blacks for minimal economic and educational gains. One of Washington's harshest critics was W.E.B. Du Bois, who also had a firm connection with Atlanta, serving as a professor for many years at Atlanta University. As a founder of the Niagara Movement and the National Association for the Advancement of Colored People (NAACP), Du Bois was in firm opposition to accommodation and incremental change. His core argument was that the Atlanta Compromise was harmful to Blacks because it failed to address serious issues such as lynching and access to civil rights. In his seminal work, *The Souls of Black Folk*, Du Bois pulled no punches in his criticism of Washington. His comments are scathing:

> Mr. Washington came, with a simple definite program, at the psychological moment when the nation was a little ashamed of having bestowed so much sentiment on Negroes, and was concentrating its energies on Dollars. . . . So Mr. Washington's cult has gained unquestioning followers, his work has wonderfully prospered, his friends are legion, and his enemies are confounded. To-day he stands as

the one recognized spokesman of his ten million fellows, and one of the most notable figures in a nation of seventy million. One hesitates, therefore, to criticize a life which, beginning with so little, has done so much. And yet the time is come when one may speak in all sincerity and utter courtesy of the mistakes and shortcomings of Mr. Washington's career, as well as of his triumphs, without being thought captious or envious, and without forgetting that it is easier to do ill than well in the world. . . . Mr. Washington represents in Negro thought the old attitude of adjustment and submission; but adjustment at such a peculiar time as to make his program unique. This is an age of unusual economic development, and Mr. Washington's program naturally takes an economic cast, becoming a gospel of Work and Money to such an extent as apparently almost completely to overshadow the higher aims of life. Moreover, this is an age when the more advanced races are coming in closer contact with the less developed races, and the race-feeling is therefore intensified; and Mr. Washington's program practically accepts the alleged inferiority of the Negro races.[5]

Atlanta in the early 1900s continued to be a center for struggles over the race issue. Atlanta was unique among New South cities in its growing Black population coupled with economic pressures and constraints that represented opportunity for a small Black elite and continual limitations for a large Black working class.[6] Blacks were limited to living in two small areas in the city. Working-class Blacks had limited economic choices beyond manual labor. Black elites were distancing themselves from the Black working class and operating many successful businesses that mostly catered to Blacks but also catered to many Whites and operated in the main commercial centers of the city. Many Black elites, following the accommodationist philosophy of Washington, actively supported the status quo, which by default kept most African Americans in a permanent underclass.

The governor's election of 1906 saw social and economic tensions in the burgeoning city come to a head. The economic success of the city and its break-neck growth presented a huge challenge to the existing social mores. David Fort Godshalk describes the challenge:

For local white commentators, two distinctive anxieties particularly stood out. As Black migrants streamed into the city and Black social progress grew more visible, many whites became uncertain of traditional racial identities and boundaries. Concurrently, growing wage work among once independent yeoman farmers and their female dependents appeared to threaten white fathers' and husbands' social status and patriarchal authority. For many whites, these twin images of white women and "strange" Black men adrift became powerful metaphors for the social disruptions and cultural dislocations wrought by Atlanta's growth. The visible commingling of the two groups in public spaces throughout the city stirred up many white men's most profound fears of racial and gender disorder.[7]

The gubernatorial candidates in 1906 played up racial fears to a fever pitch. In 1904 the Populist Tom Watson launched an attack on the Democratic establishment in Georgia. He charged that Georgia was falling victim to "Negro Domination" by this growing elite class and that the only solution was a concerted program of Black disenfranchisement. Watson, along with Congressman Thomas Hardwick and former Interior Secretary Hoke Smith, pushed relentlessly for a state constitutional amendment to achieve that goal.[8]

Smith served as the antimachine candidate for governor in 1906. He faced off against Clark Howell, editor of the *Atlanta Constitution*. Both candidates sought to maintain White supremacy and the status quo social order. The race was bitterly fought in the press, with Smith arguing that successful Blacks were on the verge of achieving social and economic equality because of the vote, and Howell, while no friend of African Americans, taking the position that the existing White primary and poll tax were enough to maintain the social order. The rhetoric and venom in the press were palpable. Stories of growing crime and drunkenness among Blacks as well as affronts to White womanhood by "brutish" and "uppity" Blacks raised tensions to a fever pitch.[9]

One of the darkest and long-ignored chapters in the history of Atlanta were the race riots of 1906. The riots started on September 22 when White mobs, responding to media reports, began attacks on Blacks and Black-owned businesses. The chaos resulted in at least twenty-five deaths, dozens injured, and tens of thousands of dollars in property damage. The riots were a direct result of rising tensions in a progressive New South city that was conflicted by economics, race, industrialization, and political control. Competition for scarce working-class jobs, housing, and business space, heightened by a sense of declining political control by Whites, created this terrible event.[10] The end result of the riots transformed race relations and resulted in the legal disenfranchisement of Blacks. The city's main business district banned Black-owned businesses. Segregation in housing became even worse. Black elites who had followed the lead of Booker T. Washington saw their gains reversed. In order to maintain those gains, most elites chose to ally with White progressives to form biracial commissions, which caused even more social division among members of the elite and the working class. Segregation of Blacks into entrenched districts such as Auburn Avenue on the fringes of the city was now the norm. Many questioned if the Atlanta Compromise was dead.

One of the best-known contemporary interpretations of the riots was Du Bois's "A Litany of Atlanta," published on October 11, 1906, in the Atlanta *Independent*. This powerful poem reflects Du Bois's gloom over the events. It also gets at the frustrations of hard work and thrift on the part of Blacks, of following the old social order, and most importantly, of the failure of Washingtonian philosophy. These events did not occur in isolation. Other race riots in the North would help to cement the creation of the NAACP in 1909. While the overall number of lynchings was in decline in the early twentieth century, White lynchings almost disappeared by the 1910s. Lynching was now almost exclusively a tool of oppression used against Blacks.[11]

Even in the face of growing segregation and hatred, Atlanta continued to be a beacon for Blacks, particularly middle- and upper-class Blacks who sought education and economic opportunity. The Black population of Atlanta nearly doubled in the first two decades of the twentieth century, from 35,727 to 67,796. By 1930 the Black population had surpassed 90,000, a third of the total number of city residents.[12] Atlanta's Black colleges and universities and the growing economic power of Auburn Avenue produced an ideal combination for attracting ambitious young Black migrants like Graham Jackson, who made the move to Atlanta in 1924 for an education. He recalled, "I said to myself, this must be the Promised Land!"[13] Atlanta had seven Black colleges, which seemed to him a "Utopia." Back in Virginia he had considered attending Virginia Union University in Richmond, but when he set foot on the Atlanta University Complex on Hunter Street, he knew he had to stay.[14] He found lodging on Auburn Avenue, later dubbed by its unofficial mayor John Wesley Dobbs as the "richest Negro Street in the World." The area around Auburn Avenue had been the site of Union camps in 1864 after the fall of Atlanta and was often called Shermantown. The 1906 riot and the subsequent passage of racially segregated zoning laws pushed downtown Black businesses out to Auburn Avenue. Martin Luther King Jr. was born in his parents' home at 501 Auburn Avenue in 1929. Other notable sites were the offices of Atlanta Life Insurance, which was founded by Alonzo Herndon, and the *Atlanta Daily World*, the first African American daily in America.

A few blocks away was Decatur Street. If Auburn Avenue was the respectable member of the Black community, Decatur was its opposite. Dive bars, pool halls, and sex workers all operated on this street. It was Atlanta's Bourbon Street in its day and of course the epicenter of White anger during the 1906 riots. Although the street served mostly Black patrons, a number of recent Jewish immigrants lived and operated businesses on Decatur. One of the crown jewels on Decatur was Bailey's 81 Theatre. Jackson found employment at the 81 as house pianist.

Employment at Bailey's 81 Theatre brought Jackson a steady source of income and more exposure and experience. The 81 Theatre opened in 1908 as a vaudeville house and transitioned into a movie house. The owners of the 81, brothers Charles and Tom Bailey, also owned two other Atlanta theaters, the Ashby on Hunter Street and the Royal on Auburn Avenue. In 1915 Charles Bailey advertised the 81 as the hub of southern vaudeville: "Did you ever work at a Real Theatre? If not, try 81, and see how it feels to work to 1,800 colored people at one time. The biggest, finest and best Colored Theater in the United States."[15] The 81's reputation was checkered among middle- and upper-class Blacks who considered the Decatur Street area a place that "decent people were not supposed to go."[16] Still, the theater saw its share of such notable blues performers as "Ma" Rainey, Ida Cox, and Bessie Smith. Gospel great Thomas Dorsey was an usher in the theater as a teenager.[17] Charles Bailey often portrayed himself as a tight-fisted manager. Some artists saw him as a White "cracker from the back woods of Georgia," accusing him of assaulting Bessie Smith and having her hauled off to jail.[18] Others described him differently. On several occasions he lent money to Black artists and refused to take IOUs. If a show performed well, he was known to pay artists well above the agreed-upon compensation. He also provided support for families of Black artists who were down on their luck.[19] Regardless of the artists' mixed views of Bailey, it is clear that the 81 Theatre served as a strong foothold for African American vaudeville in Atlanta. The 81 was the largest Black theater in Atlanta.

Jackson described how he got the job as house pianist at the 81. Bailey, "Boss" of the theatrical world of Atlanta, heard about him and hired him to play at the 81 Theatre. He was "pitted" against another piano player, Eddie Heywood, in a competition there: "It was like an elimination contest. He'd play and then I'd play and the crowd would decide who was best."[20] The 81 was the top theater in the Bailey chain, always showing first-run movies before they moved on to the smaller theaters. Another Black theater was the Paramount on Auburn Avenue; Jackson secured a three-week gig there that helped cement the young musician's place in the Atlanta music scene.[21] The Roof Garden at the Odd Fellows Building on Auburn Avenue was also considered a very respectable venue. The Odd Fellows Building was opened in a dedication ceremony led by Booker T. Washington in 1912. Dances were held almost every night there on the roof. Jackson was one of many local artists who regularly performed there.

Employment at the 81 placed Jackson into a small group of pianists and organists considered elite in the Atlanta jazz scene. The piano was the instrument of choice in the Atlanta blues and jazz scene. Other musicians considered elite were Troy Snapp, who worked with Ma Rainey, and T. Neal Montgomery and Harvey Quiggs. "Bordello and barrelhouse" musicians like Long Boy, Edgar Webb, Lark Lee, James Hemingway, Charlie Spand, and Rufus "Speckled Red" Perryman found work in the juke joints and dives in Black Atlanta. The raw nature of these establishments is shown in the lyrics of a popular Blues tune:

Down in Atlanta, G.A.
under the viaduct every day
drinking corn and hollering hooray
piano playing until the break of day.

Many of these artists would eventually migrate to northern cities such as New York and Detroit.[22] Jackson said the Bailey built or purchased a new $15,000 Kimbell 2/4 organ just because of Jackson's amazing abilities. The organ was a significant investment and remained in use in the 81 Theatre until the demolition of the edifice in 1964. At that point, it appears the organ came into the collection of an individual living in Buford, Georgia. From there the console of the Kimbell eventually came into the collection of Edd Simmons, who was active in the organ community in the late twentieth century. The remains of the Kimbell console are still owned by Simmons's children.[23]

Jackson grew up in the early twentieth century, a time of rapid change in American musical tastes. For many elites the music of choice was European symphonic or operatic. For the working class and the poor, ragtime, vaudeville, and the songs of Tin Pan Alley were most sought after. The beginnings of a distinctly American songbook and sound were emerging. For the more pious, sacred music, hymns, and spirituals were the predominant style. Jackson was chiefly exposed to sacred and spiritual music as a youngster. He recalled that his first musical memories were playing the piano and organ in a church. As his talents quickly developed, he was exposed to ragtime and popular music as well as more formal European arrangements. His musical gifts meant that he could quickly learn new music and styles of music and retain that knowledge in an almost photographic manner, often challenging listeners in his adult years to write song suggestions on slips of paper. Rarely if ever could he not play any request from memory.

By the time he was in high school, Jackson was performing traditional recitals and playing in clubs for a dime or a quarter. He was also able to quickly write and arrange new music, such as his class marching song in 1923. His arrival in Atlanta in 1924 was an example of pure serendipity in that the new musical form of jazz had made its way east and north from its origins in New Orleans. Jazz was considered by many elites to be a public menace, encouraging wild dancing, illegal drinking, and fornication. The August 1924 issue of *The Etude*, a noted journal of classical musicians, was dedicated to "The Jazz Problem," and the position *The Etude* took was crystal clear: "Jazzmania" was dangerous. Leading composers considered it vulgar or debasing, a mere caricature, distortion, and vulgarisms. For these professionals there existed a clear difference between "legitimate scoring" and "jazzing," and it came from the "wild din" of the "old-fashioned minstrel show" when performers "jazzboed" tunes.[24] Others described it as "the delirium tremens of syncopation. It is strict rhythm without melody. Today the jazz bands take popular tunes and rag them to death to make jazz" and as a "release of all suppressed emotions at once."[25]

Jackson saw jazz as the future of music, and his arrival in Atlanta was perfect timing as jazz was making itself heard. Resistance to jazz by White and Black elites was common, but ironically most of the record executives who profited were themselves elites. The combination of money and record sales quickly made that resistance falter. Jazz also opened doors for many Black artists like Jackson who could use this path to reach success. One must dig deeper to fully understand that much of the resistance to the primitiveness and vulgarity was in fact open racism. While Black elites often sought in the early twentieth century to emulate the social tastes of White elites and therefore disdained jazz, Whites saw it as a threat to the White dominant culture. Jazz was above all else the first truly American musical form that combined elements of West African, Latin, and European folk music to produce a true revolution in music.

Jackson formed his own band, the Seminole Syncopators. The Syncopators would only produce two recordings with OKeh Records in 1924 and two unpublished recordings for Gennett Records in 1930, and yet its members had long musical careers.[26] The Syncopators consisted of Jackson on piano as the band's leader, Bernard Addison on banjo, Harry Cooper on cornet, Joe Garland on saxophone, Prince Robinson on clarinet, and Happy Williams on drums. Addison would eventually work with notables such as Louis Armstrong, Jelly Roll Morton, and the Mills Brothers.[27] Cooper later formed Harry's Happy Four and performed with the Cotton Club Orchestra.[28] Garland became best known for his arrangement of the Glenn Miller hit "In the Mood."[29] Robinson would perform with McKinney's Cotton Pickers until the early 1930s.[30]

OKeh Records was one of the first labels to record both blues and hillbilly artists, starting in 1920 with the stunning success of Mamie Smith's "That Thing Called Love" and "You Can't keep a Good Man Down" and later "Crazy Love." Based primarily in New York, OKeh set up mobile recording studios in various other cities such as Atlanta, Chicago, and Dallas to record new artists. In 1922 OKeh coined the term "race records" as a more progressive method to market Black artists to Black consumers.[31] "Old time" or "hillbilly" was used to describe rural White artists. In April 1924 Jackson's Seminole Syncopators' first record, "Blue Grass Blues" (OK 40228A), was recorded in New York. The B side, "Sailing on Lake Pontchartrain" (OK 40228B), was recorded August 30, 1924, in Atlanta.[32] By 1927, OKeh and its two closest competitors had produced well over 1,300 race records.[33]

Jackson was at heart a survivor and a hustler. His impoverished childhood may have served as a catalyst for him to work hard and seek every opportunity for additional income. For a couple of years in the late 1920s Jackson operated the West Side Café at 910 Hunter, not far from the Morehouse campus. Jackson ran ads in the *Maroon Tiger*, the student paper. He promised "Home Cooking; Prices Satisfactory; Counter Service; Service Unexcelled and Private Tables." He even had a phone number listed for orders.[34]

Not content with a budding recording and performance career alone, Jackson sought out jobs performing on the local radio station WSB. The station first broadcast on March 15, 1922, and quickly became a dominant force in the Southeast. WSB was one of a handful of radio stations in the nation that regularly broadcast Black artists in the 1920s. In 1923 a live performance by Bessie Smith was broadcast from the 81 Theatre. The station aired music by Jackson and the Seminole Syncopators as well as by the Morehouse Glee Club and many Black church choirs and other groups on average at least once per week.[35] A note in the June 30, 1924, *Atlanta Constitution* states, "Graham W. Jackson's Seminole Syncopators, darktown jazzologists, who have taken Atlanta's syncopating public by storm, lived up to their reputation of being the world's greatest jazz orchestra, by giving another sizzling hour of harmony to WSB noonday circuit."

Over the next several years, Jackson would work with legendary performers of the period including Count Basie and Bessie Smith.[36] Count Basie mentions his respect for Jackson's musical skills in his autobiography.[37]

Jackson came to Atlanta to attend Morehouse College, and his roommate, Peter Dana, said Jackson decided to leave at the end of his freshman year to pursue music full time.[38] He gained a piecemeal music education during summers at Loyola, Hampton Institute, and Chicago Music College. He trained under the legendary violinist and conductor Kemper Harreld, who was the music director at Morehouse College and later at Spelman College and Atlanta University. Harreld's daughter spoke admiringly of Jackson: "Graham Jackson was a theater pianist and organist, and an incredibly multi-talented musician who also led big bands." She continued, "Oh, Graham Jackson was *the* theater pianist in Atlanta. He played at the Ashby Theater—light classical numbers, the kind of music published in an album like One Hundred Best Tunes. He was a versatile and accomplished musician, who studied periodically with my father, whom he revered."[39]

Atlanta's Black artists were becoming exposed to White audiences during this sweet Auburn renaissance. By 1927 Jackson's reputation was known outside of Atlanta, as a *Chicago Defender* article attests: "Every once in a while, this writer hears from authoritative sources of some great musical genius. . . . Graham Jackson is idolized by the whites of Atlanta. They go down to the 81st Theater just to hear him play the pipe organ, even the white press has given him columns, lauding his clever work, and admitting there are none of their race to compare with Graham Jackson."[40]

Black artists were increasingly performing in White venues, Whites were attending performances in Black clubs, and radio was introducing artists like Jackson to larger White audiences. A major transition also was happening in the world of vaudeville and the movie house—the advent of "talkies," sound films, one of the first being the infamous *Jazz Singer* with Al Jolson in blackface. Resident pianists and organists found themselves superfluous now. Adding into the equation the start of the economic upheavals of the Great Depression, many artists, Black and White, struggled for employment. Bands and artists would need to be willing to diversify and travel if they wanted to make ends meet. Most Black artists were at a distinct disadvantage since they were often limited as to where they could perform in the South. Many could only perform on the "Chitlin' Circuit," which could range from Black theaters to juke joints and dive bars.

In the early 1930s Jackson and the Syncopators expanded their radio reach onto WGST radio in Atlanta. WGST, affiliated with Georgia Tech, had recently expanded its broadcast day and signed a commercial contract with the Southern Broadcasting Company (SBC). SBC relocated the station from the electrical engineering building on campus to the Ansley Hotel downtown.[41] The new management began replacing student-made programming with profitable line-ups like the Syncopators. The contract called for Jackson to perform on average three times per day. The *Atlanta Daily World* reported in October 1932 that this was "the first time in the history of radio a Negro artist has been so honored."[42]

In a May 22, 1932, story in the *Atlanta Constitution*, Jackson received praise as a musician who was absolutely unique in his natural ability and versatility, particularly on the organ. Jackson began to cultivate his connections with Atlanta's White high society by performing at weddings and numerous other social events. He entered the music business in Atlanta at the tail end of the "colored vaudeville" wave. Jackson's transition to radio and his other gigs helped him survive this change.

In 1928 Jackson took a position as music director at Booker T. Washington High School in Atlanta. His assumption of this position gave him a steady income on the eve of the Depression. The opening of Washington High School as the first high school for Blacks in Atlanta was the culmination of many years of struggle by Black leaders to force the city to open a Black school. In 1919 the city proposed a tax increase and bond referendum. The Black community, at this point more than a third of the city's population, worked to defeat this proposal because it contained no improvements for Black neighborhoods and Black schools. Using their newfound political clout, Blacks were able to force supporters of citywide improvements to include funding for Washington High School in a 1921 referendum. The result was a victory for the Black community that paved the way for continued political influence over the next several decades.[43]

Jackson quickly received high praise for his work at Washington High School. Superintendent Mills Sutton of the Atlanta Public Schools wrote him in November 1928 to compliment a recital by his students. He called the recital "quite lovely." His principal was even more effusive in January 1929: "THERE WAS A REASON. GRAHAM JACKSON WAS AT THE

ORGAN! In Graham Jackson, the High School has one of the most accomplished organists in the South. He is a wonderfully gifted young man,—chuck full of the spirit of music."[44] In his first year at Washington, Jackson wasted no time. He quickly started a school orchestra, glee club, quartet, and harmonica club. He arranged operettas and a school song and gave numerous public recitals, such as the one praised by the superintendent.[45]

Word of Jackson's success made it back to his hometown of Portsmouth. In 1927 Jackson won the Southern Piano Championship, and praise in Portsmouth for this local boy making it big was effusive. A hometown newspaper article asserts, "One of the greatest honors a city can have is to have its citizens achieve distinction. . . . It is therefore with modest pride that Portsmouth adds its tribute to the laurels won by its native son."[46] Jackson returned home in September 1928 for a rousing concert. At this event, his former principal, W. E. Riddick, presented him with a sterling silver loving cup from the community to honor his musical prowess.[47] By 1931 his hometown paper called Jackson a "Wizard of the Musical World" and the "most versatile musician in America." This story recounts a long biographical sketch of Jackson's musical successes and calls him one of the best-loved musicians in Atlanta by "both white and colored citizens."[48]

Jackson also found love in Atlanta. On March 15, 1928, Graham married Allie Mae Allen. Allie, a Spelman girl, was a native of Atlanta. With Jackson attending Morehouse, this seemed a perfect match. Their marriage was the talk of Black Atlanta. The marriage took place at the First Congregational Church of Atlanta, the second-oldest Black Congregational church in the United States. The church sanctuary had seen a veritable who's who of Black Atlanta. Booker T. Washington attended the dedication of the structure in 1908. Former President Theodore Roosevelt visited in 1911. The congregation included Atlanta Life Insurance founder Alonzo Herndon and NAACP head Walter White.[49] Jackson also started a long residency as the organist of the church. In 1930 Jackson purchased a home at 60 C Street, directly across from Booker T. Washington High School.

Jackson was now part of the Black elite of Atlanta, whom Du Bois called the Talented Tenth. As a successful married entertainer, Jackson was ready to be part of Black Atlanta society. He began to do what Black elites did in Atlanta: become connected with social clubs and be models of racial uplift. In 1928 Jackson was dubbed Sublime Prince of the Royal Secret, 32° of the Ancient and Accepted Scottish Rite of Freemasonry. The Prince Hall Masons were a driving force in the Black community. It was considered a rite of passage among Black professionals to become Masons. Named after their eighteenth-century founder, Prince Hall, this branch of Masonry was one of few open to Black membership. By being a member, Jackson gained access to most of the business, political, and religious leadership in Black Atlanta. Among the membership of this lodge were Martin Luther King Sr. and John Wesley Dobbs. Jackson was also a member of the Elks Gate City Lodge #54 and a member of Kappa Alpha Psi Fraternity, in which he won a thirty-year achievement award in 1952.

As a Black elite, he was expected to assist other, less fortunate members of his race with racial uplift. This Washingtonian idea dated to the late nineteenth and early twentieth centuries. One gained privileged status on the basis of a record of achievements and an emphasis on respectability and values. The Black upper class conspired to mold itself into a replica of middle- and upper-class White Americans and consisted of those who possessed of a certain moral character and virtue. Given the restricted social and economic range in which Blacks could safely operate, class was rarely viewed in strictly economic terms; it embraced style, bearing, and behavior as well. What some called "low-class behaviors" were viewed as reflecting poorly on the entire race. Given that they held little real political power on their own, Black business owners in Atlanta made a deal with the White economic elites who controlled the political system. Since Blacks now constituted a third of the population of Atlanta, they promised to deliver votes in exchange for Black appointments and improved services in a still generally segregated society. Black manhood protocols among elites expected one to be poised, in control, and professional at all times. Graham Jackson Jr. said his father's mantra to him and his brother coming of age in the 1960s was to be polite, poised, well mannered, and well dressed at all times. In essence, don't give Whites an excuse to criticize you.

Jackson eventually took top billing, as the Seminole Syncopators were now called Graham Jackson and His Orchestra. In 1930 a South Carolina newspaper praised his performance in Greenville and described his "bone-thin fingers" and "drawling" style.[50] His musical repertoire continued to expand. He was performing classics on the pipe organ at the Fox Theatre and performing traditional spirituals and jazz as well. A January 3, 1932, *Atlanta Constitution* story describing Jackson's talents in a Fox Theatre performance was reverential: "Then with delighted ears and throbbing pulse, we heard the organ played as no organ had ever been played before—except when Graham Jackson is at the console. . . . These paragraphs have been written with one purpose, and one only in view. That is whenever you have an opportunity to hear Graham Jackson, seize it as an invitation to a concert by the most famous musicians of the age."[51]

This is high praise indeed, given that this is a White reporter writing in a White newspaper. A May 15, 1932, *Atlanta Constitution* story describes him thus: "He plays everything from the classics to the moaningest blues with a rhythm and sympathy that only his race can create."[52] He made his big Atlanta debut to the larger White society on May 26, 1932. This event was a fundraiser for Washington High School held at the City Auditorium. He was likely the first Black artist to headline at the City Auditorium. The program was described as "something to be remembered."[53]

The Fabulous Fox Theatre, as it would later be known, started life as a Shriners theater and ballroom. As happened with the Empire State Building, which is today a symbol of New York City, the Great Depression nearly derailed the Atlanta theater. Both began construction in 1929, and both saw years of financial ruin during the 1930s. After a few years of struggle and assistance from the City of Atlanta, the Fox under the ownership of Fox Pictures became the flagship theater of Atlanta. The Fox possessed outstanding acoustics and was known as a "live" venue. The centerpiece of the Fox was the Möller organ, the "Mighty Mo." With four manuals and forty-two ranks of pipes in five chambers, this masterpiece was for a brief period the largest theater organ in the world until it was superseded by the construction of Radio City Music Hall in New York. The Mighty Mo was and still is the star of the Fox. When a gifted organist like Jackson performed, as he did many times over the next three decades, the result defied belief. The effects at one of the Möller's premiere performances are described in a history of the Fox and its prized organ: "As the console rose out of the depths of the orchestra pit, the organ did tricks that amazed. At one moment it chirruped like a lazy canary, and a couple of seconds later it boomed out diapasons that stunned the eardrums and rolled their reverberations down into your being until your entire system quivered."[54] Jackson performed a regular radio show live from the Fox at seven o'clock in the morning.

For a year or so, Jackson rebranded himself as a small hot jazz ensemble named Graham Jackson and His Modernistics that performed in smaller venues. He also sponsored a series of amateur night competitions. It seems part of this effort was to identify new talented artists for his various musical endeavors. Jackson's fame was significant by 1934. He was now beginning to book gigs outside of Atlanta and the Southeast and perhaps overbooking. He faced legal issues in 1934 when he was accused of breach of contract and sued for $10,000. The suit, filed in February 1934, claimed that Jackson had failed to perform for two New Year's Eve events. The first, titled "Minnie the Moocher," was to be held at the City Auditorium. The second, titled "The Duchess of Harlem," was to be held at the Shrine Mosque ballroom. The suit claimed that the venues had a signed contract with Jackson and charged that he and his band never showed, forcing the event producers to refund more than a thousand tickets at great cost to them. In the end, the case was dismissed.[55]

Jackson was more and more sought after to perform for wealthy White patrons. The *Atlanta Daily World* said it this way in September of 1934: "White people go nuts over him. [He] Has personal autographs of many great White Americans set on large handsome photos."[56] On January 1, 1935, Alabama and Stanford football teams were matched in the Rose Bowl in Pasadena, California. Coca-Cola executives chartered a special flight from Atlanta to California to take fans. Jackson was hired to provide the entertainment on the flight by playing his accordion.[57] The two-day trip had a layover in El Paso, Texas. While in Texas the group took an excursion to Mexico. Once arriving in Pasadena, Jackson performed "Dixie" live at the game with a national broadcast over NBC radio. The *New Journal and Guide* praised his performance: "This was an epoch-making event, not only in the life of Mr. Jackson, but in the history of our group. It should challenge the appreciation of all Negro citizens."[58] He was often hired by Georgia Tech fans to perform on a special train that traveled to Athens for the annual "Clean Old-fashioned Hate" football matchup with The University of Georgia.

Marion Jacobson notes in her book *Squeeze This!: The Cultural History of the Accordion in America* that the accordion was invented in the 1820s in Germany.[59] The first accordions were simple small squeeze boxes that used bellows and reeds to produce sound. Over time more complex and ornate piano accordions became more commonly used. The instrument was portable and much cheaper than a piano or harpsichord, so it became a popular instrument in various styles of music across Europe. Waves of immigration brought it to South, Central, and North America. Though it was originally connected to classic European music, over time it found homes in more cultural niches such as tango, polka, and later zydeco. In the twenty-first century, the accordion is something of a musical anomaly, considered by many to be a kitschy instrument of the twentieth century, given its connections to Lawrence Welk, Frankie Yankovic, and of course the parody stylings of Weird Al Yankovic (no relation to Frankie). The early and mid-twentieth century were the high points of accordion playing, with its popularity much diminished by the 1970s and 1980s, going the way of barbershop quartets and banjos.

Jackson was a master of almost every instrument. Playing a piano accordion was a relatively easy transition from piano and organ. The first evidence of Jackson performing on the accordion is around 1930, about the time he made the transition from a house organist with the advent of sound movies. However, the accordion craze really started in Jackson's childhood. The accordion soon found a home in vaudeville. Jackson likely started using the accordion for the simple reason of utility. It was portable, and he could perform in almost any location. He could walk around among patrons as he performed. It also possessed the versatility of an organ in that one could produce a wide range of sounds and tones. Jackson said his father owned fourteen accordions in his lifetime.[60]

Accordion News magazine began publication in 1934, serving as a resource for the growing number of professional accordionists. Good, solid gigs during the storms of the Depression years could be found in small nightclubs, private parties, and events. An examination of photos shows Jackson playing several brands of accordions, among them a Bomer and a Dallape brand. His most famous accordion is the German-made Hohner L'Organla he is playing when he was photographed with FDR in November 1944 and in the famous Ed Clark *Life* photo of April 13, 1945.

Graham Jr. indicated that he and his brother, Gerald, still owned a couple of accordions each that belonged to their father. One accordion is in the Graham W. Jackson Papers collection held by the Auburn Avenue Research Library in Atlanta. The famous L'Organla was apparently sold at auction some years ago. It was purchased by John Herzig of Dover, Ohio, and placed in his collection of artifacts in his Famous Endings Museum. In speaking with Herzig, he related to the author his hopes that he did in fact hold the famous instrument. Upon examination, the item is identical in every way to the one in the *Life* photo. In the case with the instrument was an *American Heritage* magazine piece featuring a photo of Jackson. A closer look at the black case that held the accordion reveals two American flag stickers on the top of the case. The flags have forty-eight stars, as would have been the case until 1959 with the addition of Alaska and Hawaii to the union. This evidence convinces the author that this is the very accordion Jackson owned.

Swing music was a growing musical interpretation of early jazz and blues styles of the 1920s. For some, swing was a new and exciting style characterized by rapid syncopated call and response from woodwinds and horns. For others, it was a passing fad or worse, a corruption of purer forms of jazz. Kenneth Bindas explores the thesis that swing was more style than substance and concludes that it was an embrace of modernity; it was a logical evolution of musical forms based on real-life changes in American culture and society.[61] Swing made music more structured, as it did not have the improvisational nature of jazz. Many argue that this was the Whitening and mainstreaming of jazz, and the greatest beneficiaries were White band leaders like Benny Goodman and Tommy Dorsey. Jackson made clear his take and interpretation of this musical style: "Swing music is just an old commodity with a new dress on it to sell. It's just an improvisation on a primitive idea. Someone has said that modern music affects you in one of two ways—from the waist up, or from the waist down. Either you want to sit back and appreciate it, or you want to get your feet to moving."[62]

Some Black leaders criticized the continued interest in Black spirituals as an influence on swing, but Jackson countered, "They are one of the finest contributions to music that have been made by any race. They should be kept and treasured because they do remind us of a time which we have left and from which we made a start forward. . . . There is something glorious about them, and nothing humiliating."[63]

The advent of swing had favorable effects for many of the top Black artists who enjoyed steady radio play and plentiful bookings. Artists such as Louis Armstrong, Duke Ellington, and Lionel Hampton were established crossover artists who had access to White audiences. Most Black artists found their ability to book gigs in the Depression years of the swing era very challenging. They were almost always limited to small all-Black venues due to de jure and de facto segregation. They had fewer options for lodging and were paid much lower rates. The publication of the first edition of Victor Hugo Green's *The Green Book* travel guide in 1936 gave them some knowledge of safe places for food and lodging, but many artists were forced to live a hand-to-mouth existence.

On the other hand, some scholars see the swing era as an overall beneficial time for Black artists, even with the shortcomings. Peter Townsend observes,

The greater visibility and acceptance of Black musical forms is sometimes seen as part of this. Jazz, to the extent to which its influence was acknowledged in swing music, lost some of its stigmatized status. The presence in the mainstream of a form that had much to do with

African American culture tended to raise the commercial profile of Black performers. If Black musicians remained on the periphery of economic power during the Swing Era, they were nevertheless closer to the center than ever before.[64]

How does Jackson fit into swing? He was a B-list entertainer, but because of his cultivation of White patrons, he was in high demand and performing for mostly White audiences. In July 1937 Jackson and his orchestra traveled by air-conditioned train car, all expenses paid, to perform in Wilmington, Delaware, at the estate of golf pro Donald Ross. This trip also entailed a visit by the band to Derby Day at the new Wilmington racetrack that nine hundred guests attended. The sponsors of this trip were Jackson's patron R. W. Woodruff and members of the DuPont family. A photo of the group in the train car shows a smiling Jackson in the middle of the aisle surrounded by his musicians. After the Derby Day fete, Jackson and company sped by train to perform in Philadelphia that night. Just a few weeks later, Jackson's group was off by train to perform at the Edgewater Beach Hotel in Chicago.[65]

Jackson's success and performance schedule placed a great strain on his marriage. Allie Jackson was also a teacher at Washington High School. She was the head of the social studies department and active in the Atlanta social scene. She made frequent appearances in the society columns of the *Atlanta Daily World* and received praise for leading the school's Dramatic Club.[66] But a marriage to a traveling entertainer may not have been all a bed of roses. In late 1938 Allie sued for divorce from Graham. When asked for a comment on the divorce case, Allie Jackson stated, "I am glad that this is over, it has been a trying year for both of us."[67] But it was not over, as Graham contested the divorce and the case dragged on into 1939. On March 8, 1939, the jury sided with Allie Jackson and granted her the divorce. Graham was ordered to pay $27.50 per month in permanent alimony and a onetime payment of $125 in spousal support.[68] The vitriol between these two would continue for years. Jackson filed a $50,000 suit against the ex-Mrs. Jackson in March 1941. The damage claim, later dismissed, centered on Allie having Jackson arrested live on WAGA radio for failure to pay alimony.[69] While no specific grounds for this divorce are cited, just a few short months later, on June 15, 1939, Jackson wed for a second time; his bride, Miss Lurlene Baker, was a member of the music department at Washington High School. Their wedding prompted a large article in the *Atlanta Daily World* in which Baker, a native of Columbus, Georgia, is described as "an attractive and sparkling member of Atlanta's social circles."[70]

Jackson's legal issues continued. In June 1940 he was arrested on charges of sexual assault of a seventeen-year-old female Washington High School student. The assault was alleged to have occurred in a classroom of the school. Upon medical examination of the victim, the school system doctor testified that he could not say with certainty that she had been assaulted but that "something happened." The hearing lasted for more than eight hours. The female student testified that she had not cried for help but later shared the incident with a boyfriend. Jackson cried openly in court and denied that he had been intimate with the student. At the conclusion of the hearing, Judge Luther Z. Rosser did not remand the case over to Superior Court but stated he agreed that something must have happened in the classroom.[71] Rosser's father, Luther Z. Rosser Sr., known as the best attorney that money could buy, gained national fame as one of the defense attorneys in the infamous 1913 Leo Frank case.

The accusation against Jackson continued for more than a year and resulted in Jackson's dismissal from his teaching job at Washington High School. The case was reopened and brought to Fulton County Superior Court in November 1940. After the seating of the jury for the case, Fulton County Superior Court Judge John D. Humphreys dismissed the case on the recommendation of the county solicitor general. The cause of the dismissal was that a civil suit was filed against Jackson based on the incident.[72] That civil suit was heard by a jury in early 1941. The father of the girl sought $25,000 in damages from Jackson for the incident. That case resulted in a mistrial. In May 1941 a second civil case convened. Jackson sought help from well-placed White mentors and patrons as character witnesses. Among the parade of witnesses was De Sales Harrison, a Coca-Cola executive; notable real estate and banking executives; newspaper publisher Clark Howell; Pastor John C. Wright of First Congregational Church, and fellow Prince Hall Mason John Wesley Dobbs, the noted Black civic leader and grandfather of Atlanta's first Black mayor, Maynard Jackson. The best-known character witness was golfer Bobby Jones. He and Jackson had a close friendship, and Jackson often came to Jones's home to teach him piano. Jones's daughter said her father tried but only learned one song.[73] Jackson was acquitted in this case.[74] To add insult to injury, his former wife sued him that same month for failing to pay his required alimony. Jackson owed $250 in back alimony and claimed he was earning less than $10 a week due to his other legal issues and the loss of his teaching job. Allie was having none of this, arguing that he still managed to pay his house note and car note, so he must have more income than he claimed. The judge agreed and ordered him to pay her an additional $10 per month to catch up on top of his required $27.50.[75]

Though he had survived the civil case filed against him, in September 1941 he was formally indicted on rape charges. His case was heard in Superior Court on October 9. Jackson's legal odyssey saw three civil trials, two grand jury indictments, and another criminal trial in Superior Court. Jackson again called on his repertoire of well-known patrons as character witnesses and took the stand in his own defense: "Jackson sat in the witness chair with a prepared statement, and denied the charge brought against him by the young woman. Step by step, he told of his activities each minute of the time the girl claimed she was attacked in the classroom at the high school. Several persons corroborated Jackson's statements."[76] The jury returned a not-guilty verdict after ten minutes of deliberation.

Jackson survived his legal marathon but lost his teaching position as a result. Or did he? In a 1995 interview his third wife, Helen Jackson, shared a more pedestrian answer. When asked why Jackson left his teaching position in 1940, her response was that he was traveling and performing so much that finding substitute teachers was burdensome.[77] Since this happened a decade before she met him, it is very possible she had no idea about his legal problems. The question of what actually happened is perhaps unanswerable. It is certainly possible that this young girl and her family were seeking financial reward over a minor or even nonexistent incident. However, it seems more plausible, given accusations of infidelity made by Jackson's ex-wives, that something inappropriate could have happened. If that was the case, Jackson escaped conviction largely because of his public reputation and his cadre of White patrons. Misogyny of the period was not limited to White men alone. Black men who had some standing and access to powerful patrons would have had a distinct advantage over a young Black girl in so many ways. Jackson's case reflects the rampant misogyny in this period of American history, with women having access to few rights and options beyond those proscribed by the patriarchal confines of the period. One must recognize the courage and risks this young woman took in not only bringing these accusations but also remaining steadfast in her position over the course of multiple trials lasting more than a year. While her name is now lost to history, one can assume that her school community knew who she was. Did she face blowback, ostracism, or vitriol? One assumes that is a possibility.

A second area that must be examined involves the power dynamics of an adult assaulting a seventeen-year-old and a teacher assaulting a student. In the context of the time, any accusations made by a female against a male in a position of power would face much scrutiny. The exception to this maxim would be an accusation made by a white female against a Black male. With very few exceptions, a Black man facing such an allegation would risk not only conviction and prison time but also the real risk of lynching. The exploration of Black-on-Black rape accusations during this period is challenging due to a lack of primary sourcing and a dearth of scholarship. Thirty years ago historian Darlene Clark Hine noted, "One of the most remarked upon but least analyzed themes in Black women's history deals with Black women's sexual vulnerability and powerlessness as victims of rape and domestic violence."[78] David Ponton has analyzed Black-on-Black crime in 1950s Houston and plotted those reports using GIS software. He has found that the 86 percent of the victims of the crimes were women, indicating extreme gender asymmetry.[79]

A similar review of articles from the period in the *Atlanta Daily World* found only a few cases mentioned of Black-on-Black accusations. Many of them involve either Black women of some notable social status making such accusations or more commonly, notable Black men being accused. Jackson fits the latter pattern. With few exceptions, cases of notable Black men accused of assaulting Black women resulted in dismissal or acquittal. An example of a pastor accused of assaulting two women typifies this pattern. His defense was that the women invited him into their homes, and only after the older women found out about his alleged trysts with younger women were charges filed against him. One of the few convictions came in a 1932 case where the perpetrator was convicted of sexually assaulting a fourteen-year-old girl. His punishment was a $50 fine and time served. The pattern in these sources shows that most women, particularly those of lower social status and Black women, faced accusations of promiscuousness and "asking for it," a defense routinely used by men of all races.

Jackson was not only a notable Black community member with the requisite prestige associated with that. He was also able to tap into a well of prominent White patrons who vouched for his innocence. Finding a comparable case is difficult. The jury hearing his case was all White and all male, as the first female juror was seated in Georgia in 1953. Jackson's notoriety in the White community as a safe Black entertainer who knew his place in society, his connections with President Franklin Roosevelt, and the testimony of influential character witnesses made the chances of conviction very slim. The circumstances again illustrate the courage of this young woman and her family to stay the course in their accusations as rather remarkable.

3

The Ebony Echo of Cab Calloway

Jackson is best known for his relationship with Franklin Roosevelt, but the story of his first connection with FDR is complicated. Jackson himself told different versions of how he came to the attention of Roosevelt, and several people later claimed credit for introducing him to Roosevelt. What we do know is that Jackson was an astute businessman. He enjoyed many patronage relationships with wealthy Whites, many connected with Democratic Party politics. He also developed an "Old South" performance style for his orchestra that featured traditional antebellum slave songs and slave garb. Jackson's access to wealthy White patrons and his plantation style helped bring him to the attention of the nation's most powerful man, President Franklin Roosevelt. But the story is not simple.

Roosevelt came to Georgia in 1924 seeking treatment for polio. His discovery of the curative powers of Warm Springs made him a part-time resident of Georgia. Eventually he purchased the Meriwether Inn property and started the Warm Springs Institute and a foundation dedicated to the treatment of polio. It was while in Georgia that FDR reluctantly accepted nomination for governor of New York in 1928. As the Depression gripped the nation, Governor Roosevelt became the leading candidate for the Democratic nomination for president in 1932.

By 1931 Roosevelt's adopted state saw much interest in his nomination. The *New York Times* reported that the state would be fully behind a Roosevelt nomination.[1] Roosevelt Clubs formed across Georgia, the first in his own Meriwether County, home to Warm Springs. By late 1931, most counties had Roosevelt Clubs, and leaders pushed for unanimous support from the state. Always coy, Roosevelt agreed to attend a large barbeque held in Warm Springs but stated, "I would very much prefer for the occasion to be personal and not political."[2] In October he made his way to Warm Springs, encountering large crowds at many Georgia railroad stations. The largest crowd was in Atlanta and included Georgia Governor Richard B. Russell

28 · The Life and Music of Graham Jackson

Jr., an avid FDR supporter. Russell made the trek down to Warm Springs with Roosevelt. There the two discussed politics, and Russell assured FDR he would have Georgia's support if he were the nominee.[3] A crowd of more than two thousand attended the barbeque. We have no evidence that Graham Jackson provided the entertainment at this event, but we do know from news reports that the entertainment was "singing negroes."[4]

By early 1932 Georgia was firmly in the FDR camp. The state Democratic convention endorsed Roosevelt, and Governor Russell and the state delegation prepared to travel to Chicago that summer. Jackson was part of that group, hired by the delegation to provide entertainment at the convention. The train left Terminal Station in late June bound for Chicago, a desperate, Depression-wrecked city. Mayor Anton Cermak, who would die from a bullet intended for FDR ten months later, fought to host both the Democratic and Republican conventions to inject some much-needed cash into the gangrenous economy of the Windy City. In his book *Happy Days Are Here Again*, Steve Neal describes the desperate situation: "Three-quarters of a million residents were out of work and more than a hundred thousand families were on the dole. Half of the city's banks had failed, most of the Loop's great hotels were in receivership, and thousands of people had lost their homes. . . . Few cities needed more help."[5]

The convention lived up to all the hype. Held in the new Chicago Stadium, at that time the largest indoor arena in the world, the crowds exceeded 31,000 people. Crowds mobbed the city. The Georgia delegation arrived and took an active part in the convention, remaining stalwart supporters of their adopted son. Jackson's introduction to the convention crowd was by Governor Russell. He performed several times for the convention as a guest of the Georgia delegation. He also performed at many private events, including at the Blackstone Hotel.[6] He likely did not perform for Roosevelt in Chicago, as Roosevelt remained ensconced in Albany playing the traditional hands-off role of a nominee. Only after securing the nomination did he make a perilous flight from New York to Chicago to formally accept the nomination. Jackson did perform for Anna Roosevelt Dall, the daughter of FDR. Dall penned an autograph for Jackson: "To Graham Jackson, with great appreciation for all of our favorite pieces."[7] Anna was now an important confidante for her father and a go-between for her parents. It is certainly possible that she could have mentioned Jackson's performance to her father, especially given her father's well-known love of traditional American folk music and spirituals.

After Roosevelt took office in 1933, American citizens inundated the White House with homemade musical lyrics and songs. Some suggested that he use their creations to provide hope to the Depression-ravaged nation. Others boldly asked for money from FDR. One suggested he hold a competition and award the person with the best song one million dollars! In total, the archival collection held at the FDR Presidential Library contains more than 136 with an estimated total of 14,000 songs. Professional songwriters and artists also contributed hundreds of FDR-related songs. Some of these were written or recorded by notables such as Irving Berlin, Ella Fitzgerald, Judy Garland, the Mills Brothers, and Glenn Miller.[8]

Roosevelt made a triumphal return to Georgia in October 1932. Atlanta and Georgia were in an FDR frenzy as election day approached. Roosevelt arrived in Atlanta on Sunday, October 23. After brief remarks in front of thousands, he and his party motored to Warm Springs for the day and returned to the Biltmore Hotel that evening. Monday, October 24, was declared "Roosevelt Day." Huge crowds of more than 200,000 greeted him in Atlanta. Railroads offered one-cent tickets for the day. After motoring through a ticker-tape parade described as the largest in Atlanta history, he passed block after block of schoolchildren, 50,000 strong. It is possible that Jackson was in this crowd with his students from Washington High, as "all races, creeds and colors were present."[9]

He next attended a luncheon at the Biltmore with almost all the southern governors and many other Democratic political leaders. Most press reports indicate that Roosevelt retired to his suite for the afternoon to rest in preparation for a large radio address planned that evening from the City Auditorium. Many in his party, including Anna and most of the Democratic political leaders, spent the afternoon at the home of Ryburn Clay, a Roosevelt supporter and president of Fulton National Bank. Clay hired Jackson to perform for the group at his home. Jackson frequently performed for the Clay family over the next couple of decades, often at their Lazy River Farm on the Chattahoochee River. The performance was a big hit, an Atlanta newspaper reports: "Our own Graham Jackson entertained the assemblage throughout the afternoon with a program of classical and popular music, most of which were 'requests.' That he was received with enthusiasm was to be expected, but that he should be the only entertainer present, ah, that was indeed an honor."[10] So, while we have no evidence that Roosevelt heard Jackson play, we do know that Anna heard Jackson twice in 1932. FDR won Georgia with more than 91 percent of the vote.

30 · The Life and Music of Graham Jackson

Roosevelt saw fewer opportunities to travel to Warm Springs after he assumed the presidency. He made a brief Thanksgiving trip in late November 1932. He would make these annual Thanksgiving celebrations a priority, as he loved carving the turkey for the patients receiving treatment at the spring. During this visit in 1932, one of his callers was *Washington Herald* publisher Eleanor "Cissy" Patterson. Cissy was a well-known socialite and Washington fixture, a former countess and friend of Roosevelt's cousin Alice Roosevelt Longworth. She arrived in a special Pullman car to lunch with FDR. Decades later Jackson stated that Patterson connected him to FDR. In an interview in 1960 Jackson said,

> Many is the time Mrs. Cissy Patterson had me down here to entertain at parties she gave in her big house on that island they call Siesta Key. . . . In fact, it was through her that I first met President Roosevelt, only he wasn't President then. I'd graduated from Morehouse College here in Atlanta and was back up in my hometown of Portsmouth. Mrs. Patterson had me come to Washington to entertain at her parties and one time in '32 FDR was at a party. Then he was governor of New York and just thinking about running for the presidency. He took a liking to my playing, and I sure developed great admiration for him so after he became President Mr. Roosevelt told Merriman Smith (veteran UPI White House Correspondent) to hunt me up and bring me around to the White House.[11]

Let's unpack some of the claims Jackson makes here. We do know, of course, that Patterson was a wealthy socialite with connections to the Roosevelt family. We also know that Jackson and his orchestra toured much of the East Coast in the summer of 1932, with stops in Baltimore and Washington DC.[12] So far, nothing precludes this story from being factual. What does create a problem is Jackson mentioning Merriman Smith. Smith was indeed a White House correspondent. By the 1960s he was the dean of correspondents. He was a Georgia native and had started his journalistic career in the state. The problem is that Smith did not become White House correspondent for UPI until 1940, eight years later. Additionally, Jackson attended Morehouse for less than a year and never graduated. We have an anecdote that sounds entirely plausible but is factually untrue.

Given the demands of the presidency, 1933 saw only two visits by FDR to Georgia. He made a quick trip to Warm Springs in late January and stayed for about ten days. He did not return until his Thanksgiving visit in late

November 1933. This was a significant occasion, as it coincided with the dedication of the new Georgia Hall facility on the grounds of the Warm Springs Foundation.[13] This $100,000 building, meant to replace the aging Meriwether Inn, would become the centerpiece of the work of the institute. One of the key supporters of this effort was Cason Callaway.

It was when Roosevelt sought advice on construction of a golf course that this wealthy neighbor, Cason J. Callaway, drove across Pine Mountain. Callaway recommended Donald Ross to Roosevelt. Ross had designed the Highland Country Club Golf Course in nearby LaGrange, Georgia. This was the same Donald Ross for whom Jackson and his orchestra had performed in Delaware. This meeting of Roosevelt and Callaway sparked a lifelong friendship. The two were in many ways opposites, one a conservative southern textile magnate and the other a moneyed liberal New York Brahmin. But though they disagreed on many economic and political matters, they shared a deep love of public service and interest in agriculture. Callaway would be instrumental in the establishment of the Warm Springs Foundation and the March of Dimes and later would serve as a trustee after FDR's death in the establishment of Roosevelt's Little White House State Historic Site. FDR was a frequent guest at Callaway's Blue Springs Farm over the mountain in Harris County, Georgia. Many of his Thanksgiving visits in the 1930s focused on the annual Founders Day Thanksgiving Dinner at the institute. These annual dinners served as a celebration of the work of the foundation and a chance for patients to have a nice dinner, with FDR serving as host and carving the turkey. Callaway led a successful capital campaign to construct Georgia Hall on the institute grounds and attended the 1933 dinner, at which he sat next to FDR at the head table. The entertainment for the event was the Emory University Glee Club singing spirituals.[14]

Callaway was a longtime patron of Jackson, who performed at his daughter's wedding in 1940 and at Callaway's funeral in 1961. A posthumous 1964 biography, *Cason Callaway of Blue Springs* by Paul Schubert, spins a very fanciful story of FDR's visits to Callaway's home and of Graham Jackson. Schubert notes that during one of those holiday visits, Callaway invited Roosevelt and his entourage to his Blue Springs home to hear Jackson perform. FDR found his time at Blue Springs immensely relaxing. He took off his hated braces and enjoyed good food and company. Jackson's Plantation Revue included members of the Big Bethel Baptist Church choir from Atlanta. Schubert, Callaway's biographer, reports that Roosevelt was "greatly impressed" by Jackson's performance and thought, based on the group's dress, that they were actual employees at the farm. Callaway at first responded that he only hired field hands who could sing and dance but then quickly told FDR the truth. FDR fell in love with Jackson's music.[15]

This story is a great example of the mythology of the "Lost Cause" and the happy slave. It does have some factual basis. We do know that FDR made several trips to Blue Springs, and we do know that Jackson performed there several times. The *Atlanta Constitution* reported, "It was Graham Jackson, with his 'president's ensemble' of 12 singers, who furnished the entertainment on the occasion of the President's visit to the home of Cason Callaway."[16] This performance was in 1935, after Jackson had performed for FDR on several other documented occasions. One suspects that FDR might well have made a joke about the performers as field hands, and Callaway played along, or vice versa.

After the success of the 1933 Georgia Hall fundraising campaign, the Warm Springs Foundation sought a new and innovative way to raise funds for polio treatments. The result was the presidential balls. These annual events were held on January 30, FDR's birthday. More than four thousand communities across the nation participated in the first ball in 1934, raising one million dollars. Jackson was the only Black artist featured at the balls in Atlanta, held at the Shrine Mosque, Peachtree Gardens, and Standard Club.[17] Jackson continued to be in the orbit of Roosevelt's friends and supporters.

In interviews in 1995 with Jackson's third wife, Helen, writer Andrew Hill discovered who she was told brought Jackson face-to-face with Roosevelt. That person was Atlanta businessman Lawrence "Chip" Robert.[18] Robert was a successful architect and earlier a manager of the Atlanta Crackers baseball team. He got to know Jackson in Atlanta as an entertainer. Robert was likely the one who hired Jackson to perform at the Democratic National Convention in 1932. He was appointed assistant secretary of the US Treasury in April 1933 and was in charge of the Public Works Administration. Robert's appointment meant a move to Washington, but he did not leave Jackson behind. Jackson was hired on several occasions to travel to Washington and perform for parties at the Robert home. He performed in February 1934 for an event held for the president of Standard Oil and later events for FDR friends James Farley and Marvin McIntyre.[19] Based on Andrew Hill's interviews and press accounts, it seems that in July 1934 Robert brought Jackson to the White House.

Robert hired him for a party and arranged an informal visit to the White House. There, the Roosevelts maid (Lizzie McDuffie), who was from Atlanta and knew Jackson, invited him to play the piano in the President's living quarters. When FDR heard the music from down the hall, he asked who was playing. Told it was a musician from Atlanta, the President remarked that he would like to hear Jackson play at the Little White House in Warm Springs.[20]

Jackson would now become a fixture at Warm Springs. During FDR's 1934 and 1935 Thanksgiving visits, Jackson was there. Reports indicate he played three recitals for FDR over those ten days in 1934 and at the Callaway home in 1935. Jackson is quoted in a 1934 news article: "'President Roosevelt has a mighty nice tenor voice himself,' Jackson said yesterday, 'and he has a fine knowledge of music. He likes all sorts, classic, semi-classic and jazz and he's particularly fond of old college songs, requesting some that were popular before the War Between the States.'"[21] Jackson often performed alone either on piano or accordion. Other visits found him performing with choral groups and dancers. One of the young dancers who performed with Jackson at Warm Springs was noted dancer Mabel Lee. She was born in Atlanta in 1921 and lived across the street from Clark University. Lee first performed at a Jewish-owned spa at age four. She performed at the Top Hat on Auburn Avenue at age thirteen. Jackson was her music teacher at Washington High School in the late 1930s and took her with him to entertain at Warm Springs for FDR. In 1940 Lee moved to New York, where she became a nationally known dancer for the next several decades. She appeared in dozens of films, performed internationally, and appeared on Broadway, dancing into her eighties.[22]

Life magazine photographer Margaret Bourke-White chronicled the relation of FDR to the pageantry of a Warm Springs Thanksgiving in 1938. The spread shows photos of wide-eyed young patients seated next to FDR as he carves the turkey. But much more is gleaned from the subtexts of the photo essay, in photos of Lizzie McDuffie and cook Daisy Bonner, sans last name, smiling Black servers and Pullman porters, and an unidentified Graham Jackson performing for Will Moore and Cissie Lord at Warm Springs. As writer John Edwin Mason puts it so well, Bourke-White gives an unintended and unadulterated look at Jim Crow racism: "Inadvertently, Bourke-White produced photographs that documented the casual rituals of racial subordination in stark, matter of fact detail." In discussing the depiction of Jackson, Mason writes, "If it's the same man, it's the sort of ironic coincidence that historians love. The differences in the way he's depicted in photos from 1938 and 1945 are stunning. Wearing the mask of a fool in one; embodying dignified grief (with which *Life's* White readers would identify) in the other."[23]

The developing friendship between Jackson and FDR serves as a window into personal and political views on race in America. Roosevelt's progressive New Deal policies were in many ways revolutionary and groundbreaking as economic and social policies. But the one area where Roosevelt was reluctant to tread was in confronting the issue of race in America. John Kirby argues, "The New Deal, in effect, provided what most race liberals had so desperately wanted in the twenties—a reform program to which they might attach their concern for Negro rights."[24] This established the future link between reform and racial liberalism. But FDR never championed civil rights or pushed for desegregation. Rather, his approach was one of creating an equal-opportunity society.[25] Some New Dealers, such as Norman Thomas and Harold Ickes, agreed that education and economic reform could end racial divisions, and many New Dealers, including FDR, defined the "Negro problem" as an economic problem.[26] Blacks saw an increase in appointments to federal jobs under FDR. What was also different was that most appointments were nonpolitical and based on training and merit. They were not Democratic Party appointments. Most were middle-class, college-educated, well-trained professionals.[27]

Roosevelt had little contact with Blacks other than as servants until he arrived in Georgia in 1924 and as he became a national political figure. Certainly his relationship with Graham Jackson, whom he referred to often as a friend, was one-dimensional. Jackson often spent private and intimate moments with Roosevelt and other notables but always in the context of an entertainer, not a confidante. Roosevelt spent the most time with his valet and maid, Irvin and Lizzie McDuffie. Lizzie claimed that she did influence the president on Black issues on rare occasions, particularly concerning Black servicemen arrested in a Houston riot and perhaps in more Black appointments to the postal service and WPA. But these were infrequent at best.[28]

The main roadblock to intervention by FDR and his long-standing refusal to push federal antilynching legislation was his reliance on the largess of powerful southern Democrats in Congress. Blacks lacked voting strength and political voice to outweigh the power of reactionary outcries from southern racists. Since the core of the New Deal was economic, Nancy Weiss observes, "it was absolutely vital for the President to respond to the concerns of the southern senators and congressmen who could determine the fate of his legislative program."[29] This served as an ongoing source of conflict between the president and the first lady. Eleanor Roosevelt was much more liberal on the issue of race and often clashed with and pushed her husband to go further. One area where Eleanor was influential was in increasing the number and variety of Black artists and entertainers who frequented the White House.[30]

November 29, 1935, found FDR in Atlanta for the dedication of the new Techwood Homes federal housing project. Shortly thereafter he stopped for a brief visit at the Atlanta University complex to make some brief remarks in front of a crowd of twenty thousand Blacks. Large crowds also greeted him when he made a visit to Fisk University in Nashville. These visits reflected his desire to be accessible to Blacks, whom he counted on as voters in tight races in northern states.[31]

4

Atlanta Goes Mad with the Wind

The premiere of *Gone with the Wind* in December 1939 was a groundbreaking event for Atlanta. The madness generated first by the novel and then by the movie created a national spectacle like never before in the city that Sherman had burned. Atlanta high society saw this as a once-in-a-lifetime opportunity to cash in on the mania of the film's release there. Business and political leaders wanted to put Atlanta's best foot forward and bring much-needed national attention to the city that had suffered during the Depression years and skirted insolvency. First-term Mayor William B. Hartsfield, a Jackson patron, took center stage and served as ringmaster for the event. Hartsfield, who would serve as mayor for more than two decades and is the namesake of now the world's busiest airport, made the campaign for the premiere in Atlanta his personal crusade when he took office in 1937. He went as far as to send engraved invitations to southern governors and other dignitaries across the nation. He promised an event like no other. By all accounts he exceeded even his own expectations.

Loew's Grand Theatre in the heart of downtown was transformed into a living replica of beloved Twelve Oaks. Large banners and portraits of the stars of the film graced Atlanta's storied main thoroughfare, Peachtree Street. Belles and dashing young men in Confederate gray graced glamorous balls. Aged Confederate veterans were paraded out as living testaments to the Lost Cause of the gallant Old South. Atlanta and the larger South saw valor and redemption for a lost way of life that was destroyed by evil Yankee meddlers and villains. All seemed right with the world. The long struggles of the Depression seemed forgotten.

All was right with the world if you were a White southerner. African Americans were universally banned from any participation in this celebration except as servants and entertainers in slave garb. Even one of the stars of the movie, Hattie McDaniel, who won an Oscar for her portrayal of Mammy, did not attend due to Atlanta's segregation laws. But while most

Blacks were a repressed population that was largely ignored and often reviled, they were also affected by the hoopla surrounding the film. Atlanta was on the cusp of a transformation into a modern, international, diverse city. Much of this transformation happened because of the growing influence and political power of African Americans.

The Black community generally looked at the novel and movie *Gone with the Wind* with trepidation and concern. Many recalled the 1915 *Birth of a Nation* premiere and its open racism and hatred and feared a repeat. In Thomas Cripps's book *Slow Fade to Black* he argues that the infamous movie amounted to a malicious conspiracy that fomented and heighted racism and led to the rebirth of the Ku Klux Klan. With its use of White actors in blackface, lynchings and terrorism of Blacks, and glorification of the KKK, *Birth of a Nation* inflamed race relations and caused incalculable harm to Blacks.[1]

An examination of the press coverage of the Atlanta premiere of *Gone with the Wind* shows that many in the major Black press struggled at times to openly condemn the film in a unified voice. Some of the major communist press did call it to task on both racial and capitalistic grounds. Ben Davis Jr. of the *Sunday Worker* argued that the movie incited racial hatred and showed happy, White southerners ruined by the end of a feudalistic slave economy.[2] David Platt, a writer for the *Daily Worker*, wrote extensively, comparing *Birth of a Nation* and its impact on race prejudice with *Gone with the Wind*. His thesis was that *Birth of a Nation* had succeeded in its author's intent in creating White abhorrence for Blacks.[3] One scholar quotes a news article of the day:

> The New York Amsterdam News reported on the guarded and speculative mood in the African American community in Atlanta following the *Gone With the Wind* premiere: "[T]he 'spirit of the Old South' filled this Queen City of Dixie and left the local colored population with mixed feelings." The festivities included two monster "Gone With the Wind balls' . . . and a number of Negroes were hired to perform the services which, in those times, were done by slaves." The reporter noted that the "inquiries at the Negro theatres in town as to whether the film would be brought to any of them resulted in a unanimous no!"[4]

John Clarence Wright perhaps sums up feelings among many in the Black press in his review of the film in the *Atlanta Daily World*: "As Atlanta goes mad with the wind, one hundred thousand of her citizens should become more thoughtful than ever of the course that must be pursued to gain their rights as free men and citizens in a land where the spirit of secession and slavery still lives."[5]

New York Urban League President James Hubert feared that the movie would win the war for the South. He complained that the movie would make northern Blacks suffer like their southern brethren. Noted African American civil rights attorney William L. Patterson pulled no punches in his review of the film. In no uncertain terms, he states, "It has lied about the Civil War period shamelessly. It has distorted and twisted the history of an era which saw democracy fighting for its life against the inhuman system of slavery. . . . Gone with the Wind is a weapon of terror against Black America."[6] For many Black leaders and civil rights supporters, the excitement and popularity of the film was a major setback for the limited but hard-won progress made in the 1930s under Roosevelt's New Deal policies. Reports of widespread picketing and boycotts in Chicago, New York, and London appeared in the *Chicago Defender* and the *New York Amsterdam News*.

The architect of the film, producer David O. Selznick, struggled from the start with what he himself termed the "Negro problem." Selznick, a Jew, grappled at times with the open race-baiting dialogue of the novel in its abundant use of racial slurs and depictions of the "good" Blacks as happy slaves who craved guidance from firm White hands and "bad" Blacks as unruly brutes who must be tamed. One writer likened the film to the history of Judaism as told from Hitler's perspective. Selznick responded that he was keenly aware of what was happening to his fellow Jews in Europe and "cannot help but sympathize with the Negros in their fears about material which they regard as insulting and damaging."[7] Over time Selznick came under intense pressure to modify the language of the novel to avoid the worst of these depictions and avoid making an "anti-negro" film. However, most of the racial slurs remained, the one concession to the censors and Black critics being that the N-word was omitted, with Whites using the more (presumably in Selznick's view) acceptable term "darkies."

Selznick International Pictures started to receive a steady stream of letters from concerned groups about the film. Walter White, the NAACP secretary, was particularly concerned that the film be historically accurate and fair in its depictions of African Americans. White offered to provide historical assistance and recommended that a "Negro, who is qualified be hired to check on possible errors."[8] In the end Selznick and his team were able to charm White and much of the Black press by crediting their concerns with the elimination of the N-word from the film. The stark reality was that the near revolt by many of the Black actors and ultimately the pressure of censors had more to do with the term's removal. Selznick was able to tone down some of the criticism of the film with this one gesture.

Planning was moving forward in Atlanta at a fevered pitch. For Atlanta's White society, this was a rare chance to correct what many saw as erroneous beliefs long held by many about the South. Mayor Hartsfield took charge of various business and society interests and directed them toward one goal, celebrating the virtues of the Old South while simultaneously trumpeting the advances of the New South. It is important to put into context how provincial and isolated Atlanta was in this period. This was not yet the international Fortune 500 city with the world's busiest airport, the "city too busy to hate," or the host of the Olympic games. For most of the MGM executives and Hollywood elites, visiting Atlanta was like visiting a foreign country. The thought of entrusting the premiere of such a financial investment to a relatively backwater city was frightening to MGM executives and Selznick. And to make matters worse, most of the all-star cast did not relish the thought of an Atlanta premiere at all. Clark Gable refused to attend if his friend Hattie McDaniel could not participate. McDaniel talked him into going. The irony was that McDaniel's father, Henry, was a Union veteran of the Civil War who suffered terrible injuries that plagued him all of his life.[9]

For the White power structure, this event was an economic godsend. The challenge for White moderates, David Stephen Bennett asserts, was to "promote the movie without promoting the more overt White supremacist ideologies of the Klan."[10] He contends, "Atlanta's newspapers struggled to balance the values of the city's rural communities and the values of a growing urban business elite, they found themselves frontline defenders in a cultural war over *Gone with the Wind*'s racial and historical authenticity, as well as the historical authenticity of Margaret Mitchell's work."[11]

A major African American participant in the premiere was the Reverend Martin Luther King Sr. "Daddy" King was the pastor of the Ebenezer Baptist Church. Michael Luther King was born into poverty and sharecropping in rural Stockbridge, Georgia. He moved to Atlanta in his teens to seek an education at Morehouse College and more importantly, respectability. King Sr. answered the call to ministry and eventually took over the pastorate of his father in-law's church, Ebenezer Baptist. By the time of his famous son's birth in 1929, King Sr. was emerging as a race leader in Atlanta and the highest-paid African American pastor in the city. Such was his stature and perhaps hubris that after attending an International Baptist Conference in Germany he returned home and announced that he was changing his and his young son's first name to Martin in honor of Martin Luther.

King Sr. took on leadership roles in challenging Jim Crow in Atlanta. He explained, "I became a chronic complainer. I grumbled about all the conditions I saw segregation imposing on Negroes, and I talked too loud about it and got on a lot of people's nerves. . . . I wondered why some reasonable whites and Blacks couldn't just sit down and bring a swift halt to all of the dumb kinds of things segregation represented."[12]

King Sr.'s first stab at challenging Jim Crow was a voter registration effort in 1935. His political awakening came although he was a successful young pastor who was paid well, dressed well, and provided well for his family. While a large crowd marched to Atlanta City Hall for the effort, only a small number registered to vote. In 1936 King took up the issue of equal pay for African American teachers in Atlanta. The result of this controversy was King Sr.'s realization that many in the African American community did not want to cause trouble over the complaints of relatively well-paid and well-educated teachers.

Graham Jackson also found much opportunity by participating in the premiere. His Plantation Revue group, already performing antebellum spirituals and dressed in slave garb, were a natural fit. Jackson and King Sr. were close in age and were Black elites. They both lived and worked on Auburn Avenue and shared a connection with gospel music and the city's African American choirs. It is clear that they also shared similar backgrounds, coming from poverty and being migrants to Atlanta in the 1920s. Furthermore, both men were consummate showmen and shrewd businessmen who enjoyed the spotlight and sought ways to further their brands. Jackson was focused on his entertainment brand, and King Sr. was in the process of raising funds to expand Ebenezer and keep it the city's alpha African American church of the day. Graham Jackson Jr. recounted that as a youngster he and his family shared many Sunday lunches with the Kings at various upscale restaurants. In 1940 Jackson was the first to play a new Wurlitzer pipe organ installed in King's Ebenezer Baptist Church.[13]

King Sr. saw opportunity in the 1939 premiere of *Gone with the Wind*. He quickly seized the moment to ensure that he would be out in front as the leader of African American participation in the spectacle. His church choir was to perform, and he would take center stage as well, playing the guitar in accompaniment. His ten-year-old son, the future leader of the American civil rights movement, would be in that choir as well, in full slave regalia, along with Jackson and his Plantation Revue.

The reports in the White press concerning the pomp and circumstance of the premiere were glowing. The headlines that described the events touted Hollywood stars parading on Peachtree and estimated the turnout at 600,000 people, which was double the population of the city. Mayor Hartsfield declared a three-day city holiday, and Governor E. D. Rivers declared a state holiday on the day of the premiere. Between the arrivals of the stars of the film at the airport, the parades, balls, and other associated events, Atlanta celebrated in style.

Jackson and the Ebenezer Choir performed on Thursday, December 14, 1939, at the Junior League of Atlanta ball held at the Atlanta Auditorium. All the singers were in traditional slave attire. A photo in the Atlanta History Center collection shows ten-year-old Martin Luther King Jr., wearing a white hat and slave garb, singing in the choir. Other photos of the event show Graham Jackson in overalls playing the accordion with a large smile on his face. *New York Times* reporter Meyer Berger described choir members wearing "antebellum plantation garb, wide-brimmed straw hats, bright cotton shirts and dresses, and red bandanas."[14] The printed schedule for the ball had the following text for master of ceremonies Clark Howell to read in introducing the choir: "Tonight, we want to give you a glimpse into the past—and visit an old plantation on a warm, fragrant June evening. Can you smell the wisteria? Can't you hear those darkies singing? They're coming up to the Big House."[15] In Herb Bridges 2011 book, *Gone with the Wind: The Three-Day Premiere in Atlanta*, the only photo of Jackson and his fellow African American entertainers is labeled "local Atlanta entertainers."

The White press praised the performance. An article in the *Atlanta Constitution* praised Jackson's performance under the blatantly racist headline "In the Evening (or the Morning) Darkies Sing."[16] The reaction of the Black press and community was mixed. Some took a very pragmatic view that exposure of Black talent and good wages were positive steps for the race. Others reported a big backlash in the community, especially toward King Sr.'s participation. Karen Kruse Thomas describes King's participation as a classic example of "Deluxe Jim Crow." The term was coined by the *Baltimore African American* in 1927 in reference to high-end but segregated Pullman cars for well-to-do Blacks. Thomas offers this as an example of how Black leaders of the period were torn between pleasing their own constituency and White leaders at the same time.[17] John Wesley Dobbs, a leader in the

Atlanta Black community and grandfather of Atlanta's first Black mayor, Maynard Jackson, was aghast that King participated and said, "It is unconscionable that they cooperated."[18] King faced further repercussions from the Atlanta Baptist Ministers Union. In a meeting the following week the group censured King for his participation. King was unfazed, later stating, "Not everything we do is political."[19]

The conservative Black-owned *Atlanta Daily World* took a nuanced approach in its criticisms of the novel and film. It was consistent in its promotion of Black business interests and its commitment to gradual uplifting of the race and mindful of maintaining good relations with the White power structure. The editors viewed the promotion of the Lost Cause as an excuse to ignore the devastating history of slavery and murder of Blacks in the name of a New South promotion of Atlanta. The celebration of the supposedly happy relations between the master and the enslaved ignored the realities James Firth describes: "African slave trade and the old marts where mothers were torn from their babies like animals" and "cotton fields, human prostitution and the grinding of human bones and blood into liquid currency."[20]

Jackson suffered no adverse effects from his participation, in large part because his primary source of income was performing for White audiences. He remained in high demand for performances across Atlanta high society. His talents so impressed businessman Henri T. Dobbs Sr. that he purchased Jackson a new Italian-made accordion. Jackson was effusive in his praise of the benevolence of Dobbs in granting this gift. The accompanying photo of Jackson with his wide grin and new instrument is a classic example of the happy minstrel imagery of Black entertainers of the period.[21] His entertainment success continued into the early 1940s with Plantation Revue performances at various high-society venues such as the Kiwanis Convention, Capital City Club, and Piedmont Driving Club.

Gone with the Wind retains a central place in Atlanta history. The seventy-fifth anniversary saw the unveiling of a major display on the premiere at the Atlanta History Center. The Atlanta History Center and the City of Atlanta reached an agreement to relocate and restore the Atlanta Cyclorama painting to a new multimillion-dollar facility in Buckhead. Margaret Mitchell's home, "The Dump," was saved from collapse and is now a museum on her beloved Peachtree Street. Pittypat's Porch, a themed restaurant in downtown since the 1960s, continues to draw patrons from around the world. All this interest continues to be associated with Atlanta, which is ironic, given Atlanta's status as a major nexus for African American music, industry, and culture. This is the strange legacy of *Gone with the Wind* in Atlanta. At times Atlanta has moved on from the film and its premiere, but at other times Atlanta still embraces that contradictory moment in its past. W.E.B. Du Bois, who spent much of his academic career in Atlanta, wrote the seminal *Black Reconstruction* in 1935. In the final chapter, "The Propaganda of History," he addresses many commonly held misconceptions about African American history. At its core, he argues, the White South had practiced cultural denial of the realities and brutalities of human slavery.[22] *Gone with the Wind* is the apex of that cultural denial.

5

"A Good Chief Petty Officer"

The coming of war in 1941 brought a profound and rapid change to the very fabric of American life. This change would manifest in many forms, but the social and economic impacts would be felt most quickly and profoundly. The common assumption is that all Americans felt outraged and frightened by the prospect of war and were quick to enlist, but one group of Americans expressed reservations. African Americans had reservations based on unfulfilled past promises, particularly during and after World War I. Though the Roosevelt administration was slow to acknowledge it, a real and justifiable morale problem existed among African Americans. As the war progressed in 1942 and manpower shortages became critical, the morale issue had to be addressed. Adding fuel to this fire was the unity of the Black press in supporting a "Double V" campaign, for victory over fascism abroad and racism at home. This complicated situation found tradition in conflict with pragmatism.

The issue of general morale was of keen interest to the Roosevelt administration from the start of the war. Given all the preparation for war in the late 1930s and the beginning of the 1940s, such as armament increases and even the draft, a plan for morale was sorely lacking.[1] Donald Rugg argues in 1942 that while morale certainly spiked after Pearl Harbor, it was not a given that it would remain high: "Just as the Japanese attack on Hawaii was no single, isolated incident, but part of a larger Axis plan of aggression, so our morale was not suddenly born, full-grown like Minerva, as a consequence of this attack."[2] Kenneth Clark goes further and focuses on Black morale:

> Marginal men have marginal morale. And in our society the American Negro has been made socially and psychologically marginal. It is, therefore, impossible to approach the problem of civilian morale among Negroes during a time of national emergency without a clear

picture of the usual everyday struggle of Negroes in their attempt to participate in and contribute to the society which is now threatened. The basic factor underlying Negro morale appears to be a deep-seated frustration complicated by bitterness and resentment. Other related factors are undoubtedly hope, psychological conflict, suspicion, and a more or less fatalistic apathy and indifference, this latter particularly among the masses of the more underprivileged and exploited Negroes. In order to understand the nature of the frustration among Negroes, one must realize that Negroes are a part of the general population who in time of war are stimulated to exert maximum effort for the common victory. The Negro, like other loyal Americans, responds naturally to these stimuli. He wants to do everything within his power to show that he too is an American with rights to preserve. By and large, he is prone to forget past injustices in his attempt to come to the aid of his threatened country. But in his very attempt he finds himself still balked. The building of an adequate morale in the Negro group entails a sudden, dramatic, and honest reversal of the present American policy of racial exploitation and humiliation. Such a program adopted and prosecuted in good faith by the government of the United States would change almost immediately the present pattern of Negro morale from the negative and confused to the positive and dynamic.[3]

Clark, perhaps best known for his later work that demonstrated the effects of racism on Black children, articulates some of the key issues that needed to be addressed to improve morale among Blacks: "The evidence is overwhelming that Negros as a whole were disillusioned by the events of the last war."[4] These broken promises were now serious issues in the Black community.

One of the few "victories" for Black morale was the signing of Executive Order 8802 in May 1941 by FDR. This order was intended to eliminate racial discrimination in defense industries. FDR reluctantly signed the order to head off a planned march on Washington organized by A. Phillip Randolph and the Brotherhood of Sleeping Car Porters. Fear of public unrest and possible work stoppages convinced Roosevelt to sign. This was a victory on paper, and resistance and lack of enforcement resulted in many in the Black press questioning the effectiveness of the order. To them, it was clear that only through concerted efforts by various pressure groups such as

46 · The Life and Music of Graham Jackson

the Urban League, NAACP, and the Black press could the order be enforced and morale raised.[5]

Black militancy was on the increase in the early 1940s, much more than had occurred prior to World War I. Surveys of Blacks showed that they were still experiencing rampant discrimination and housing shortages for defense work. Many Blacks expressed alarm at the internment of Japanese Americans. One survey in 1942 showed that 50 percent of respondents believed they would be no worse off under Japanese rule.[6] E. Franklin Frazier states in 1942, "The traditional relationship of loyalty to Whites has been destroyed, and race consciousness and race loyalty have taken its place."[7] Y. W. Bell argues in 1944 that segregation was a luxury America could no longer afford. It would result in loss of efficiency, money, and most importantly, blood.[8]

One of the most influential contemporary interpretations of the issue of race is Gunnar Myrdal's *An American Dilemma: The Negro Problem and Modern Democracy*, published in 1944. In this massive work Myrdal makes the clear argument that the aims of Jim Crow and the aims of the war were fundamentally incompatible. He called out America for fighting fascism and race-based intolerance while practicing them at home. "Caste is becoming an expensive luxury of white men," he argues.[9]

Migration for promised defense jobs in the North and West became an important goal for many southern Blacks. Even with all the disappointment generated by lack of enforcement of federal laws, lack of housing, and unequal wages, this migration would alter the demographics of the nation. By 1950, half of Black men in their twenties lived in a different region than their places of birth. For Whites this number was 25 percent. This mass migration was not without its problems. Cities of the Midwest and North, which saw spikes in Black populations, experienced more discrimination and racial unrest.

The summer of 1943 saw the peak of racial unrest during the war years. Greater numbers of Blacks in uniform led to more verbal and physical attacks on Blacks. Crowded buses increased tension among Whites newly mingling close to Blacks. Racial gang conflict ran rampant in cities like Newark, Philadelphia, Buffalo, and Chicago. The most infamous of these racial attacks were the "zoot-suit" riots in Los Angeles that saw White mobs attacking Blacks and Mexican Americans with impunity as local and military police did nothing to intervene. A White mob of three thousand shipyard workers attacked fellow Black workers in Beaumont, Texas, largely over fears of losing their jobs. The result was two dead, seventy-five injured, and thousands of dollars in lost war production and damage. Riots and mobs of disgruntled White workers would make similar attacks in Mobile, Alabama, and Chester, Pennsylvania. All told, more than 242 racial incidents in forty-seven cities occurred.[10]

The worst rioting in 1943 was in Detroit. All the factors of unrest were present. Touted as the headquarters of the "Arsenal of Democracy," Detroit was woefully unprepared for the influx of 50,000 blacks and 500,000 Whites who rushed in to man the defense industries. With an acute shortage of housing and transportation and no plan on the part of city leaders to address racial tensions, the city seethed with unrest. Fights on buses, at schools, and on playgrounds became the norm. The powder keg exploded on Sunday, June 20, when crowds seeking relief from the heat clashed at Belle Isle amusement park. The clash quickly spread to the entire city. At first, local and state officials refused to ask for federal assistance. By the time troops arrived Monday night to secure the city, thirty-four were dead, more than seven hundred were injured, millions of dollars in property were damaged, and thousands of hours were lost in war production. Troops would remain in the city for months keeping a fragile peace.[11] In August a smaller, though still serious, riot in Harlem resulted in five dead and over five hundred injured. Worried about his dependence on southern Democratic leaders in Congress, Roosevelt refused to take a public position in racial issues, though some in his administration begin to work fervently behind the scenes to address the crisis.[12]

Morale among Blacks was guided by the actions of prominent Black leaders and the Black press. At the outbreak of the war, the Negro Newspaper Publishers Association decided to publicly support the war effort but not give up on its call for civil rights. Many argued that this dichotomy was a continuation of the dual life that Blacks had been living for decades. Just a few months later the *Pittsburgh Courier* launched the "Double V" campaign. Other papers quickly followed. The *Baltimore Afro-American* soon introduced the closed Black fist as a symbol of Black unity. Critics, both Black and White, feared these actions might hurt the war effort and incite more racial violence. Roosevelt complained in May 1942 about what he considered to be seditious articles in Black newspapers. The Army confiscated newspapers on posts so that Black soldiers could not read them.[13] The Office of War Information (OWI) estimate showed that over four million Blacks read Black newspapers each week, a staggering thirty-three percent of the Black population, of which a large percentage was functionally illiterate. In other words, among literate and educated Blacks, that readership percentage would be well over fifty percent.[14]

The Negro Newspaper Publishers Association eventually built enough creditability with military officials that in July 1943 they began to partner to promote the war effort. Vice President Henry Wallace met with association officials, and the OWI created a Public Information Bureau in Europe staffed by Blacks to report on Black troops. At the end of 1943 the first Black reporter officially began to cover the White House. All of this happened without censorship of the press and with the continued publication of stories critical of the administration and the military.

The OWI played a critical role in the administration's attempts to maintain Black morale during the war. It became clear very early that administration officials had little understanding of Black concerns. OWI anthropologist Phileo Nash, an expert in minority group relations, knew that most Whites were woefully uninformed about racial tensions. He conducted a series of surveys of Blacks to produce data to help guide the administration. An insight he discovered was that if the administration intervened quickly in small racial incidents, it could prevent larger racial riots. As a result, Nash's boss, Jonathan Daniels, working directly for FDR, was successful in quelling all major racial incidents from July 1943 to VJ day in August 1945.[15] "Considering the grave dangers facing the country . . . it is desirable and necessary to de-emphasize our many longstanding internal dissensions and to close ranks," is how the OWI suggested that they move forward.[16] The end result would be a focus on pamphlets, radio, film, and public statements to maintain morale, albeit not the much more difficult task of addressing of substantive problems. This approach was criticized for largely ignoring serious inequities and focusing mainly on favorable public relations outcomes.

The Roosevelt administration had been planning for war since the late 1930s. These plans involved a gradual rearmament program and growing coordination and cooperation with Britain. That cooperation increased rapidly after war started in 1939 with programs such as the lend-lease of military equipment and ships. Internally, one of the big areas of planning was in manpower allocation. That allocation was to be accomplished through use of volunteers and conscription. The Selective Service Act of 1940 contained clear provisions that prevented discrimination, but those provisions were rarely enforced in the beginning. The administration stated publicly that the Army would draft Blacks proportionally, and they would be assigned to all branches in segregated units. Of the population of draft-age men, eighteen to thirty-four, Blacks made up 9 percent, about 1.5 million.[17] From the start this system was never fully implemented. When local draft boards began operating in 1941, they drafted Black men but then refused to induct them, claiming that separate facilities were not yet constructed. This led to a growing number of young men who lost employment thinking they would be shipped out soon but spending many months in limbo.[18] P. L. Prattis states in 1943, "Both the Army and the Navy have dealt the morale of the Negro soldier and sailor a soul crushing blow" by refusing to allow them to serve.[19] Over time some 300,000 young Black men were cooling their heels, which led to an increase in the drafting of older and married Whites by 1943 and a sense of fear and resentment among southern Whites at this growing group of young Black men.[20]

Even inducted Blacks faced a stiff barrier to service: literacy. The basic literacy requirements of military service resulted in a high number of Blacks and lesser number of rural Whites, classified as 4-F, rejected for service because of physical, mental, or moral reasons. Secretary of War Henry Stimson freely admitted that these literacy standards were designed to reject most Black inductees.[21] The few Black officers inducted were only assigned to the medical corps or as chaplains in existing Black units.

By mid-1942 the Army was beginning to suffer manpower shortages. The primary instrument used for classification was the Army general classification test. As a result of the shortages, the Army lowered the literacy level to a fourth-grade education and instituted a thirteen-week basic literacy training course. This intensive course was highly successful, resulting in an 84 percent passing rate among Whites and an 87 percent passing rate among Blacks. Selection into this course was based on the policy of accepting 10 percent of "intelligent illiterates" into service based on the visual intelligence classification test, which helped identify men who could benefit from literacy training.[22]

While the Army was willing but reluctant to induct Blacks, the Navy was a totally different story. The Navy had a long history of Black sailors in limited numbers. The few Blacks who served were largely messmen or stewards. However, in the early twentieth century the Navy started to replace Blacks with those of Asian descent, largely Filipino, believed to be more pliant and less disruptive to naval order and traditions. During the interwar years, the number of Blacks serving dwindled to less than three thousand. Even at the outbreak of war in 1941, that number had climbed to only five thousand.[23] The secretary of the Navy, Henry Knox, himself a businessman with little knowledge of naval procedures, relied heavily on advice from admirals. These by-and-large conservative traditionalists resisted, much like the generals in the Army, any talk of inducting Blacks into any posting outside of the steward service. Knox told FDR that the challenge of building a two-ocean Navy was so daunting that if he was expected to integrate the Navy racially as well, he would resign.[24] On July 2, 1941, Knox created a committee to inquire as "to the existing relationship between the United States Navy, United States Marine Corps and the Negro race."[25] The committee met three times. The majority report on December 24, 1941, concluded that "the enlistment of Negroes (other than as mess attendants) leads to disruptive and undermining conditions."[26] A minority opinion opposed this position and argued that limited-service billets must be considered to avoid damage to national morale and harmony.[27]

The NAACP was monitoring the situation of Black service in the Navy. Shortly after Pearl Harbor, it contacted the secretary of the Navy asking for the acceptance of Black recruits. Knox's response was that no change in policy was to be made. The NAACP then contacted FDR directly. FDR punted the question to the Fair Employment Practices Committee for comment. The committee chairman conferred with the Navy but told FDR that while he recommended some additional use of Black sailors, he had no jurisdiction to intervene. As a result, FDR finally decided on January 9, 1942, to recommend to Knox that the Navy "might invent something that Colored enlistees could do in addition to the rating of messman."[28] In response, Secretary Knox asked the Navy General Board to devise a plan to place up to five thousand Blacks in positions other than as messmen. The board again demurred, stating that doing so "would inevitably promote race friction and lowered efficiency."[29] When FDR received this response on February 5, he pushed back and ordered further study in locating duty posts for Blacks. Even with presidential support, the Navy General Board and the chief of naval operations remained resistant, advising that it was both unwise and inadvisable to proceed. However, if this action was taken, they recommended the employment of Black sailors in shore duty and in construction battalions only. The response concludes, "Segregation is an essential part of administration, and hence Negroes could not be used in any general service billets in the Fleet."[30]

Roosevelt's response shows a hint of anger at the naval brass for a lack of appreciation for the larger issues of public relations and manpower. It is also likely that FDR wanted to curry some favor in the Black press over the failed attempts to see Doris Miller, the mess attendant hero of Pearl Harbor, publicly recognized for his heroism. Roosevelt would personally order the awarding of the Navy Cross to Miller in May 1942. Some have argued that FDR was exploiting Miller to distract Blacks from the limited progress made in military service.[31] At a meeting with Secretary Knox, FDR had ordered the implementation of Negro recruitment. The Navy announced on April 7, 1942, that Blacks could begin enlistment on June 1 for general service billets.

It had been a tough couple of years for Graham Jackson. He had lost his teaching job at Washington High School because of his arrest for an alleged assault against a female student. He had endured more than a year of legal challenges in the case, both civil and criminal. In the end he was acquitted of the criminal charges and found not liable for the civil suit. He tapped into the deep well of White clients and patrons who served as character witnesses in his defense. Among those witnesses were publisher Clark Howell, a Coca-Cola executive, and noted golfer Bobby Jones.[32] Although he was vindicated and found innocent in November 1941, he had spent a great deal of money on his legal bills and his reputation was sullied. Now a full-time performer, Jackson was hustling to make ends meet without the stable income of his teacher's salary. He still booked high-profile gigs in April 1941 for the Democratic Party of Georgia and Governor Talmadge and at Augusta National Golf Club.[33] He also continued his Plantation Revue for weddings and other social events.

The coming of war had a profound impact on all of America. The Rose Bowl game, scheduled for New Year's Day 1942 in Pasadena, California, was cancelled. The Army quickly ordered soldiers to bivouac on the football field. Just weeks after Pearl Harbor, the entire West Coast was rife with rumors and fears of attack. One result of these fears was the infamous decision to order the internment of Japanese Americans in states on the Pacific Coast. Ironically, one of the stars of the Oregon State football team was Jack Yoshihara, who came with his family to the United States at age three. Within days of Pearl Harbor, Yoshihara was banned by the government from participating in the Rose Bowl game. His coach and teammates were incensed. Within months, he and his family were sent to Minidoka War Location Center.

Both teams, Duke and Oregon State, desired to play the Rose Bowl game. Many of the young athletes expected to volunteer to serve in the US military but wanted to play the bowl game first. Duke coach Wallace Wade worked quickly to host the game in Durham, North Carolina, at the home stadium of Duke University. Duke officials decided to plan several events

Figure 1. Graham Jackson with accordion, 1942 Rose Bowl dinner, Durham, North Carolina. University Archives Photography Collection, David M. Rubinstein Rare Book and Manuscript Library, Duke University, Durham, NC.

for the players and coaches. One of the events was a Christmas dinner held at the University Union. Oregon State players were feted with gifts from local merchants and a huge dinner of southern favorites. Graham Jackson was the primary entertainer at this dinner. It was his second time providing entertainment at a Rose Bowl event.[34]

Decades later Jackson reminisced about his decision to enlist. He wanted to be a pilot when World War II started: "Oh in those early World War II days, they didn't let 'n-s' as they called them then, enter the Army Air Corps schools. I remember how hard I tried to get into flying. I know I could have been a good pilot, but they thought it would be dangerous to have colored folks flying all over the country." Turned down, he went to the Navy recruiter in Atlanta. He recalled, "I told the officer, he'd heard about me playing in the White House, that I didn't want one of those suits that most sailors wore. I wanted pants to be like 'normal pants,' and I wanted some brass buttons on my coat." The Navy was short of its quota, "and there were all of these colored boys standing outside seeing Graham Jackson joining up. A big ranking officer came into the room where I was and said, 'All right Jackson, we've decided that you would make a good chief petty officer.' All of those boys who would not join up came flooding into the place and I was made a recruiting officer right here in ATL."[35] Jackson had a flair for a turn of phrase and perhaps some exaggeration.

It is likely that Jackson found out about the Navy's plans to induct Blacks in a May 7, 1942, press release in the *Atlanta Daily World*. This item reported that the Navy was looking for "Race" musicians to form naval bands. NAACP head Walter White had advocated for formation of "good Negro bands" on battleships to ease relations between Blacks and Whites as shipmates.[36] This press release spoke glowingly of the administration's plans to induct Black Marines and sailors. The Navy would hold auditions, and those selected would be sent to the Great Lakes Training Center for four weeks. Jackson's naval discharge papers show he enlisted on May 16, 1942, as a musician second class. News of his enlistment spread quickly. The *Atlanta Constitution*, referring to him as the South's Cab Calloway, praised his musical skills and predicted success with the forty-five-piece band he was to lead at the naval preflight school in Athens, Georgia, where he was assigned.[37] On May 28 Jackson performed for a statewide parley of naval recruiting personnel held in Atlanta.[38] By June an Associated Press wire story appeared in numerous papers touting that Jackson was now a chief specialist tasked with recruiting Black sailors. The headline states he had quit a $200 weekly income to recruit for Uncle Sam.[39]

The Great Lakes Training Center saw a rapid transformation. Isolated Camp Berry was quickly renamed Camp Smalls in honor of the Black Civil War hero Robert Smalls, an enslaved person who was pressed into service in the Confederate Navy as a ship's pilot. He later stole a Confederate vessel and delivered it to the US Navy, making good his escape from bondage. Smalls's reward was the rank of commander in the US Navy, and he later served as a member of Congress from South Carolina.[40] The naming of the training center after Smalls was a blatant attempt to distract the Black press from the continued racial segregation in the Navy. The officer appointed to run the camp was Lieutenant Commander Daniel Armstrong, son of the founder of Hampton Institute in Virginia, one of the first Black Colleges. Armstrong was an enthusiastic champion of inducting Blacks into the Navy. However, his management style was paternalistic. He saw Blacks as needing special training and discipline. As a result, he often clashed with educated Blacks and Black leaders over how best to train Black sailors. In a somewhat patronizing manner, Armstrong instituted an arts program at the camp featuring murals and paintings of prominent Blacks in history as morale boosters for incoming sailors. This was criticized for showing Blacks in very limited roles.

Camp Smalls remained in use as a segregated training facility for a couple of years. Its first use would be to train Black naval musicians. All told, more than five thousand musicians, many who would later be noted performers, passed through its doors. This was a who's who of Black jazz and swing artists such as Dave Bartholomew, Von Freeman, John Coltrane, and Lou Donaldson. The bands that would form from this group were considered among the best military bands in the world at the time.[41] Given that music was one of the few areas where Blacks were allowed to excel as professionals in America and the large pool of available Black artists, it was no surprise that the Navy had little problem filling these billets. What became a problem was the relative lack of educated and technically skilled Blacks who were volunteering. As in the Army, a high percentage of volunteers had little formal education and often were illiterate. Naval officials puzzled over this condition, seeming to forget the image of the Navy in the Black community as a bastion of racism. One solution that helped alleviate this problem was the appointment of Black recruiting specialists like Jackson.[42]

Jackson is credited with being the genesis of the recruitment of Black musicians. Howard Funderburg, one of the early Navy volunteers, described Jackson's role: "So, the President had spoken, and from there, they went to . . . Graham Jackson in Atlanta. And then they formulated this plan and put any number of chief musicians [White] who'd had years in the Navy all out across the United States to recruit Black musicians. That's how they got in."[43] In the same interview Jackson proudly stated that everyone was "utterly baffled" by his ability to recruit so successfully.[44]

Atlanta embraced Chief Jackson's new role with excitement. The first round of Black sailors inducted into the service were greeted with pomp and circumstance. A ceremony was held at the Royal Theatre on Auburn Avenue on Sunday, June 7, 1942. Jackson was the master of ceremonies. John Wesley Dobbs gave a short address, and a naval band performed patriotic music. The oath was administered by radio broadcast from Washington to induction sites across the country.[45] The rapid success of Jackson's efforts brought quick praise from naval officers. It was reported that the Navy had high confidence in his efforts and that he was already exceeding expectations. He embarked on a tour of Georgia and performed statewide for Black and White audiences as a part of his duties.[46] He was stationed at the Naval Air Station, Atlanta. By the end of June he assisted in opening a recruiting substation in Decatur, Georgia.[47]

July saw Jackson tapping into his pool of notable Black citizens of Atlanta. He recruited a team of twelve volunteers to assist in his recruitment efforts, among them Black business leaders, newspaper reporters, and advertising executives. Potential recruits were to contact these community leaders to begin the process of induction. These recruiters reported directly to Jackson.[48] July also saw Jackson supporting the purchase of war bonds. This was an area in which Jackson would excel over the next three years. The Atlanta Million Dollar War Bond Breakfast was a huge success in bond sales.[49] WAGA radio station began a daily *War Bond Jamboree* broadcast as well. Jackson was featured performing live daily from Five Points in the heart of downtown at 12:30 p.m. He was praised not only for "helping his nation fight this war by volunteering, but he also pays tribute to other members of his race who are fighting for their country."[50] For this first year of recruitment, the Navy left activities generally in the hands of the "carefully selected" Negro recruiting officers with little guidance, allowing for a personal contact approach to recruiting.[51]

Even though recruitment of Blacks in limited roles such as musicians was a success, overall recruitment efforts were floundering. The goal of having 10 percent of the Navy made up of Blacks was nowhere in sight. The total in late 1942 was around 2 percent of the total enlisted manpower. This is in large part due to the Navy's refusal to participate in the Selective Service and to rely on volunteerism. Even with all these efforts, it was clear that the quickly expanding Navy could never fill its billets, White or Black, without switching to a draft. A further complication was the practice of many southern draft boards having separate draft calls based on race or refusing to call Blacks at all. The chair of the War Manpower Commission stated plainly that these separate calls were simply untenable and resulted in a backlog of Black registrants numbering in the hundreds of thousands awaiting orders to report. He feared that White draftees might soon sue in court to challenge this situation.[52] Jackson knew that changes were coming and ran a series of advertisements in newspapers extolling in detail the pay and benefits for anyone ages seventeen to fifty with a reading knowledge of music to consider enlisting. One ad reads, "In view of the fact that married men as well as most single men will in the very near future be called to service in the armed forces, why not take advantage of this opportunity to follow your profession and serve your country at the same time?"[53] The upshot of these concerns was Executive Order 9279, dated December 5, 1942. In it Roosevelt ordered the end of recruitment and enlistment. Moving forward, the Navy, like the Army, would rely solely on draftees. By early 1943, on paper, the Navy had agreed to a wide dispersion of Black sailors in service. FDR was very direct to Secretary Knox: "You know the headache we have had about this and the reluctance of the Navy to have any Negroes. You and I have had to veto that Navy reluctance, and I think we have to do it again."[54]

Figure 2. Graham Jackson with unidentified Navy officer, Atlanta, 1940s. Graham W. Jackson Sr. and his service in the Navy, plaques and photographs, box 8, folder 4, series 7, Graham W. Jackson Sr. Papers, Archives Division, Auburn Avenue Research Library on African-American Culture and History, Fulton County Library System, Atlanta.

Jackson's role as a recruiter might soon come to an end, but his role as an entertainer and war bond salesman was taking off. Lieutenant Commander S. A. Jones, his superior, praised Jackson effusively: "I should like to state that Jackson is indeed a star performer. His presence at our recruiting rallies has been responsible for getting together exceptionally large gatherings in several Georgia communities."[55] Jackson also performed each Sunday evening at an Open Door Canteen set up on Peachtree Street downtown. Jackson would take requests from servicemen. Most musical requests were not upbeat lively music. No, it was more often or than not classical, soothing, or melancholy. A soldier just needed to hum a few bars and Jackson would play it on the organ.[56]

Christmas Day 1942 found Jackson performing an organ concert at the Municipal Auditorium with famed jazz artist Louis Armstrong. Like many Black artists, Armstrong participated in many USO and war-bond events across the nation. Armstrong and his band performed at the White House for FDR's sixtieth birthday party on January 30, 1942. Armstrong held a series of national broadcast concert events as well. The 1942 Christmas concert featured holiday songs from all the Allied nations. This was not a random playlist of songs. The State Department distributed lists of songs to celebrate an anticipated Allied victory.[57] Crowds grew so large speakers were set up at Hurt Park across the street for attendees to listen in. The lights in the fountain at Hurt Park were set to change with the music.[58]

Jackson started the night performing many of these pieces on the organ. Armstrong's band included former Seminole Syncopators Joe Garland and Al Prince. An article in *Phylon* magazine in 1945 describes the evening:

> The night that Louis Armstrong played was a grand patriotic occasion. Attorney Walden [a local Black attorney] urged the need for buying bonds; his clipped, dry speaking could barely be heard in the huge auditorium and was in contrast to the floridity and extravaganza that it interrupted. Graham Jackson, home-boy of Atlanta, a good pianist and accordion player, now recruiting officer for the Navy, appeared in the gleaming white uniform of a petty officer and gave a canned recruiting spiel. Then he turned and pumped old Satchmo's hand, exchanged a bit of jive talk; went over to the piano stool that Louis Russell gladly gave over to him, and showed his virtuosity on the keyboard. He was more enthusiastic here than while making his speech, and so was the crowd.[59]

Jackson was one of many Black artists and entertainers who heeded the call to support the war effort. Some, like Jackson, enlisted; others, like Armstrong, regularly raised money for the war effort. One of the best known to also enlist was the Brown Bomber himself, Joe Louis. He was an inspiration for Black Americans; his victories as a boxer as well as his perception by White America as a safe Black, not a troublemaker, made his decision to enlist in the Army huge news across the nation. At first, Louis was assigned to a segregated cavalry unit based in Fort Riley, Kansas. Through serendipity, Louis was successful in helping the careers of Black officer candidates, one of whom was Jackie Robinson. Later military officials tasked Louis with traveling to training camps to entertain and teach recruits fighting skills. Like Jackson, Louis was successful and quickly promoted to technical sergeant. Louis gave up an estimated $40,000 a week income for his basic service pay.

Louis was asked why he chose to support the war effort, given the discrimination Blacks faced at home. He responded, "There ain't nothing wrong with us that that Mr. Hitler can fix."[60] And when asked when he would fight a professional match again he answered, "I'm interested in winning only one fight now, and that's the war."[61] Louis was so universally

58 · The Life and Music of Graham Jackson

popular that Army reports of his activities began to omit his race in their reporting.[62] This did not sit well with critics who saw the omission as white-washing on the part of the Army.

Another noted African American entertainer who made a huge impact on the war effort was Hattie McDaniel. Oscar winner McDaniel had chosen not to attend the 1939 premiere of *Gone with the Wind* in Atlanta because of Jim Crow. Regardless of this, she chose to join with other Hollywood actors to do her part. In early 1942 McDaniel was elected as a member of the Hollywood Victory Committee. The committee was composed of notables such as *Gone with the Wind* costar Clark Gable, Jack Benny, Claudette Colbert, Bette Davis, and Gary Cooper. The goals of the committee were to support the war effort through music and entertainment. McDaniel was proud of her selection by her peers and promised that this was a serious undertaking: "This honor I accepted gratefully and humbly, realizing that the honor, while personal, also served to bring honor to the thirteen million Negroes in America—our country."[63]

McDaniel took charge of an interracial subcommittee on entertainment for Black troops, often holding meetings at her home. From the beginning, she and the subcommittee were frank in their observations that segregated military camps were depriving Black soldiers of most access to entertainment and therefore hurting morale. Within just a few months more than 250 artists performed in eighty-one USO shows. Shows by this biracial group of artists were often lavish affairs with dozens of entertainers, dancers, and on occasion, exhibitions from Joe Louis. McDaniel worked tirelessly at her job, often going directly from a movie set to entertain the troops. McDaniel served as a captain in the American Women's Volunteer Service. One of the largest home-front volunteer organizations, the service trained more than 325,000 women in a plethora of support jobs. In 1943 McDaniel was given an honorary appointment as a first lieutenant in the 28th Army Regiment and commendations from the Red Cross and the Women's Army Air Corp Auxiliary.[64]

Even before the war, Roosevelt administration officials were concerned about the effective allocation of needed resources. FDR had served as assistant secretary of the Navy in the Wilson administration and experienced economic and resource mobilization close up. The real genius behind the Defense Savings Bond program was Secretary of the Treasury Henry Morgenthau. He developed the first US savings bond program in 1935 to provide a simple and safe vehicle for any American to invest in and to provide a pool of surplus revenue for New Deal program funding. As war clouds approached, the administration sought a specific solution for ramped-up defense spending. This solution was the E series Defense Savings Bonds.[65]

Roosevelt announced this new program on April 30, 1941. He called for "One Great Partnership" in defense savings.[66] The goals of this program were manifold. On the surface, the primary goal was to provide much-needed funding for defense spending. Secondary to that albeit just as important was the goal to provide a mechanism for increased savings to assist in slowing spending to lower inflation and in preventing shortages of needed war materials. A third goal of the program was to provide a means for "small savers" to be unified in support of possible war. To make this small savings program even more accessible, Treasury also introduced defense stamps. These small-denomination stamps cost as little as a dime, making them accessible to those with little income, even children. The brilliance of this accessibility, coupled with a sense of national unity and patriotism, fit right in with the larger plans for war propaganda activities. In the spring of 1942, the name of the program changed to War Savings Bonds.

In January 1943 Jackson received his first commendation for his efforts in selling war bonds. All told, he received six commendations. In *Pledging Allegiance: American Identity and the Bond Drive of World War II*, Lawrence Samuel considers Jackson the most notable promoter of war bonds among Black Americans.[67] The state chair of the war savings staff credited Jackson with selling more than $300,000 in war bonds and stamps, an impressive total.[68] Jackson's success made him a desired commodity for the Navy. A week after winning his citation, he received orders transferring him to Richmond, Virginia, to work directly for Commander H. G. Chandler, recruiting inspector for the Southeast region.[69] In February Jackson was transferred to Baltimore, Maryland. While there he performed at a war bond rally at the Emerson Hotel with the Coast Guard band and Hollywood notables Constance Bennet, Lanny Ross, and Bert Lytell. The end of March saw him transferred to Macon, Georgia.[70]

Jackson's return to Georgia fully coincided with the Navy's switch to using Selective Service inductees alone. This meant his recruitment efforts could only focus on seventeen-year-olds and men over thirty-nine, a change that meant he would mostly perform for bond rallies and concerts. Yet even with his commendations and success, Jackson still faced issues of racial discrimination in attempting to carry out his naval duties. Jackson sought a telephone in his home so potential recruits could contact him directly. Southern Bell Telephone Company refused his requests. It took two letters from the Navy in April and May to force the phone company to act.

The Navy expressed grave concerns that Southern Bell had refused to give him phone service and stated that as a naval recruiter it was vital that he have it.[71] Even with these challenges, Jackson still managed to send fifty-six seventeen-year-old volunteers off to training in April 1943.[72] In August he reached his highest single month number with seventy-five volunteers sent to various training schools around the nation.[73]

In May, Hollywood royalty arrived in Atlanta to raise money for the Red Cross. Bing Crosby and Bob Hope were tireless in their efforts to support the war thorough entertainment. The two embarked on a six-week cross-country tour with stops in Chicago, New York, Washington, Birmingham, Nashville, and Atlanta.[74] On May 30 Crosby and Hope held a golf match at Atlanta's Capital City Golf Club to raise money for the Red Cross ambulance corps. The crowd exceeded 10,000, with some estimates putting the number at 18,000. Regardless, it was the largest crowd for a golfing event in Atlanta's history. Jackson performed at the event luncheon and later had an opportunity to perform with Crosby in an impromptu session in the locker room of the Capital City Country Club.[75] In June, Madame Chiang Kai-shek, wife of the Chinese leader, made a visit to Macon. Madame Chiang was a graduate of Wesleyan College and had not returned to her alma mater in more than thirty years. Jackson greeted her as she exited the train and played "Dixie" on his accordion.[76]

As 1943 progressed, tough budget choices were resulting in less money for the OWI and Treasury. Added to that, bond sales were showing signs of sagging, perhaps due to market saturation. Initial bond campaigns focused on patriotism, and much of the basis of purchase had been economic. Bonds were a sound investment for the purchaser. As a result, Treasury decided that the focus of the campaigns must hinge on emotion and entertainment.[77] James Sparrow argues, "Mass participation was essential in 'total war.' . . . Not only would it unleash vast financial resources, but it would also habituate civilians to their patriotic obligations."[78] The new approach was well coordinated and planned eight "victory loan drives" from December 1942 until December 1945. These events exceeded expectations and negated more draconian measures considered, such as salary caps and forced savings plans. By adopting payroll deduction and blurring the meaning of volunteerism, these high-pressure drives and patriotic promotions allowed persuasion to supersede compulsion.[79] They allowed the patriotic participation of men, women, and children on the home front in the war effort. Studies conducted at the time illustrate the public's reasons for participation. The most common response was the determination to provide soldiers

Figure 3. Actor Jane Withers smiles at Graham Jackson at a 1944 bond drive dinner at the Hotel Colonial in LaGrange, Georgia. Dorothy Allen (*left*) and Paula Copeland sit on either side of Withers. The photographer was Snelson Davis. From the Nix-Price Collection (MS-4), Troup County Archives, LaGrange, GA.

with the money they needed to win the war.[80] James Kimble has called this successful approach to massive war financing an example of "militarized propaganda."[81]

Jackson received his second "citation for distinguished service in behalf of the war savings program" in December 1943. This citation was for his hard work in the third war-loan drive. An article in the *Atlanta Constitution* states, "In voluntary performances since his enlistment, Jackson has visited every part of the state of Georgia, as well as nearby cities in other southeastern states. About one-third of his audiences have been Negro—at a bond rally one rainy Sunday afternoon in Newnan, a slim crowd of 88 persons subscribed $54,000; a total of $17,000 was bought by children at one Negro junior high school."[82]

Jackson continued to receive praise from naval officers for his recruitment and bond efforts. Captain J. V. Babcock, commander of the Georgia Tech naval unit, had high praise for Jackson, saying, "I am proud to have Graham Jackson in the uniform of my service, the Navy. He is a credit to that service." He continued, "I can state without reservation that I have never encountered one man whose conduct and activities had such a fine influence on his community." Finally, he praised Jackson's skills as an entertainer, saying that "most of the nation's entertainers on the platform and radio might well emulate" him.[83]

Black morale continued to be of concern in 1944. As the war entered its third full year, the segregated nature of military service, use of Blacks largely as shore labor, and lack of good leadership by paternalistic White officers were taking their toll. Racial strife among naval personnel resulted in clashes at Saint Julien's Creek, Virginia, in June 1943. Not long afterward, several Black alleged agitators in a construction battalion in Trinidad were court-martialed. The most violent incident by far was the July 1944 Port Chicago explosion. This horrific ammunition accident resulted in the deaths of 320 sailors, two-thirds of that number Black. Just weeks later, with no new safety measures in place, Black sailors were ordered to resume activities at the docks. Most refused, and 258 were subject to court-martial. Fifty were charged with mutiny and faced fifteen years in prison. All eventually received clemency.[84]

Several changes occurred in 1944 because of these growing concerns as well as continued manpower shortage issues. Following the death of Secretary Knox on April 28, 1944, FDR appointed Under Secretary James Forrestal to the position of secretary of the Navy. Forrestal was much more progressive than Knox and was a member of the National Urban League; he saw the issues of segregated training and billets as simply detrimental to efficiency and fair play. Forrestal made quick changes that presaged the 1948 executive order by Harry Truman ending segregation in the military.[85]

The first change Forrestal implemented was the immediate use of Black sailors in fleet auxiliary ships. Forrestal stated to FDR, "From a morale standpoint, the Negroes resent the fact that they are not assigned to general service billets at sea, and White personnel resent the fact that Negroes have been given less hazardous assignments."[86] FDR supported this plan, which fixed the total number of Blacks assigned to 10 percent of the crew. Over the next several months, commanders at sea reported no difficulties and berthed Black sailors randomly among the crew. Black officers also were receiving training for commissioning. At first these officers were training in the segregated facilities at Great Lakes or in the Navy's V-12 training programs at various colleges across the country. By 1944 the costs of these separate facilities due to duplication of services was too much. In July 1944 the Bureau of Naval Personnel ordered the end of all separate advanced-training facilities. Going forward this training was fully integrated.[87]

The Navy produced a pamphlet to educate White officers in how better to lead Black sailors. *The Guide to Command of Negro Personnel* was businesslike in its approach to the race issue:[88]

> It must be recognized that problems of race relations do exist and that they must be taken into account in plans for the prosecution of the war. In the Naval Establishment they should be viewed however solely as matters of efficient personnel utilization. . . . In modern total warfare any avoidable waste of manpower can only be viewed as material aid to the enemy. Restriction, because of racial theories, of the contribution of any individual to the war effort is a serious waste of human resources. . . . The Navy accepts no theories of racial differences in inborn ability, but expects that every man wearing its uniform be trained and used in accordance with his maximum individual capacity determined on the basis of individual performance.[89]

The overriding message of this pamphlet was that racial theories and discrimination were impeding military efficiency and were a blatant waste of manpower and materials. Old excuses concerning White sailors' feelings or lack of capacity by Blacks were no longer a paramount concern. The keys to success were good training and good leadership. The message mirrors that of the rationing programs of the war: racism aids the enemy in the same way waste of resources does.

Another progressive step by the military was the production of films to educate service members and later the general public on issues of race. By 1944 the OWI had produced several films, the best known and most widely released being the *Why We Fight* series produced by Frank Capra. Capra had served in World War I as a math instructor. He reenlisted in February 1941 at the height of his success as a director. His task was to produce this series so young Americans would understand what they were fighting for.[90]

The purpose of the 1944 film *The Negro Soldier* was to boost Black morale and educate White troops. Capra was indifferent to making the film, but a call from Secretary of War Stimson, who discussed the ongoing discrimination against Black soldiers, convinced Capra. In reality, Capra had little direct participation in producing the film and largely left it to director Stuart Heisler to produce.[91] The movie was produced at a high technical level and portrayed Blacks as middle-class, neat, and orderly. The script was written by a Black writer, Carleton Moss; sociologist Donald Young wrote a list of dos and don'ts to include in the film. Thomas Cripps and David Culbert argue that the film brought about the end of the "race movie" in America.[92] This is ironic, given that the Army was attempting to maintain segregation but in the end produced a film that logically promoted integration.

A less-known companion film is *The Negro Sailor* (1945). Following the Army's rationale, Navy officials desired a film that could accomplish similar goals of Black morale and White tolerance. The film, directed by Henry Levin, follows the induction of a young Black man into an integrated Navy. Blacks are depicted as professional, middle-class, and above all, patriotic. The goals of the film, like the pamphlet and the changes to assigning billets and training, all reflect the new direction of the Navy under Forrestal.

By the summer of 1944, Jackson had received a fourth citation for his war-bond work. He was honored at a special showing of the film *Desti-nation Tokyo* at his old stomping grounds, Bailey's Royal Theatre on Auburn Avenue. In the crowd were wounded black servicemen from Lawson Army Hospital in nearby DeKalb County. Admission for this event was the purchase of five dollars in bonds or stamps.[93] That same month he also performed at a testimonial dinner for W.E.B. Du Bois at a gala in Atlanta. Jackson led the crowd in singing "Auld Lang Syne" in honor of Du Bois.[94]

September found Jackson performing at the Biltmore Hotel for actor Bette Davis, who was in Atlanta to visit a wounded "friend" and celebrate his birthday. Davis's relationship with this mysterious soldier was a source of much interest in the press. One reporter paid Jackson to give him details on this private event. Davis called Jackson's performance was a big success.[95] Davis was, like Jackson, a huge supporter of the war effort. She helped found the Hollywood Canteen in October 1942. She served drinks to soldiers side by side with notables like Greer Garson and Marlene Dietrich. It was at the Canteen that she met and started the ongoing relationship with Corporal Lewis A. Riley, the mystery man.

Davis was also a strong opponent of segregation. When opening the Canteen, she entered on the arm of African American actor Rex Ingram and quipped, "The Blacks got the same bullets that the Whites did and should get the same treatment."[96] Davis entertained groups of African American soldiers many times and happily posed with them for photos. The *Chicago Defender* began weekly features on Davis's work with African Americans, though this was never mentioned in the White press.[97]

October and November found Jackson still in high demand. In celebration of Navy Day, Jackson performed for an audience of more than three thousand at his former place of employment, Booker T. Washington High School. One of Jackson's longtime White patrons and friends, Ralph McGill, editor of *The Atlanta Constitution*, gave the keynote address.[98] Jackson again entertained injured servicemen from Lawson Army Hospital in November. The event at the Piedmont Driving Club, sponsored by the *Atlanta Constitution*, featured circus performers as well as Jackson playing his accordion. A serviceman who lost one leg in combat jumped up to dance leaning on his crutches to one of Jackson's songs.[99] A few weeks later Jackson took part in a production called "Here's Your Infantry." The purpose of this show was to demonstrate the skills and training of the infantry and raise money. It was the kick-off of the sixth war-loan drive in Atlanta. The event was at Ponce de Leon Ball Park, home of the Atlanta Crackers baseball team. Jackson was the main speaker at the event.[100] He closed out the year performing at an Atlanta Women's Club Christmas dinner for servicemen. This event also had fortune-tellers, jitterbug dancers, and a full turkey dinner.[101]

Jackson continued his breakneck travel pace in the new year. The sixth war loan drive wrapped up at the end of 1944. With Germany in retreat and the bombing of mainland Japan by US planes, many in the administration feared donor fatigue. These fears were unfounded, as the end total of $21.6 billion was raised. The Georgia state chair of the American Legion had high praise for Jackson's efforts, especially given his race: "I do want to call to your attention in this letter to you the splendid work rendered by Graham Jackson. It would have been outstanding for a White man to have performed as he did but for a Negro, with no decent places to stay or eat as I found the situation to be, it of course was doubly outstanding."[102] Plans for the next war loan drive, the seventh, were in the works. Ironically, that drive started just days after VE Day.

Among the highs and lows of 1945 for Jackson and the nation were the Allies' victories over Germany and Japan that would end the worst conflict in human history but also sorrow that the architect of victory would not live to see it. Warm Springs and FDR's beloved Little White House were seared into the collective memory of the nation, and the symbol of the nation's mourning would be in *Life* magazine: the tear-filled visage of Graham Jackson playing the accordion.

In total, Franklin Roosevelt made forty-one trips to Warm Springs from 1924 until his death in 1945. In the early years, before his 1928 election as governor of New York, he spent much of his time in Georgia. The first few years he focused on his own recovery, but he eventually started working

66 · The Life and Music of Graham Jackson

with patients who showed up because of stories of his recovery. In 1927 he purchased the Meriwether Inn property and started the Warm Springs Institute and Foundation. In 1932 construction of his secluded cottage, the Little White House, was completed. Though his visits slowed once he assumed the presidency, he tried to continue his traditional Thanksgiving visits.

Roosevelt made his penultimate trip to Warm Springs in November 1944. He enjoyed a restful break from Thanksgiving until December 18. This visit was a continuation of the long tradition of Thanksgiving dinners overseen by FDR at the dining room in Georgia Hall on the grounds of the institute. The dinner was an engaging affair. Graham Jackson was the entertainer for the evening. He started out leading songs on the piano and then on the accordion.[103] The evening was even more exciting because Bette Davis was in attendance. Davis had rented a home in Phenix City, Alabama, just across the Chattahoochee River from Fort Benning. Davis desired to be close to her beau, Corporal Riley, who was stationed there at the time. She took to life in the Phenix City quite well, reportedly joining her neighbors on coon and possum hunts.[104]

The invitation to Warm Springs was a happy happenstance. Davis had campaigned for FDR in 1944 and wanted to meet him in person. She attended an event at the White House in October, and Roosevelt, upon spotting her in the crowd, approached her to apologize that she was treated in such a common manner. During the conversation she mentioned she would be in Georgia for the holidays. Roosevelt immediately responded with an invite to Warm Springs. Davis jumped at the chance and accepted the invitation, bringing her beau along.[105]

None of Roosevelt's staff knew of the off-the-cuff invite and were quite taken aback when she arrived after the thirty-five-mile drive from Fort Benning. As she entered the dining room of Georgia Hall, she made a beeline for the head table. This ruffled the feathers of Basil O'Conner, the head of the institute, and William Hassett, FDR's press secretary, who felt she monopolized FDR's time. She was apparently unmoved by the angry glares directed at her. Many feared that photos of Davis next to FDR would be used against the president to hurt his image.[106] Two of the photos show Jackson performing for the president and Davis.[107] These are the only extant photos that show Jackson and Roosevelt together. In one, Jackson stands behind FDR and Davis, smiling and playing his accordion. Davis is looking directly at Roosevelt with a smile on her face. Davis's relationship with

Figure 4. Graham Jackson performing for Franklin Roosevelt and Bette Davis at Warm Springs, October 1944. Graham W. Jackson Sr. and his service in the Navy, plaques and photographs, box 8, folder 4, series 7, Graham W. Jackson Sr. Papers, Archives Division, Auburn Avenue Research Library on African-American Culture and History, Fulton County Library System, Atlanta.

Corporal Riley would soon come to a predictable conclusion when he was sent to Europe and the romance ended.

A *Life* magazine reporter describes the majesty of Jackson's performances at Warm Springs:

> As we filed into the room Graham Jackson made his appearance.... Above his immaculate uniform his round, friendly face shone. He seated himself at the chapel piano, which suddenly looked oddly defenseless. (I have been told that after Graham Jackson's appearance it had to be sent away for complete overhauling). His playing, debonair and gay, achieved exactly the right, if unexpected note. The serving

boys straightened with pride, their wrists seeming to ease back up into their sleeves, we even managed to forget the disquieting presence of the secret service men who stood at strategic places along the wall. The President entered. He came in as we came in, in his wheelchair.[108]

Beyond his traditional Thanksgiving celebration, FDR also wanted to visit Warm Springs so he could spend time with his longtime love, Lucy Mercer Rutherford. She traveled over from her home in South Carolina and spent five days with FDR. They would plan another fateful visit upon his return to Georgia in March 1945. These reunions happened in large part because of the intervention of Roosevelt's daughter, Anna, who facilitated the visits because she felt her father was lonely.

The death of Roosevelt on April 12, 1945, is chronicled in great detail by scholars. Numerous books have described the last days of FDR, with a particular focus on his health issues in the last year of his life.[109] Some accounts are more fanciful than others, but the broad details of his last visit to Warm Springs are generally agreed on. Roosevelt returned from the physically exhausting trip to Yalta in late February 1945. After a few weeks of further exhausting work, he was ready for the peace and quiet of Warm Springs. He arrived in late March so weak and frail that many of the regulars in town noticed. When he exited the train to his waiting car, his head lolled backward as the agents lifted him into the seat. His cardiologist, Howard Bruenn, ordered total rest. When he was not reading dispatches, he spent the first several days mostly chatting with his two cousin companions, Laura Delano and Margaret Suckley, and taking long, slow rides around Pine Mountain. On April 1, Easter Sunday, Roosevelt and his party attended services at the institute chapel. Worshipers saw Roosevelt's hands shake and his glasses fall to the floor. On April 5 Roosevelt met with Philippine President Sergio Osmena to discuss plans for independence for the island nation after the war. His real joy came on April 9, when Lucy Rutherford made the long drive to Warm Springs from South Carolina. He was so excited to see her he ordered the Secret Service to caravan him over to nearby Macon, hoping to intercept her. Lucy had with her the artist Elizabeth Shoumatoff and photographer Nicholas Robbins. "Madame" Shoumatoff was there to complete a portrait of FDR, commissioned by Lucy as a gift to Lucy's daughter, Barbara. On April 12, 1945, while posing for this unfinished portrait, Roosevelt suffered a cerebral hemorrhage and died a short time later.

Graham Jackson recorded his memories of FDR's death a few days later. On April 19, 1945, Jackson sat down with Ella May Thornton, the state librarian of Georgia, to record and transcribe his memories of FDR's death. Jackson combined a narrative of the events surrounding FDR's death and departure from Warm Springs intermixed with an accordion performance of Dvorak's "Going Home," which Jackson had performed as the hearse bearing the deceased president passed in front of Georgia Hall. This recording was produced on a record album. Another song on the album is one that Jackson composed with FDR called "How Sweet Is the Air."[110] Eleanor Roosevelt read the account and noted, "The simplicity and real affection which shone through the whole account gave it a really beautiful literary quality."[111] A second account of FDR's death was written in a letter by Institute staffers Betty Brown and Hazel Stephens and mailed to a relative of Stephens who was serving in the Pacific.[112] All three, Jackson, Brown, and Stephens, had prepared to take part in a minstrel show for the president scheduled for 5:30 p.m. on April 12.

Stephens was the recreation director at the institute. FDR's secretary, Grace Tully, requested a minstrel show for "The Boss." William Rogers notes, "It was an all patient cast except for three specialties; two dancers from Atlanta and Graham Jackson."[113] In the recording by Thornton, Jackson explains, "Last week I had a call, just like dozens that have come to me during the last twelve years when Mr. Roosevelt was there, that I was wanted at Warm Springs to take part in an entertainment program."[114]

Jackson reminisced about the last time he performed for FDR, in November 1944: "He looked so broken. I was alone with him one whole evening on that visit. 'Graham,' he said 'I am so tired. Play to me and let me rest.' And so I knelt with my accordion, on the floor by his side, just like this in the living-room in the Little White House. I stayed there for a long time with my arms touching those terrible braces."[115]

The next part of Jackson's account is problematic. Jackson claims he reached Warm Springs at 11:35 a.m. on Thursday, April 12. He states that he approached a crossroad, and "Mr. Roosevelt passed in front of me, driving his own car. He saw me, raised his hand and called out 'So you got here. I'll see you later. I'm going home now.' The last words I ever heard him speak."[116] This statement is contradicted by every other available contemporaneous account of FDR's last day. These accounts indicate that Roosevelt awoke at 8:30 a.m. but remained in bed until later that morning because the message pouch from the White House was delayed due to fog and would not arrive until after 11 a.m. Bruenn examined FDR and noted that he reported a slight headache and stiff neck. Further, Bruenn telephoned Dr. Ross McIntire in Washington to give him a report on the president's health. FDR ate breakfast in bed, as was his custom, and then at 11 a.m. he asked his valet, Arthur Prettyman, to assist him with bathing and shaving so he could get dressed. Once that was completed, he was wheeled into the living room to complete some work and continue posing for Madame Shoumatoff. He remained there until about 1 p.m., when he suddenly complained of a terrible headache, slumped in his chair, and was carried into his bedroom. With him in the room or nearby were Shoumatoff, Laura Delano, Margaret Suckley, his cook Daisy Bonner, his valet Arthur Prettyman, and the Navy messman Joe Esperancilla. None of these accounts indicates that FDR left the house at any time on April 12, as Jackson claimed. Furthermore, while FDR had taken several drives on this visit, all were with others driving for him. His cousin Margaret's diary indicates that his driver Monty Snyder always drove him, and on March 30 she states that he formerly "had taken pride in driving his own car, [but he] no longer felt up to it."[117]

Was Jackson's recollection simple, wistful memories of a previous encounter accidentally included? Or was this a deliberate attempt to further connect himself to FDR? While the answer may never be known, we do know that Jackson gained a great deal of notoriety after the publication of Ed Clark's photo of him in *Life* magazine.[118] This original recording was donated to the Library of Congress. It seems certain that Jackson had hoped to sell copies of the recording. A handwritten note on the original transcript by Thornton, dated January 12, 1959, indicates that she felt that the music should have been featured more on the record.

The next part of Jackson's account mostly line up with the Brown and Stephens letter. Jackson stated that after changing out of his uniform in his cottage into his costume, he was driving to the playhouse when he heard the announcement of FDR's death on the radio. He rushed in and shared the news with the wife of the institute's chief surgeon, Charles Irwin. The Brown and Stephens account claims that Jackson told Stephens, who then called Mrs. Irwin to get confirmation. According to their account, this happened around 5:10 p.m. The first press dispatches of the death went out at 4:47 p.m. for broadcast.[119] The Brown and Stephens account also states, "Graham always brings the President red American Beauty roses. The American Beauty roses were probably the first flowers to reach the Little White House. Captain Ford of the 4th Service Command, who also helped us with the show, took them up."[120]

Figure 5. FDR's hearse passing Georgia Hall in Warm Springs, April 13, 1945. Reprinted hand-colored print of Franklin Delano Roosevelt arriving at Georgia Hall, Warm Springs Institute for Rehabilitation, Warm Springs, Georgia. *Atlanta Journal-Constitution* via Associated Press.

The high point for Jackson in his connection to FDR in public life was his *Life* magazine photo. Geoff Dyer, in his book *The Ongoing Movement*, describes the powerful imagery of this photograph. "Because Jackson is Black, Clark's picture dips into the deep wells of Negro spirituals which Dvorak believed contained all that was needed for 'a great and noble school of American Music.'" He continues, "My God! What a picture! Everything about it—the music, Jackson's race, his uniform—make it a classic, even definitive *Life*-like image."[121]

His iconic photo of Jackson was mentioned in Clark's 2000 *New York Times* obituary.[122] The 1977 television miniseries *Eleanor and Franklin* erroneously portrays Jackson performing at the Warm Springs train depot, not the institute. Jackson spent the remaining three decades of his career maintaining his connection with FDR.

Author Jodi Kanter beautifully dramatizes the relationship between FDR and Jackson in her book *Presidential Libraries as Performance*:

Interlude: A Legacy in Song—Graham Jackson Brings Roosevelt Home

Comin' to Georgia was comin' home for me. Didn't move from Virginia until I was grown, but somethin' about it, the heat, the land, the way people acted toward you. And of course the music. I was a theater organist in Georgia, which meant I got to help create the sound and the feel of the mostly made up places where the plays took place, help bring them to life. I loved it, I really did. In fact, of the places where I played organ, Georgia is a lot more home to me than Portsmouth ever was. But not to him. Bein' from the east, he never could get into the swing of things down here. They sent him here to relax, you know, to help the pain, and the man just kept on workin.' Relaxin' just wasn't a part of his nature, I guess.

I wouldn't say we were friends, not friends exactly. Not quite "friends." But I respected him. A man grows up with more money than Daddy Warbucks and he dedicates his whole life to givin' the guy who gets the sorriest deal a better one. How are you goin' to not respect that? Oh, I know, there's folks that say he just wanted the government meddlin' in people's lives, makin' all the decisions, controllin' all the money. But I'll tell you, when he got here there were a lot of people who needed some meddlin' pretty bad.

So when we started talkin' about the song and he asks, would I work out a new version with him, well to tell the truth I thought he was pullin' my leg. But when I figured out he was serious, well a'course I said I'd do it. It was based on a line from Dvořák he loved and we called it "Goin' Home." We wasn't quite finished with it, but finished enough, I guess. He died in Warm Springs on April 13, 1945. The day that funeral train went by was one of the saddest days of my life. We'd just been with him so long, he was like our family, even if he wasn't quite our friend. I couldn't see her, his wife, she was way back inside the train, and I didn't really want to see him. So I just closed my eyes and started to play the song. I was thinkin' about home—not Georgia, not Virginia but, you know, the larger home, the whole United States. I thought about the kind of home he had wanted it to be and the kind of home I had wanted it to be. I kept playin' and cryin,' playin' and cryin.' I was wishin' I was inside a theater so my playin' could bring up the curtain on that place.[123]

6

"A Negro Musician of Fine Character with an Excellent War Record"

Atlanta and the South were on the cusp of fundamental social and economic changes after the end of World War II. Huge social forces were released by the mobilization efforts of the war. These changes created backlash from conservative Whites who feared social and economic equality with Blacks. Atlanta took a different path from the rest of Georgia, exacerbating the tension over race as well as growing the power of Atlanta as a regional and later an international city. This rural-versus-urban struggle defined politics in Georgia for the remainder of the twentieth century. The end of the White primary and the civil rights efforts of the Truman administration would reap real advances for African Americans and galvanize White resistance.

Graham Jackson found the need to redefine himself as well. In June 1945 he was summoned to Washington, DC. He performed for President Truman at a musical event at the Statler Hotel on June 2. This was a farewell dinner given by the White House Correspondents Association in honor of recently departed press secretary Stephen Early. The event, scheduled for four hours, lasted six. Jackson was the first entertainer to perform for President Truman. The next day he received his sixth citation for his efforts in raising money for war bonds. This citation was presented to him by Secretary Morgenthau himself. Jackson was credited with a grand total of more than two million dollars raised in his naval career.[1] The press release states, "For distinguished service to the War Bond program, Secretary of the Treasury Henry Morgenthau Jr. has personally awarded Chief Petty Officer Graham W. Jackson of Atlanta, Georgia, the Treasury's War Bond Achievement Citation."[2]

In July, Jackson performed with members of the Tuskegee Airmen in a special bond show. Titled "Roger," this was a cleverly written variety show

Figure 6. Graham Jackson with Secretary of the Treasury Henry Morgenthau Jr., June 3, 1945, Washington, DC. Acme Photos Collection, Prints and Photographs Division, 20540-473, Library of Congress, Washington, DC.

that featured all sorts of skits, songs, and parodies. Jackson was the headliner of the show in Norfolk, Virginia. The day started with a parade through the city. Jackson performed live over ABC radio. The show was a smash hit, exceeding expectations when it raised more than $400,000 in bond sales.[3] In August 1945 Jackson was invited to perform at the American Negro Musical Festival in Saint Louis. In front of a crowd of sixteen thousand, Jackson re-created his iconic performance of "Going Home" as part of a memorial service to the late president. Other performers included actor Paul Muni and Lionel Hampton and his band.[4] Honorably discharged from the Navy on September 8, 1945, Jackson returned to the civilian world as a more seasoned and now more famous entertainer.

In 1947 Jackson remodeled his home in Atlanta as a replica of the Little White House. Jackson, with the blessing of his friend Mayor Hartsfield, successfully petitioned the city council of Atlanta to rename his street Whitehouse Drive. Jackson wrote a letter to Eleanor Roosevelt announcing his remodel as a personal tribute to President Roosevelt with "absolutely no commercial angles involved."[5] While it was true that he never charged ad-

Figure 7. Graham Jackson in uniform, with actor Paul Muni, Chicago, 1945. Graham W. Jackson Sr. and his service in the Navy, Plaques and Photographs, box 8, folder 4, series 7, Graham W. Jackson Sr. Papers, Archives Division, Auburn Avenue Research Library on African-American Culture and History, Fulton County Library System, Atlanta.

mission to his home, he did use images and photographs of it ubiquitously for the remainder of his career. Jackson's brand was now seen through the lens of his connection with FDR and the *Life* magazine photograph. He also worked hard to perform for as many future presidents and dignitaries as he could and to use those performances in his promotional literature. But none of this paid his bills. Themes of the next three decades of his life were ongoing financial issues, another divorce, and more alimony.

In the spring of 1947, Jackson's hometown honored him for his work. The Chestnut Street YMCA in Portsmouth, Virginia, held a ceremony honoring Jackson. One of the letters of support for this honor was from Coca-Cola executive Robert W. Woodruff: "As one of his longtime friends, I am happy to have this opportunity to join with the Young Men's Christian Association and the citizens of Portsmouth in paying tribute."[6] Jackson had a long connection with Coca-Cola executives, having performed at many company events over the years. One of the character witnesses in his 1940 criminal trial had been a Coke executive. His friendship with Woodruff would become important to him in the 1950s.

Figure 8. Graham Jackson's home at 60 Whitehouse Drive, Atlanta. Home and Studio of Graham Jackson Sr., Plaques and Photographs, box 8, folder 1, series 7, Graham W. Jackson Sr. Papers, Archives Division, Auburn Avenue Research Library on African-American Culture and History, Fulton County Library System, Atlanta.

Coca-Cola, like many multinational corporations, was in the process of rapid growth in the postwar period. A booming economy and a growing Black middle class made many corporations begin to consider more targeted marketing to Black consumers. Migration and higher wartime wages had caught the attention of advertising executives. In 1943 David J. Sullivan published a seminal essay in *Sales Management*. The article gave a prescriptive list of what not to do to market to Blacks. He recommended strongly that advertisers avoid stereotypical Black imagery such as "buxom, broadfaced, grinning mammies" or "a Negro eating watermelon, chasing chickens, or shooting craps."[7] In 1944 Sullivan published powerful statistical information showing the real strength of Black buying power, that Blacks often spend more per capita on certain categories of items and that Black buying power was two and one-half times that of South America.[8]

The architect of Coca-Cola's new approach to Black advertising was Moss Kendrick, an Atlanta native and Morehouse graduate who founded his advertising agency in 1944. His tenacious style was to approach major corporations and pitch this untapped market to them. Kendrick's pitch to Coke was very simple, to treat Black consumers as American consumers. E. Deloney Sledge, Coke's director of advertising, gave this plan the green

Figure 9. Man and woman holding Coca-Cola bottles at a counter in an unidentified bar or restaurant, Pittsburgh, Pennsylvania, June 1956. Beside the woman is a Coca-Cola advertisement for Coke in bottles that features accordion player Graham Jackson. Photo by Charles "Teenie" Harris, 1908–1998. Heinz Family Fund, 2001.35.7068. Photograph © Carnegie Museum of Art, Pittsburgh, Charles "Teenie" Harris Archive.

light. Kendrick hired Black musicians, entertainers, and sports figures to launch this campaign, and Jackson was one of the Black entertainers he hired. Jackson's smiling visage appears holding a Coke bottle in one hand while he plays his accordion with the other. Jackson signed a five-year contract in 1953 and was paid $500 for the use of his image and testimonial.[9] Among other celebrities Kendrick hired were Lionel Hampton, Duke Ellington, Count Basie, Jesse Owens, and Reese "Goose" Tatum of the Harlem Globetrotters.[10]

Jackson had a long-standing relation with Kendrick, who had been Jackson's student at Washington High School. In 1950 Kendrick was a guest on Jackson's radio show, during which he and Jackson swapped stories of Kendrick's youth.[11] In 1953 Jackson was the keynote entertainer at the Coca-Cola fiftieth anniversary celebration in Montgomery, Alabama. In 1954 Jackson was the official entertainer for the Coca-Cola Company at a Coke business conference. Jackson and Kendrick were photographed together giving the Coca-Cola Coach of the Year award to A. S. Gaither of Florida A&M University.[12] This award was a part of a larger strategy of Coke to build goodwill in the Black community.

Jackson's patron and Coke executive Woodruff was savvy on the issue of race and Coke. At its heart, it was simply an issue of creating a good atmosphere for business in Atlanta. Woodruff and Atlanta Mayor William Hartsfield worked tirelessly in the 1950s to make Atlanta the city "too busy to hate." Woodruff contended that the image of the Old South was a cruel lie. He was a supporter of many Black causes, such as the National Urban League, Tuskegee Institute, and United Negro College Fund. Woodruff was unquestionably a patriarch, owning a large plantation in rural southwestern Georgia staffed by Blacks. However, he saw racism as cruel, unnecessary, and detrimental to his business interests.[13] Critics point out that the use of Black celebrities implies that only the best and brightest can be featured in a Coke ad, while White ads had long featured average people.[14] In 1955 the success of the Black celebrity campaigns led to an expansion. Kendrick wanted to feature "everyday people." Many of these ads feature attractive Black college students like their White counterparts. These ads were featured in Black newspapers and Black magazines such as *Ebony* and *Jet*.[15]

Jackson spent his life navigating the Jim Crow caste system of the South. He managed by dint of hard work, talent, and showmanship to become relatively successful for a Black entertainer of this period. He seemed consistently to focus on being an entertainer and to scrupulously avoid public stances on controversial political issues. He became well respected by many Blacks and cultivated powerful White patrons who employed him and publicly sang his praises. In World War II he was an earnest patriot who was one of the first to volunteer for naval service. The growing White resistance movement of the late 1940s and early 1950s led to his targeting by the Ku Klux Klan.

In 1944 the White establishment recoiled at the Supreme Court's decision in *Smith v. Allwright*. This decision outlawed the long-standing practice in many southern states of all-White primary elections that were dominated by one-party rule and meant that general elections were largely moot. This exclusion of Black voters was ruled unconstitutional, opening the door for Black voters and moderate and progressive Democratic candidates. Resistance to the ruling manifested in attacks on Blacks who attempted to vote and a resurgence of the KKK. The Supreme Court ruling, coupled with the Truman administration's civil rights initiatives such as the desegregation of military and civil service, encouraged open resistance.

The Klan leadership of the late 1940s consisted of confidence men and grifters. More than a dozen Klan organizations existed across the South. Many of these organizations and their leaders faced prosecution and investigation by the FBI for several crimes such as tax evasion, fraud, and theft. FBI confidential reports describe the situation: "The field was now open to anyone who wanted to capitalize on the Klan name to promote his own brand of intolerance. . . . These various Klan organizations have not been stable. Constant bickering within and between Klan groups, mergers, reorganizations, and the shifting of membership and leadership from one organization to another had become normal procedure."[16]

The growing resistance movement in the South served as a catalyst for the resurgence of the Klan and Klan-related marches and violence. In 1948 the resurgent Klan appeared across rural Georgia. In February a rally in Swainsboro brought out two hundred robed Klansmen to march and claim they would rededicate their lives to protecting White women and maintaining the traditions of segregation of the races.[17] Longtime Klan foe and patron of Jackson, Ralph McGill of the *Atlanta Constitution*, took the Klan and White southern racists to task in a series of scathing critiques. In a March 4, 1948, column he responds to a recent cross burning in Wrightsville, Georgia:

> What the South has got to learn is that the rest of the nation regards the Southern position as wrong. . . . The South, by its failure to correct the injustices within the segregation pattern, while our laws said that the education, travel, and courthouse justice should be equal within that system, has created the state of mind in the rest of the country which makes our predicament one [for] which they have no sympathy at all. . . . But what honest person can insist that there is not justification for some of the national coldness towards us when the Ku Klux Klan burns a cross on the courthouse lawn in Wrightsville, Ga., on the eve of a primary?[18]

Other editorials titled "The KKK Still Seeks Suckers" and "Into the Hands of Our Enemies" point out how rank-and-file Klansmen were being played by their own leaders and that Klan actions were providing ammunition to those who condemned the South and segregation. In an editorial titled "Ignoring the Hooded Hoodlums" the newspaper praises African Americans who voted in the primary election in Twiggs County in the face of cross burnings and "bed-sheeted bigots." And finally, in an editorial titled "The Klan—a Traitor to the South" the paper calls all these incidents surrounding the intimidation of Black voters treasonous.[19] The Klan continued its agitation, and in August 1948 it formally endorsed race agitator Herman Talmadge for governor. Talmadge won election in November 1948.

80 · The Life and Music of Graham Jackson

The same patterns of Klan activity continued into 1949. In July the mayor of a small hamlet in southwestern Georgia, Iron City, was in a shootout with Klansmen he claimed were attacking his home. The FBI began an investigation into this incident as well as threatening letters purportedly mailed to local residents by Klansmen. The shootout had all the drama of a Hollywood blockbuster. Mayor Drake, a longtime Klan foe, had only one arm. After exchanging fire with the mayor, one of the Klansmen went to the local sheriff to swear out a warrant for assault. The mayor and his supporters arrived at the jail, and a high-speed pursuit ensued. The Klansman, a Florida electrician named Bill Hendrix, fled across the border into Alabama with the mayor and party in pursuit. Hendrix traveled thirty-eight miles to Dothan, Alabama, where he surrendered to local authorities and asked for protection from Drake. Hendrix was charged in Georgia with attempted murder and kidnapping of Mayor Drake. Hendrix and other Klansmen brought charges against Drake for the same offense. Much of this incident centered on Drake's opposition to Talmadge and his efforts to have the city council pass an antimask ordinance. In the end the ordinance passed, and Drake lost his race for mayor and was fined for discharging a firearm on a public road. The grand jury declined to indict any of the Klansmen.[20]

Jackson was politically active after the war. He was a favorite performer among the Atlanta Jewish community and regularly ran ads in the *Southern Israelite*, an influential Jewish publication. In 1948 and 1949 he was a named sponsor of National Brotherhood Week, which advocated for acceptance of all individuals regardless of race or religion. This national campaign during the 1930s and 1940s was one of the first of its kind to address interfaith and racial issues.[21] In 1950 Jackson arranged and performed campaign songs for the Atlanta NAACP membership drive. The drive was significant in that Atlanta Black voting power was becoming very influential.[22]

Klan activity continued across rural Georgia. In April 1950, a White Methodist pastor in Unadilla, Georgia, was threatened for agreeing to preach at an Easter service honoring a long-serving Black pastor. Ralph McGill excoriated those making the threats, calling them "yellow rats" and declaring "now the rat-souled gang has set itself up as more powerful than the meaning of Christ."[23]

The Seminole County High School senior class invited Jackson to perform in Donaldsonville, Georgia, at a benefit concert. Donaldsonville is the county seat, not far from Iron City. Jackson performed many concerts of this type a across Georgia and the Southeast. The senior class overwhelming voted to invite Jackson. The March 31, 1950, announcement in the *Donaldsonville News* praises him effusively:

> Graham Jackson has captivated millions of listeners by his marked ability and humbleness. He was the late President Roosevelt's favorite entertainer, the man who played "Going Home" when the immortal body of Roosevelt left Warm Springs, Georgia, the man who so unselfishly played for the crippled and blind children of Georgia. He requires no lengthy introduction to music lovers. He is known already. His unique ability allows him to play, from memory, anything ranging from "Mule Train" to the "Warsaw Concerto."[24]

It is important to take note of the description of Jackson offered by this small-town Georgia newspaper. No mention of his race is made. He is called "the man," and his accolades are many. The students are the ones requesting him. "'Many of us have heard him. More of us want to,' is the cry that has hit the ears of Seminole County Seniors."

On April 12 Jackson was notified by telegram that the concert was cancelled for "circumstances beyond our control." As it turns out, Klan members made threats to the school board and local merchants of a violent "boycott" if the concert happened. While school officials refused to comment, it was an open secret, according to news reports, that the Klan was behind this action. It is likely that the cancellation was precipitated in part by the incident in Unadilla.

The paper that was so effusive before suddenly seemed concerned about the race issue: "On Monday morning, cards signed by the 'Citizens Committee, Seminole County' were mailed and distributed in the county calling attention to the fact that Jackson was a Negro and urging that protests be raised against his appearing here."[25] The message on the cards was threatening and full of racist and Cold War rhetoric:

WARNING

A Negro by the name of "Graham Jackson" has been hired by some of our White high school teachers to have a concert at the Donalsonville high school. Have White entertainers gotten so scarce that we must hire negroes to entertain our White children? This is just a start the next thing will for sending negro and whites to school together. We protest this type (of) entertainment and demand this stop. This is the communist plan to mix negro and white, Paul Robeson the negro

82 · The Life and Music of Graham Jackson

communist will be singing next. This negro was hired to come here without the consent of the school board. Write or call your board member and protest. Let's stop this now.

Citizens Committee
Seminole County[26]

The cancellation caused indignation among many in Atlanta. An editorial in the *Atlanta Constitution* of April 13, titled "Another Victory for Hate," was clear:

> Once again, a decent community has been victimized by unnecessary fear. Once again a few un-American, un-Christian goons and their misguided allies in indecency have held up the entire state of Georgia to shame. . . . Graham Jackson, a Negro musician of fine character with an excellent war record . . . has played for literally thousands of audiences and is in much demand because of his skill and personality. The whole town was behind the benefit and had planned to participate, but in neighboring communities where the Klan scum has some minor strength, there was resentment. This is evil.[27]

Jackson received much support from the public over this incident. A White supporter, A. S. Perrin, mailed him a check for the amount lost in the concert. Several letters of support published in local papers condemned the Klan and called for swift action. An editorial in the *Sylvania Telephone*, a small paper in southern Georgia, compared the Klan to the Gestapo of Nazi Germany and further condemned the state for failing to intervene.[28] Ironically, some months later the Donaldsonville paper ran a front-page story and a photo of Jackson with Governor Herman Talmadge. Cryptically, it seemed to skewer the recent protests and cancellations:

> WELL, LO AND BEHOLD, just who is this? One of them is Herman Talmadge who seeks re-election as Governor of this state. The main plank in his platform is segregation. He yells "anti-n-" at the top of his voice. Let's see who else is in the picture. If our eyes do not deceive us, it is Graham Jackson, the negro artist, who was recently barred from giving a concert in Seminole County on the grounds that it was a mingling of the races. Many of the same group that kept Graham Jackson from appearing before a white audience are supporting Herman Talmadge. From the above photo, it seems that the Lion and the Lamb have lain down together.[29]

Figure 10. Graham Jackson with Strom Thurmond and Herman Talmadge (*center*), date and location unknown. Graham W. Jackson Sr. and noted local and national individuals, Plaques and Photographs, box 8, folder 6, series 7, Graham W. Jackson Sr. papers, Archives Division, Auburn Avenue Research Library on African-American Culture and History, Fulton County Library System, Atlanta.

In many ways the threats made against Jackson produced more work opportunities, particularly among business and state leaders. Many clearly saw the threats as an injustice to a highly respected Black entertainer. Just a few weeks later he performed for a convention of Georgia county commissioners. In May he was a headliner of the Greater Atlanta Music Festival. He served as master of ceremonies at Morris Brown College's Herndon Field at an event cosponsored by the *Atlanta Constitution* and the Georgia Music Educators Association. High school musicians in the thousands performed at three stadiums, with more than 40,000 people in attendance.[30] In June Jackson was the headline performer for a community health screening at which more than 2,500 people received free chest x-rays to screen for tuberculosis.[31]

Atlanta was practicing more moderate racial policies that ran counter to the rural tactics of the Klan. In 1948 the city hired eight Black police officers.[32] Their beats were limited to Black neighborhoods, but this was seen by moderates and Black leaders as a giant step. In 1950 Jackson served as jury foreman on a mixed-race jury in Fulton County Superior Court.[33] In 1952 he used his city hall connections to be appointed as a "special" police officer. This reserve force's task was to patrol neighborhoods, much

84 · The Life and Music of Graham Jackson

like a modern neighborhood watch. Jackson took credit for breaking up numerous fights and preventing three car break-ins in his neighborhood. He stated that before his patrols, "thugs frequently would catch unwary pedestrians, particularly elderly Negroes, and 'lay a razor on their necks.'"[34]

Jackson was now in his late forties, a seasoned performer with regional fame and a modicum of national recognition. One goal he always craved in his professional career was real national fame and stardom. For all his breakthroughs into radio in the 1930s, his image as Roosevelt's entertainer, and his patriotic service in World War II, he was still a national footnote. He dominated radio successfully in the Southeast. Numerous stories in the press in the late 1930s and early 1940s seemed to portend that his big break was coming soon on the silver screen. But reported auditions with talent scouts and meetings with producers never panned out. Now he eyed television as the next great breakthrough. An opportunity came in 1951 that might have been that breakthrough he had been seeking, to perform on Ed Sullivan's *Toast of the Town*.

The invitation came because of Jackson's connections with Georgia Governor Herman Talmadge. Jackson performed many times for the governor and his father, Governor Eugene Talmadge. The younger Talmadge sent a letter to Sullivan recommending Jackson: "Ed, we have a wonderful performer down here. You could cover up the piano with a big heavy cloth on it, and he can play as you have never heard someone play."[35] The irony of Sullivan following the advice of the segregationist governor cannot be lost. Jackson flew to New York and performed on June 17, 1951. His pay of $750 is perhaps the largest single payment he ever received for any one performance.[36] Video of the performance shows Jackson being invited to teach several New York Yankees baseball players how to play Saint Louis blues on the piano.[37] Then Sullivan asked him to play the piano and accordion simultaneously. Jackson appeared with a typical Sullivan variety of entertainers. The headliner was Sullivan's friend Arthur Godfrey, who had his own show but made appearances on *Toast of the Town* from time to time. Metropolitan Opera soprano Blanche Thebom performed as well. Burlesque comic Pinky Lee came next. Lee was known for various stints on television, including hosting the *Gumby Show*. Actor, writer, and professional heckler Pat C. "Patsy" Flick also performed along with dancer Nanci Crompton.

Sullivan and Talmadge would not remain on friendly terms for long. Sullivan had advocated for Black entertainers and athletes for years. As a young sportswriter in 1926 for the *New York Evening Graphic*, Sullivan attacked New York University for agreeing to bench Black players in a game

Figure 11. Graham Jackson performing on Ed Sullivan's *Toast of the Town* television show, June 17, 1951.

against the University of Georgia. He recalled, "For the next week I castigated NYU's immorality and suggested that their Hall of Fame be torn down and transferred to some other university with a higher regard for a boy's dignity."[38] Sullivan challenged the expectations of network executives and sponsors on radio and his long-running television show. In 1950 Sullivan argued that television played a critical role in taking the struggle for civil rights directly into living rooms. "Discovering" a lesser-known Black artist like Jackson was right in Sullivan's wheelhouse. Sullivan revered less-known artists such as Peg Leg Bates, Pigmeat Markham, and Tim Moore of *Amos 'n' Andy* fame, and he was the first to introduce the Harlem Globetrotters to White viewers. The *Pittsburg Courier* praised Sullivan for presenting Black entertainers as an integral part of his show with no hint of bias.[39]

Sullivan was not the only impresario on television who was willing to challenge southern notions of propriety. Steve Allen, Ted Mack, and Arthur Godfrey also took pride in booking Black artists. Governor Talmadge aimed his ire at Godfrey in January 1952 when Godfrey presented a mixed-race barbershop quartet called the Mariners on his show. Talmadge reacted to this affront to segregation with a blistering attack on Godfrey and threats of a boycott across the South. Talmadge was angry that Blacks might perform with scantily clad White women and that Black and White children might perform together on a "socially equal basis."[40] Godfrey responded strongly: "I'm sorry for his Excellency, Governor Talmadge, but as long as

Figure 12. Graham Jackson with NBC's *Today Show* host Dave Garroway in Warm Springs, 1958. Stuart A. Rose Manuscript, Archives, and Rare Book Library, Emory University, Atlanta.

I am on the show the Mariners are going to stay with me. We also have some colored boys in Korea. I wonder if the governor knows that!"[41] CBS supported Godfrey, as did his friend Ed Sullivan, who called Talmadge "stupid and vicious" and went further in his own column: "The statement made by Georgia Gov. Talmadge that Negroes should be barred from TV is a complete contradiction. When we used Atlanta Negro pianist Graham Jackson, Gov. Talmadge sent a very warm letter of congratulations, lauding Jackson as an outstanding citizen of Atlanta. Figure it out."[42] Sullivan said he preferred to recognize Jackson's patron Ralph McGill as a more accurate spokesman for the South than Talmadge.[43] This back-and-forth had taken an even stranger turn. Talmadge invited Jackson to perform at the governor's mansion to mark the start of the legislative session. Shortly after that, Talmadge named Jackson the official entertainer of the governor of Georgia.[44] In the end, Jackson appeared only once on Sullivan's show but made more television appearances in the decade.

In May 1956 NBC's *Today Show*, hosted by Dave Garroway, broadcast live from Atlanta's downtown Hurt Park. Jackson was one of the headliners of the show. In total, he performed eight songs during the three-hour broadcast. The show also featured a Rich's Department Store fashion show, a tour of the Atlanta Cyclorama, and an interview with former governor

Figure 13. Graham Jackson with Eleanor Roosevelt at a March of Dimes event in Warm Springs, 1958. Graham W. Jackson Sr. and noted local and national individuals, plaques and photographs, box 8, folder 6, series 7, Graham W. Jackson Sr. Papers, Archives Division, Auburn Avenue Research Library on African-American Culture and History, Fulton County Library System, Atlanta.

and now Senator Herman Talmadge.[45] In January 1958, to celebrate the twentieth anniversary of the March of Dimes polio campaign, *The Today Show* broadcast live from Warm Springs. This major celebration included interviews with Eleanor Roosevelt and Warm Springs Foundation president Basil O'Conner. The show originated from Roosevelt Hall on the campus of the Warm Springs Institute. Jackson performed "Going Home" as he had in 1945.[46]

Jackson performed on radio for nearly three decades. In 1949 he began a long association with WERD radio in Atlanta. WERD was significant because it was the first Black-owned station in the nation. The station started in 1948 under White ownership. After experiencing management shakeups that led the station to go off the air, it was purchased September 1949 by Jesse B. Blayton Sr. He had moved to Atlanta in 1922 to work in the insurance business. In 1930 he joined the business faculty of Atlanta University and continued his work expanding Black business interests in the city. Blayton was one of the few Black certified public accountants in the United States and a successful consultant who seized the opportunity to purchase the defunct radio station. He relocated the studio from Broad Street downtown to the heart of the Black business district on Auburn Avenue. He stated that his purpose was "to put on programs which will aid in creating more goodwill between the races here."[47]

WERD received consistent high praise for its community efforts throughout the decade. The FCC praised its unique status as a source of racial understanding and reconciliation. The station was a model of interracial programming and staffing. The lineup featured a who's who of Black leaders and entertainers in the community. William Boyd, chair of political science at Atlanta University, served as a news analyst. Professor Baldwin Burroughs of Spelman College served as dramatics director. The station featured live interviews with Black notables who passed through Atlanta such as Joe Louis and Cab Calloway. Graham Jackson was one of the featured artists with a thirty-minute show each morning, Monday through Saturday. His show originated from his home studio at 60 Whitehouse Drive.[48]

Jackson broadcast a mixture of musical numbers and interviews on his program. Many of his interviews were interspersed with songs or hymns that were important to the guest or the topic of the interview. Part of his shtick involved his canary, Mario. The bird was trained to sing along with Jackson and his organ. Jackson placed a microphone next to the cage to capture the songbird's melodies. In May 1952, seven-year-old Gladys Knight was his guest. Knight leaped to national fame on *Ted Mack's Original Amateur Hour. Jackson dedicated a special *Sunday Serenade* broadcast to welcome her back to Atlanta. A photograph shows him greeting her at Terminal Station with his accordion as she returned from New York.[49] In November 1953 Jackson performed in the "Biggest Show of '53" at the Atlanta City Auditorium. The headliner for this show was Nat King Cole.[50] Cole organized a series of appearances across the nation under the "Biggest Show" moniker. These were integrated shows with Cole, other national headliners such as the Duke Ellington Orchestra, and local talent like Jackson. The November performance was only a few months after Cole suffered a near-fatal bleeding ulcer.[51]

Jackson performed for his third US president in late 1953. Dwight Eisenhower, a friend of Coke executive Robert Woodruff and golfer Bobby Jones, often vacationed at Augusta National Golf Course in eastern Georgia and visited there twenty-nine times during his presidency. After his election in 1952 the club decided to construct a special cabin for Ike on the tenth tee.

The cabin was a seven-room, three-story cottage with a basement designed for Secret Service use. It is known as Mamie's Cabin or sometimes the Eisenhower Cottage and was completed in late fall 1953. On November 7 Jackson traveled to Bethesda, Maryland, and performed for Eisenhower at the famous Burning Tree Golf Club. A few weeks later Eisenhower departed Washington at 9 a.m. on November 24 and flew to Fort Benning, Georgia, and then traveled by car across the state to Augusta to spend Thanksgiving at the cottage. On Friday, November 27, Jackson performed for Eisenhower at the cabin. In later press releases Jackson called these "Command Performances," though it is unlikely that Eisenhower requested Jackson's attendance. Jackson's history of performing at Augusta National and his connections with Woodruff and Jones seem the most likely reason this performance was arranged.[52] In January 1954 *Jet* reported that Jackson was now the "official" musician for Eisenhower when he would visit Augusta.[53]

Jackson was asked in a 1957 interview by journalist Ernest Rogers about many of the well-known individuals he had performed for over the years. He happily responded and added what the favorite song of each was. Woodruff, head of Coca-Cola, loved the hymn "Just a Closer Walk with Thee." Chip Robert, the Atlanta businessman who introduced Jackson to FDR, enjoyed "Happy Days Are Here Again," and longtime patron Cason Callaway asked for "You Tell Me Your Dream." President Harry Truman listened to "Missouri Waltz," and for Ike and Mamie Eisenhower the song was "Blue Ridge Mountains." Georgia Senator Richard Russell called for "High Noon" and Senator Herman Talmadge for "Home on the Range."[54]

Jackson remained no stranger to legal scrapes. He had faced lawsuits and divorce in the 1930s as well as his infamous trial and civil suit over an alleged sexual assault on the campus of Washington High School. He managed to survive those legal problems using his charm and a plethora of well-known White character witnesses. In early 1951 Jackson filed a civil suit against five musicians who had performed with him for decades. Jackson claimed that the musicians ran ads for gigs using his name without his knowledge. Guitarist Frank Sawyer responded that the suit arose from a misunderstanding. Sawyer stated that he usually served as the band's manager and simply placed the ad to seek work for all of them, but Jackson claimed it was a conspiracy to defraud him and sought $25,000. A hearing was held on March 30 in Fulton County Superior Court, with the intention of the case going to trial in June. The suit was quickly dismissed by the court as groundless.[55] On June 19 the American Federation of Musicians Local 416 in Hornell, New York, voted unanimously to suspend Jackson

90 · The Life and Music of Graham Jackson

for six months and fine him $150 for violating union rules that required him to bring the issue to the union before filing suit. Jackson appealed the suspension and eventually was cleared by the national union.[56] It is unclear when Jackson joined Local 416, an integrated union in upstate New York. Prior to 1945 most musicians unions across the nation were segregated and separate.

In the summer of 1952, Lurlene Jackson filed for divorce. As with his first divorce, the contested grounds dealt with charges of infidelity. Lurlene charged that Jackson was "indiscreet" with his secretaries. Further, she alleged that he failed to show her any attention and often kept a large crowd of people at their home at all hours of the day and night. She also charged that he had organized a realty company to keep their finances a secret from her. She sought $500 per month in alimony, attorney's fees, and a division of property. She claimed Jackson earned from $25,000 to $30,000 per year. Jackson's response was pure Jackson. He claimed the case was "all a conspiracy, born of professional jealousy to destroy his reputation."[57]

The case dragged on for a year. In October 1952 at a contentious hearing, the two sides faced off. Lurlene was granted temporary $50 monthly alimony payments pending a jury trial. Jackson's legal team vigorously assailed her claims concerning his income, introducing tax returns showing his net income in 1951 was just $1,491.58. Lurlene openly laughed in court when this statement was presented. Jackson then worked his charm on the judge, spinning a tale of woe as to his financial straits. He claimed that was the worst year he had in twelve years, that his bank account often had between three to seven dollars in it, and that at best he might clear $60 from a $300 gig. Lurlene's attorney engaged in a blistering cross-examination seeking to establish that Jackson was hiding funds and could not possibly own two homes on his reported pay. He hammered repeatedly at Graham for owning a $4,500 Cadillac. Jackson was long known to drive only the biggest and best Cadillacs.[58] A jury trial finally settled the issue in June 1953. Jackson was ordered to pay $125 per month alimony plus $350 in attorney's fees and court costs.

In April 1956 Lurlene went back to court seeking $750 in unpaid alimony.[59] In September 1957, Jackson was found in contempt and ordered to pay the $750. Jackson pleaded with the court, claiming his phone was about to be cut off, but he did admit under cross-examination that he still owned a 1954 Ford and a 1956 Cadillac.[60] He was back in court in 1961 for failure to pay alimony again. This time he was ordered to pay an additional $25 per month until his debt was caught up. It appears he struggled to pay his alimony commitments for most of the rest of his life.

Lurlene continued her teaching career after the divorce. In 1962 she remarried and took the last name Garland. In 1990, suffering from dementia, she was living in the care of a nephew, and her life came to a sad end. Her nephew returned home to find his screen door kicked out and his aunt missing. She was found dead in a nearby creek. Investigators found no signs of foul play and suspected she wandered off and fell into the creek and drowned.[61]

As with his first divorce, Jackson wasted little time in remarrying. Thirty days after the divorce from Lurlene, on July 2, 1953, Jackson married Helen Catherine Balton. Jackson reportedly met Helen around Easter of 1953 while he was performing in Birmingham. Helen was a 1951 graduate of Miles College in Birmingham. She was twenty and Jackson was fifty-one. She was a teacher, the child of William and Gertrude Balton of Birmingham. Gertrude was a few months younger than her new son-in-law. William Balton worked for many years as a chauffeur, and according to census data, Helen had several siblings. Her older brother was attending business school as part of the National Youth Administration in 1940. In 1949, when Helen was attending Miles College, her father was employed in the lab at nearby Roberts Field, now Sumpter Smith Air National Guard Base. While both of her parents had little education, she and several of her siblings were able to attend high school and some college.

Helen described in a 1995 interview with Andrew Hill, a writer and former student of Jackson, how that courtship happened and how Jackson was able to set her parents minds at ease: Her mother "demanded that Graham bring me back to Birmingham because she didn't approve. And he did the next day. We knew at that point we were married. It didn't matter. And Graham was traveling back and forth. He wouldn't be here that much anyway. So I went back to Birmingham and stayed two months. And Graham, instead of coming to Atlanta, he came to my parents' house. Every other night, he would fly in from a job to Atlanta. They got to know him and loved him."[62]

On October 27, 1954, Graham Washington Jackson Jr. was born to Graham and Helen at the new Hughes Spaulding Pavilion Hospital in Atlanta. This state-of-the-art hospital for Black Atlanta was the result of a concerted effort among White business leaders and philanthropists to provide needed health care to the growing Black population of Georgia. Attorney Hughes

Spaulding, its founder and namesake, credited a conversation he had in 1946 with Margret Mitchell for the genesis of the idea. Mitchell's longtime laundress Carrie Holbrook, an African American, was dying of cancer and had no viable health care options. Mitchell donated $1,000 toward the project. The result of this campaign was a new 130-bed hospital to serve Black residents.[63]

Press reports about the Jacksons' son's birth indicate that the hospital switchboard was jammed with congratulatory calls, requiring additional workers to be sent over from the White Grady Hospital to assist.[64] Jackson was naturally ecstatic with the birth of his namesake, finally becoming a father at age fifty-two. For Jackson, whose own father disappeared from his life at age three, the chance to be a father must have brought great joy. When Graham Jr. was about six months old Jackson proudly showed him off to friends during a visit to Portsmouth. Jackson shared how his son was a "dream come true" for him. "God must have had a hand in this," he shared with friends as tears came to his eyes. Observers noted that this joy must have gone far to fill an emptiness in Jackson's life given his challenging childhood. Jackson shared how he had always dreamed of being a father.[65]

On March 13, 1958, a second son, Gerald Wayne Jackson, was born to Graham and Helen. Helen went into labor while Graham was performing in Montreal at the Sheraton-Mount Royal Hotel. Jackson quickly hopped on a flight and made it back in the nick of time.[66] Helen Jackson considered Graham to be a wonderful and doting father. Part of the reason was his rather advanced age when he became a father:

> Graham Jr.'s first car was given to him by his father at age 12 or 13 when he finished St. Paul of the Cross. That was 8th grade. He kept that one for three years, and he got his second car in high school. By the time he was in college where he attended Georgia State and Morris Brown, he got his third car. And Gerald, when he finished 8th grade at St. Paul of the Cross, he got his first car. He got his second car in high school, and his third car in college. By the time they finished college he [Jackson] had bought them three cars each. Now, as I look at it, he was trying to provide what he knew because of the age . . . his age. Because when he died he was 79, and Graham and Gerald were about 18 and 21. So that was young. And I think, as I look back on it now, he was trying to provide them with some of the happiness he would have given them later in life. He felt that he was getting older. But when he started giving them the cars he was not that old.[67]

Figure 14. Graham Jackson and his choir. Graham W. Jackson Sr. and singers, box 8, folder 3, series 7, Graham W. Jackson Sr. Papers, Archives Division, Auburn Avenue Research Library on African-American Culture and History, Fulton County Library System, Atlanta.

    Jackson clearly faced enormous financial pressure now that he had two young children as well as continuing legal issues with alimony payments. He began a collaboration with Westminster Records in 1956 and worked with noted organists Dick Leibert, chief organist at Radio City Music Hall, and Ann Leaf, who was often called "America's First Lady of the Organ." Leibert wanted to record on the "Mighty Wurlitzer Organ" of the Byrd Theatre in Richmond, Virginia, because of its lush sound. Leibert invited Jackson and Leaf, and these collaborations resulted in several Westminster albums among them. Jackson released *Solid Jackson* in 1957. The album features a number of standards such as "Sweet Georgia Brown," "Caravan," and Jackson's own "Shortnin' Bread Stomp." *Organ* magazine called these "outstanding records."[68] In 1958 he released an album of spirituals to much acclaim. Also published by Westminster Records, this album featured the Graham Jackson Choir, with arrangements by Jackson of several classic spirituals. The cover photo continued the plantation revue theme he had used successfully for several decades. The photo shows Jackson and the choir members

94 · The Life and Music of Graham Jackson

in slave-type garb in a boat in a swamplike setting complete with Spanish moss. This motif was still a popular one. The album was lauded by critics for its musical style, and news media described Jackson on the Wurlitzer organ as "brilliant" and "superb."[69] The album was re-released in 1967 under the title *Every Time I Hear the Spirit*.

Black spirituals have a long history and tradition dating to the earliest days of America. A blending of traditional African and Afro-Caribbean sounds with the hymnology of the first and second Great Awakenings, enslaved and free Blacks developed a distinctive style before the Civil War. Churches became almost totally segregated after Reconstruction, and Black spirituals continued to develop a distinctness. Black groups such as the Fisk Jubilee Singers popularized the style in the late nineteenth century. White artists dating back to Stephen Foster appropriated many of the key styles of the genre. By the 1920s the rise of ragtime, blues, and jazz incorporated many of those musical elements, especially call and response and syncopation. Spirituals played a prominent role in the civil rights movement starting in Montgomery in 1955. Martin Luther King Jr. considered the great spiritual singer Mahalia Jackson to be his muse, often calling her to sing to him over the phone in especially dark times.

7

"The Familiar Strains of Dixie, Played by Graham Jackson"

Graham Jackson entered the fourth decade of his career facing challenges. The musical landscape was rapidly changing. Rock and roll and Motown dampened interest in old standards and the American songbook, two of Jackson's strengths. Organ and accordion music lost popularity on radio and in record sales. As Jackson approached his late fifties, he faced real legal and financial challenges and had no nest egg for retirement. Staying current on his alimony payments seemed at times impossible. In August 1961 he received notice that his bank account was overdrawn on two occasions. In December 1963 he received legal notice that his home was facing sale for unpaid loans. Somehow he caught up, but again in 1966 he received a letter from an attorney pleading with him to pay $200 toward his house note. Jackson responded, "Your letter is encouraging, but I need a little more cash money to satisfy you and Mr. Whitman which I hope to have in a few days."[1]

Jobs were scarce. Many of Jackson's old patrons were dying. He was now called in this decade to perform at funerals for these notables, patrons such as Cason Callaway in 1961. One constant that continued was his association with FDR. With very few exceptions, on April 12 Jackson would make the trek to Warm Springs to perform at memorial services for the late president. He was there in 1952 to perform next to Shoumatoff's *Unfinished Portrait* of FDR when the painting returned to be displayed at the Little White House. He was there for *The Today Show* live broadcast in 1958. In 1960 he performed for his fourth president, Senator John F. Kennedy.

Kennedy's road to his victory in Georgia in 1960 started early in his political career. In 1956 southern Democrats championed JFK's nomination for a place on the Stevenson ticket as vice president. This support might seem at first glance odd, given that Kennedy was a northeastern liberal scion of a powerful Boston political dynasty. However, Guy Paul Land argues, Kennedy satisfied two key problems conservative southern Democrats faced, that is, maintaining party loyalty and unity and at the same time not exhibiting the "taint of active liberalism."[2] His personal charm, combined with his middle-of-the-road approach to controversial issues such as civil rights, made him the most palatable choice of conservative southern Democrats. Though he received most votes from southern delegates, in the end the nomination went to Estes Kefauver of Tennessee. Kennedy was a gracious loser and immediately set to work campaigning vigorously for the Stevenson-Kefauver ticket.

Though denied the vice presidency, and with a subsequent Democratic loss to Eisenhower, Kennedy gained the label of party stalwart and began to strategize for the top spot in the 1960 campaign. He and his staff quickly developed a southern strategy that would use a White bloc of southern Democratic votes combined with his existing northeastern liberal bloc and a midwestern labor bloc.[3] This combination was seen as the key to victory in 1960. To implement the strategy, Kennedy started a series of speechmaking trips across the South in 1957. He visited Georgia in the spring of 1957 and gave the commencement address at the University of Georgia.

Once Kennedy secured the nomination in 1960, his team decided on one campaign visit to Georgia. They would not go to "liberal" Atlanta. Rather, they chose a traditional and safe venue for JFK, Roosevelt's Little White House. David K. Adams argues that the Kennedy campaign made liberal use of FDR and New Deal imagery and motifs throughout his campaign, so much so that Adams notes direct parallels between the optimism of "New Frontierism" and a call for a bright future and FDR's constant optimism.[4] Kennedy faced some early criticism from the grand old lady of the party, Eleanor Roosevelt. Placating her concerns was also a clear part of this FDR strategy. What better way to accomplish all these goals than to stand next to the *Unfinished Portrait* in front of the Little White House with Graham Jackson at his side playing the accordion?

The visit was a whirlwind. On October 10, 1960, JFK's plane landed in nearby Columbus, Georgia. After Kennedy made brief remarks, the motorcade made the short drive to Warm Springs. After they toured the grounds, Kennedy and party assembled on the front porch of the home in front of a packed crowd of supporters. Jackson opened the ceremony by playing a new song called "I'm Going up to Washington." Kennedy ruffled a few racist feathers by greeting "Mr. Jackson" when thanking the platform party and then departed by open car for nearby LaGrange, Georgia. Schoolchildren lined the streets of LaGrange as JFK motored to Callaway Airport. The

"The Familiar Strains of Dixie, Played by Graham Jackson" · 97

Figure 15. Presidential candidate John F. Kennedy speaking to a crowd at the Little White House in Warm Springs, October 10, 1960. *Atlanta Journal-Constitution* via Associated Press.

author's parents, local high school students, were in that crowd. Kennedy again raised racist eyebrows when he had the car stop so he could shake hands with a local Black principal who was on the roadside with his pupils.[5] After making more brief remarks he departed for South Carolina. The entire visit from landing to departure lasted about three and one-half hours.[6]

Kennedy's murder in 1963 elevated Lyndon Johnson to the presidency. By early 1964 Johnson made history in advancing a civil rights agenda while simultaneously seeking to win that year's election as president in his own right. Though he officially was undecided as to his plans for the Democratic nomination, Johnson knew that to seal passage of the monumental Civil Rights Act of 1964 and win the nomination and the general election, visits to the South were required. A Texan with his own baggage as a solid-South White Democrat, LBJ possessed the moral and regional credentials to force practitioners of massive resistance to accept the inevitable and move on

98 · The Life and Music of Graham Jackson

from the issue of segregation. He planned a cross-states visit that would allow him to bring his message directly to the people of the South and force reluctant southern politicians to appear in public with him. Johnson's approval ratings were high, and he intended to use them to his advantage. His visit to Georgia in May 1964 was the opportunity for Jackson to perform for his fifth president.

Johnson and party arrived in Atlanta late on Thursday, May 7. After spending the night at the Dinkler-Plaza Hotel, formerly the Ansley Hotel, Johnson gave a short live television address from the hotel. He then proceeded by vehicle in an impromptu parade through downtown. Crowds in the tens of thousands cheered. The visit is significant in that Johnson directly addressed civil rights in his remarks to the legislators and the crowd:

> Because the Constitution requires it, because justice demands it, we must protect the constitutional rights of all of our citizens, regardless of race, religion, or the color of their skin. For I would remind you that we are a very small minority, living in a world of 3 billion people, where we are outnumbered 17 to 1, and no one of us is fully free until all of us are fully free, and the rights of no single American are truly secure until the rights of all Americans are secure. Democratic order rests on faithfulness to law. Those who deny the protection of the Constitution to others imperil the safety of their own liberties and the satisfaction of their own desires. So we now move forward under that Constitution to give every man his right to work at a job.[7]

The strong medicine LBJ delivered was enthusiastically accepted by the crowds. The *Atlanta Constitution* predicted on the morning of his arrival that he could expect a "warm and hearty greeting from the state of Georgia."[8] The *New York Times* reported, "The display of enthusiasm was all the more extraordinary because he used the occasion to reiterate his strong commitment to action on civil rights—and was applauded for it."[9]

Graham Jackson was front and center in the crowd. He was able to position himself close to LBJ because of his celebrity and through his connections with the Atlanta mayor's office and the governor. Jackson also communicated with members of the Secret Service that day, some whom he knew from his time at Warm Springs. His connections allowed him to play two quick songs for LBJ. The Secret Service officers suggested he play "The Yellow Rose of Texas" and "Happy Days" for the president. A photograph shows Graham at the front of a throng of people shaking hands with the president.[10]

Figure 16. Graham Jackson reaching to shake hands with Lyndon Johnson in Atlanta, May 7, 1964. Bill Wilson Photo Collection, VIS 99.83.16, James G. Kenan Research Center, Atlanta History Center.

Despite his moments near the spotlight, changing tastes in music and fewer bookings meant that Jackson had to hustle once again to make ends meet. He found steady employment over the next two decades performing nightly in antebellum-themed restaurants. This was not inconsistent with Jackson's decades of plantation revue–themed performances. A number of these establishments started in Atlanta after the buzz surrounding the *Gone with the Wind* craze of the late 1930s. They had several common threads: glorification of the Lost Cause mythology of the Old South, caricatures of Blacks as mammies or Uncle Remus characters, and a harkening back to the simplicity of the good old days.

Michael Kammen argues in his classic work on American culture, *Mystic Chords of Memory*, that collective memory is a socially constructed artifice that is largely shaped by the dominant culture to stimulate a shared sense of the past.[11] The danger of subscribing to collective memory is that it can empower the dominant culture and demean or ignore other cultural understandings of the past. The irony of the growth of the establishments like those where Jackson performed is that they were in ascension as the racial and social realities of the region were in flux and change; the nostalgia of these restaurants would comfort locals, attract tourists, and perpetuate racial stereotypes.

One of the first of these to open was Mammy's Shanty on Peachtree Street, just north of downtown. Opening around 1930, it predated publication of *Gone with the Wind*. The imagery used in the ads and menus for the restaurant represents sickening examples of tropes and stereotypes of Blacks. The restaurant extended to Pappy's Plantation Lounge and the Pickaninny coffee shop, and it had Uncle Tom's roast turkey on the children's menu. We have no evidence that Jackson performed at Mammy's Shanty. The restaurant gained national infamy in 1968 when a receipt from it was discovered among assassin James Earl Ray's effects left behind after he fled the country. Ray had London broil on March 23, 1968, at Mammy's, just days before he murdered Martin Luther King Jr. in Memphis.[12] It seems no surprise that Ray would enjoy the décor of the Shanty such as Black women in head scarves and wooden name tags on twine around their necks. The place closed in 1972.

Another antebellum establishment opened in nearby Smyrna, Georgia, in 1941. Aunt Fanny's Cabin was like Mammy's Shanty but claimed to be much more authentic. The structure was touted as a former slave cabin, and the recipes and notions sold were all based on the recipes of a purported former "slave," Fanny Williams. Isoline Campbell MacKenna, the founder of Aunt Fanny's, used a relocated 1890s tenant shack from her nearby family farm. "Aunt" Fanny had served as a cook for the family but was born around 1870 and had never lived in the cabin. Like Mammy's, Aunt Fanny's featured many of the same tropes and stereotypes such as mammy servers and singing and dancing Black children. Jackson performed there in 1955 for an Air Force party sponsored by the nearby Lockheed Corporation.[13] A 1984 *Washington Post* story describes in detail the practice of young Black boys with menu boards and slave-garbed waitresses. The *Post* describes Aunt Fanny's as the South finally choosing to laugh at itself and the spectacle as a caricature of its old self.[14] The business closed in the early 1990s. The city of Smyrna opted to purchase the building and relocate it based on the belief that it had been a slave cabin. Upon relocating it, historians determined it was constructed in the 1890s. It served as a local history museum and venue.[15] Recently its racist history resulted in its closure. The City of Smyrna placed it for sell, indicating it would likely be demolished if it was not purchased and relocated. In the summer of 2022 the building was demolished.

Another long-standing racist fixture was the Dobbs House restaurant in the terminal of Atlanta Municipal Airport, which some people once suggested naming Scarlett O'Hara Airport and now is named Hartsfield-Jackson for two former mayors. The Dobbs House featured an Uncle Remus greeter sitting in a chair by the entrance of the restaurant. Alfonso Smith worked for many years as this character. He was straight out of central casting, the spitting image of James Basket's Uncle Remus in Disney's 1946 *Song of the South*. Many consider the film the most controversial and racist Disney movie ever produced. It was based on Atlantan Joel Chandler Harris's "Uncle Remus" stories. While the film is set during Reconstruction, its use of Black vernacular and racist imagery was challenged upon its release. Ironically, Basket won a special Academy Award for his performance, the first African American man to do so, and the song "Zip-a-Dee-Doo-Dah" won the Oscar for best song.[16]

By 1955 Black media and leaders were openly critical of the Dobbs House. As air travel increased in the decade, more and more Black patrons began to complain about the establishment. *Jet* magazine ran a story on March 17, 1955, featuring a photo of a smiling Smith in character next to a bale of cotton. The story states, "Negroes, using airport facilities during stopovers, have termed the sight 'disgusting.'"[17] In 1956 Martin Luther King Jr. was on a layover in Atlanta traveling to Virginia. After mechanical issues delayed his flight, he got a voucher for a meal from the airline. Upon entering the Dobbs House, he quickly faced discrimination. He wrote in a letter, "After getting in the Dobbs House I was taken to the back and offered a seat behind a dingy compartment which totally set me off from other passengers. I immediately refused, stating I would rather go a week without eating under such conditions."[18] Fresh off his victory in Montgomery, King considered legal action but decided against it. After being denied service again in 1959, King contacted attorney Donald L. Hollowell to make plans to file suit. However, another suit from a Black traveler from Birmingham Alabama, *Coke v. City of Atlanta et al.* (1960), resulted in a federal court order to desegregate the restaurant.

In the late 1950s a chain of restaurants opened in Atlanta named Johnny Reb's. There were four Atlanta locations. The exteriors were shrines of neo-Confederate imagery, including full-size figures in gray and butternut (many Confederate soldiers wore home-dyed uniforms that were more tan than gray), a cannon, and the ubiquitous Confederate battle standard, known colloquially as the "Rebel flag." The flag had gained prominence as a symbol since the 1954 Supreme Court *Brown* decision to desegregate schools. The Georgia legislature voted in 1956 to change the state flag to include Confederate battle standard symbols as part of a "massive resistance" to desegregation. This remained the flag of Georgia until 2001.[19]

Another factor that influenced the design aesthetic of the restaurants was the pending hundredth anniversary of the Civil War and a revived interest in Confederate history and symbols. One of the nation's largest Confederate memorials, Stone Mountain, was purchased by the state of Georgia in 1958. Home of the world's largest bas-relief carving, the face of the mountain depicts Jefferson Davis, Robert E. Lee, and Stonewall Jackson on horseback. The carving was started in the 1920s as the brainchild of a member of the United Daughters of the Confederacy and a KKK member. The original sculptor chosen was none other than Gutzon Borglum of later Mount Rushmore fame. The project languished over the years, but the purchase by the state was another step in the massive resistance programs of the 1950s. The park officially opened on April 14, 1965, the hundredth anniversary of Lincoln's assassination! Work on the carvings was completed in 1972. The park has remained controversial as an homage to White nationalism and Lost Causeism ever since.[20] (Full disclosure: the author's parents married in November 1965 and honeymooned at the park.)

The Johnny Reb's chain was the brainchild of Stanley "Tubby" Davis, who entered the hospitality industry in the early 1940s with a small eatery in downtown Atlanta. Over time he would develop the Johnny Reb's marquee as well as the better-known chain of David Bros. cafeterias, which covered several states across the Southeast and remained in business until the early 1990s. The Marietta location, off the four-lane US Highway 41, was the largest and known as Johnny Reb's Dixieland. The views from the parking lot were of Kennesaw Mountain Battlefield to the north and the skyline of Atlanta to the south. The establishment was the world's largest Confederate restaurant in 1959. A March 30, 1959, *Atlanta Constitution* story describes it this way: "Stepping into the lobby, you are greeted by many clever effects in Southern-type décor. A spinning wheel sits to the left of an open fireplace. A smiling Negro girl sits on the right, churning milk into butter and buttermilk."[21] Jackson's residence as house musician was an upfront part of the announcement of the restaurant: "The familiar strains of Dixie, played by Graham Jackson at the organ . . . the folksy interior of the old farm house . . . the food and hospitality traditional in the South."[22] Jackson's head shot was front and center in the story. The menu featured a portrait of Nathan Bedford Forrest, Confederate general and founder of the KKK. Steaks could be ordered "Shermanized (burned to a crisp), Lin-

Figure 17. Johnny Reb's Dixieland Restaurant, Marietta, Georgia, circa 1960. Tracy O'Neal Photographic Collection, 1923–1975, N10-23_a, Special Collections and Archives, Georgia State University Library.

conized (warm, red heart), and Stonewalled (rare)."[23] The restaurant spared little expense when it came to advertising. Various ads with Jackson would appear almost daily in the *Atlanta Constitution*. Some of the ads continued in this folksy Confederate vein in the 1960s: "Where you win the war between the steaks!" "Stop shootin' Stonewall.... It's time for music," and "Old time barbecue and watermelon cutting."

Just as with many of the other antebellum establishments, the Johnny Reb's chain faced mounting pressure to desegregate. In July 1962 the NAACP held its annual convention in Atlanta. NAACP protesters targeted the downtown Johnny Reb's for picketing. Newsreel footage shows Black protesters holding signs while a White man in a Confederate uniform, presumably an employee, holds a sign reading, "Everybody loves Johnny Reb's Ice Cream."[24] Many Atlanta restaurants quietly desegregated by 1963, with most doing so after passage of the Civil Rights Act of 1964. Atlanta Mayor Ivan Allen Jr. was a leading voice for ending legal barriers in the city and avoiding major civil rights conflicts and confrontations. By the late 1960s he wooed major-league sports teams—the Atlanta Braves, Hawks, and Falcons—to Atlanta largely because the Atlanta business community was viewed as progressive on the issue of race.

Restaurant owner Stanley Davis also had a fast-food Johnny Reb's Chick, Chuck, and Shake just north of the Dixieland location. Since chicken was the top seller at this location, he hired a Georgia Tech engineering student to construct a massive fifty-six-foot-tall metal chicken at this location. Known colloquially as "the Big Chicken," this roadside oddity quickly became a well-known attraction and geographical marker. The mechanism that moved the beak and rolled the eyes was so loud that it shattered windows in the restaurant. The Big Chicken outlived the restaurant. In 1974 the building was sold to become a Kentucky Fried Chicken franchise. At first, KFC wanted to remove the monstrosity, but local outrage saved it. By the 1990s it suffered severe storm damage. Finally in 2017, KFC undertook a $2 million renovation of the structure, restoring the moving beak and rolling eyes.[25]

Another way Davis sought to popularize his restaurant chain was the release of an LP in 1964 titled *Johnny Reb's Presents: The Battle of Atlanta and Other Civil War Songs: By Graham Jackson*. Released to mark the one hundredth anniversary of the Battle of Atlanta, the album was produced by Johnny Reb's Records. The cover features a photograph of a cannon at Kennesaw National Battlefield. The reverse features a drawing of Graham Jackson playing the piano. The songs, all performed and arranged by Jackson, are vintage southern songs of the Civil War period. Side 1 features "The Battle of Atlanta." This is how Jackson describes the arrangement on the notes: "I'm not trying to tell the story of the Battle of Atlanta in facts, I'm trying to tell it the way I hear it emotionally—with music."[26] Side 2 contains various regional songs of the period. Jackson had a financial stake in the success of the restaurants and the records, as he owned 525 shares of stock of Davis Brothers Enterprises.[27]

In 1967 another temple to the neo-Confederate religion opened in downtown Atlanta. Named after Scarlett O'Hara's aunt, Pittypat's Porch tried a more modern take on the romanticized vision of *Gone with the Wind*. The founder of this establishment was an immigrant, Anton (A. J.) Anthony. He envisioned opening an Italian restaurant, but according to the restaurant's history, he read an article that Atlanta lacked enough truly southern cuisine, as expected by the growing number of tourists visiting the city. The results do resemble an idealized plantation fantasy world. Gone are the overt racist tropes and stereotypes, replaced with the look and feel of an antebellum home and big on the charm of southern hospitality. It has a large veranda on which to sip mint juleps, a large staircase a la Tara or perhaps a Carol Burnett spoof of Tara, and funeral-home paper fans for menus. *Gone with the Wind* imagery and posters are everywhere, and the menu includes "Carpetbagger" steak.[28]

Graham Jackson left Johnny Reb's and started a residency at Pittypat's when it opened in October 1967. Perhaps there was something of a free-agency bidding war over his services, or maybe he wanted to work closer to home. That second theory might be borne out by this backhanded shot at Aunt Fanny's and Johnny Reb's Dixieland: "We wanted a place downtown to express the true Southern hospitality to Northerners without driving 20 miles out of town."[29] Whatever the reason, Pittypat's ads picked up with the same shtick and imagery of Johnny Reb's, and Jackson was the centerpiece: "Ya'll drink and eat as you please without limit. Dance with Graham Jackson."[30] "Y'all" was often misspelled in the ads and on the menus for several years. This was a sure sign that a nonsoutherner was operating the restaurant. Jackson remained at Pittypat's until shortly before his death in 1983. He was praised by many for his performance, as a reporter observes: "Suddenly the organ explodes into 'Dixie,' and the crowd stands reverently for the past, clapping their hands and waving napkins over their heads."[31] One patron wrote to Jackson, "We were very much impressed with your talents, but were equally impressed with your pleasant and bubbly personality and the pleasure that you seemed to receive while making so many people happy."[32]

Journalist and Iowa native Walter Higbee recounts a visit to Pittypat's in the 1970s as follows:

> About halfway through our meal, a distinguished, gray-haired Black gentleman took his seat at an enormous organ in the center of the room. I later determined this was Graham W. Jackson. . . . Soon after taking his seat on the organ, Mr. Jackson commenced to playing some sweet antebellum tunes, Stephen Foster and the like. But soon his intensity on the organ increased. It occurred to many of us that he was recreating the War Between the States on that organ. . . . Finally came Appomattox and the most grand of all, the war ended with the playing of Dixie. At that moment, all of the Southerners in the room (most everyone there) leaped to their feet and emitted a raucous rebel yell. I nearly choked on my hush puppy.[33]

Just as before, Jackson released an album of performances at Pittypat's Porch. The songs and arrangements on this album, as well as the notes on the album cover, are identical to his previous *Battle of Atlanta* release, so this was really a re-release of his previous album. The cover features a drawing of Jackson's face next to a drawing of the recently completed carving of Davis, Lee, and Stonewall Jackson on Stone Mountain. The reverse features photos of Graham Jackson in a white dinner jacket and tie at the organ.

Jackson's association with these paragons of the Lost Cause and massive resistance are troubling when viewed through a modern lens. Jackson increasingly faced charges of Uncle Tomism and worse, a continuation of the horrors of minstrelsy. The irony of a Black artist being associated with Confederate nostalgia is complicated. Jackson was a product of his time. He was a conservative businessman and entertainer. He came of age in a time when Black artists endured all sorts of indignities in making a living. He was a disciple of Booker T. Washington's call for gradual and incremental change in the social structure of the United States.

Minstrelsy and blackface had mostly died out by the 1960s, but White desires to support the illusion of the content and happy Black were paramount in maintaining massive resistance. This clash created a "bearable cognitive dissonance that outlasted enslavement."[34] Jackson was not the only artist painted with the taint of minstrelsy. His contemporaries such as Louis Armstrong, Sammy Davis Jr., and Nat King Cole all faced criticism from Black society that they were sellouts. They too were hard-working and talented artists who managed to breach some of the walls of Jim Crow. Jackson was never a radical, even while he was a groundbreaker. That is the paradox of Graham Jackson and his choices of musical styles. He certainly had a love for traditional spirituals. Based on his own words, he seemed to have a love for Confederate songs as well: "I'm too busy to get into race. Music has no color, race, or creed. If I can play Chopin or St. Louis Blues in Atlanta, I can play them in Boston or Europe."[35]

8

"He Is an Honorable Man. Isn't That Enough?"

By the middle of the 1960s Jackson was an elder statesman entertainer. His residencies at Johnny Reb's and Pittypat's Porch made him something of a historical footnote to a past era. His FDR luster remained, and he stayed a yearly fixture at Warm Springs on April 12, but even FDR's dominance of American memory was in decline. The last connections with the Roosevelt family were disappearing. In June 1962, now herself an elder stateswoman of the Democratic Party, Eleanor Roosevelt made her final visit to Georgia. Though it is not generally known, she held few fond memories of the state. She detested the backwardness of Warm Springs almost as much as Franklin reveled in it. She rarely visited and then only when it was politically expedient. One of the few memories she enjoyed was naming the new Black school in Warm Springs after her in 1936, the final Rosenwald school built. The Rosenwald Fund was a significant philanthropic organization that constructed hundreds of Black schools across the South in the early twentieth century. To compound the bitter memory otherwise, she was told after her midnight arrival in Warm Springs on April 12, 1945, that Lucy Mercer was present at Franklin's death, something that was not made public until several years after Eleanor's death. Her relationship with Jackson was limited at best. She saw him perform at the White House and at Warm Springs and nodded with thanks as she passed his tear-filled visage at Warm Springs on that terrible morning. He communicated by letter to her a few times, and she acknowledged his account of FDR's death.

Her health was failing by 1962. She suffered from anemia and a recurring case of tuberculosis. Eleanor was now seventy-eight; her daughter, Anna, was caring for her. This did not stop Eleanor, always a champion for human and civil rights, from accepting an invitation to speak at commencement ceremonies at Atlanta University and accept an honorary doctorate degree.

108 · The Life and Music of Graham Jackson

Her visit on June 4, 1962, was her final one to Georgia. While there, Graham Jackson visited with her briefly and performed a quick song. Eleanor penned him a note of thanks and signed it, "I often think of you with pleasure. I want to thank you for all the pleasure your music gave my husband."[1] Eleanor died in November 1962.

Jackson was like many Blacks of his generation, relatively conservative and somewhat uncertain about the tactics of the younger generation of civil rights leaders. Jackson was steeped in the philosophical approach of Booker T. Washington as a young man and still tended to adhere to that bootstraps mentality. Much of his outward appearance and attitude in his later years reflected that way of thinking. He was struggling financially in the late 1950s and the 1960s, but he never seemed to show it. In public he was always dressed in a suit and tie and wearing expensive cologne. In 1964 Jackson created a Glee Club at the new Drexel Catholic High School in Atlanta. His expressed goal was to include all the students and teach them the fundamentals of music. But his bigger goal was to make these students ambassadors for Blacks in the turmoil of the 1960s.

Black Catholics in Atlanta saw the consecration in 1954 of Saint Paul of the Cross Catholic Church. The church was completed in 1961. Drexel Catholic High School opened in 1962, funded by the Atlanta Diocese of the Catholic Church. The school facility was in Collier Heights, an affluent White neighborhood that was transitioning into a mixed neighborhood, just north of Atlanta. Writer Andrew Hill was one of the students who participated in the Glee Club at Drexel. He recalled,

> This was a time, right before civil rights that Black people were trying to put their best foot forward, to make a good impression. . . . He [Jackson] wanted to contribute to something that was going to be a part of this ongoing energy, image making that was taking place. He spent the first couple of weeks having each of us come up to the piano and sing something we knew. . . . As far as I know he used almost everyone in the school to be part of that Glee Club. . . . Then he began to teach us complicated pieces. . . . Later I was a classical music disc jockey on the West Coast, and I heard the Xerxes Largo, and I thought, Oh my God, we sang this! . . . It was very important to him that this was an inclusive Glee Club, and that it was excellent.[2]

The Glee Club performed at several events in Atlanta over the next few years. Jackson took a position teaching music and served as organist at the church. The school, just as it was starting to flourish, was closed in 1967, after graduating three senior classes. The school was closed because Atlanta schools were finally in the process of total desegregation. Most of the students transferred to Saint Pius X Catholic High School.

In 1964 Helen Jackson decided that she wished to convert to Catholicism. This was problematic for Graham, given his two divorces. Helen explains, "This was not Graham. This was me. Maybe there's something we can do different in his life. So I suggested that we go to the Catholic church because they don't believe in divorces. And that's why we left and went to the Catholic Church. We were married 28 years, and he played for the Catholic church for 25."[3]

In order for Graham to be able to take communion as a Catholic, he needed a papal dispensation to officially annul his previous marriages. Helen said the priests at Saint Paul worked for months to complete that process, largely because of their respect and love for Graham:

> When we got this letter from the Pope saying that it had been dissolved . . . he sent this long decree saying why . . . it came during the day. Father called me—I was doing supply teaching at Harper [high school] to come by the church, and Graham would be there. He showed me what the Pope had said, and he said, "We're going to remarry you right now." So I had Graham and Gerald I had picked up from school and the priest—that's all the people who were there.[4]

Jackson was not overtly political most of the time, yet his name is associated with one of the significant songs of the civil rights movement. "We Shall Overcome" is entwined with the civil rights movement largely because of the influence of the Highlander Folk School in Tennessee and Zilphia Horton, who worked at the school. In 1947 the song was introduced to students at the school. Later, well-known recordings of the song would be produced by the likes of Pete Seeger and Joan Baez. But one of the first public broadcasts of the song was by the Congress of Industrial Organizations in a series of fifteen-minute radio programs aired in 1950. The programs aired across the South as part of union organizing efforts. The artist performing this song was none other than Graham Jackson.[5]

In 1969 Jackson partnered with Atlanta business leader and fellow Morehouse man T. M. Alexander Sr. to produce a record album entitled *The Black Man's Revolt of Protest and Progress and Poems of Inspiration, Despair, and Courage* (NRCA 204). Alexander was a successful Auburn Avenue insurance broker and real estate developer, active in Republican politics, and a friend of Martin Luther King Jr. His company provided liability insurance for civil rights marchers and vehicles for almost two decades. He also served in many city, state, and federal advisory roles.

Contrary to the album's title, this was more an example of racial uplift than an advocacy for Black Power or revolution. Alexander saw this as a key part of his efforts to educate young Blacks on the real story of Black history in America. He, like many older Black leaders, preferred to work within the system as opposed to younger leaders who were pushing for more radical solutions. This was a spoken-word album in which Alexander desired to "treat power as a force rather than color. We should debunk the idea that either white power or Black power is something to boo or be feared."[6] Jackson arranged and performed background organ music for the album.

Another connection that Jackson had to civil rights had to do with a room in a café. Frazier's Café Society was a Black landmark in Atlanta. Opened in 1946 on Hunter Street on the west side of Atlanta and only a few blocks from Jackson's home on Whitehouse Drive, this elegant café served the Black community for decades. In the early 1950s the larger back banquet room was dubbed "the Graham Jackson Room" in honor of Jackson's achievements. In the 1960s both Frazier's and nearby Pasqual's restaurants served as hubs for civil rights group meetings. NAACP and Student Nonviolent Coordinating Committee (SNCC) meetings were common at Frazier's, usually in the Graham Jackson Room.[7] Two of the most significant meetings held in that room were on March 5–6, 1965. SNCC and other civil rights organizations were mired in the voting rights protests in Selma, Alabama. There was great debate as to how to proceed. SNCC and some other groups sought to plan a march from Selma to Montgomery to demand equal voting rights in Alabama. King and the Southern Christian Leadership Conference were cool to the idea. SNCC leaders held a two-day executive committee meeting in Frazier's to decide the course to take. The result of that meeting was the firm decision to proceed with the planned march on Sunday, March 7, 1965. As we know, that march ended with the infamous attack on the marchers by Alabama state troopers that was broadcast live across the nation that Sunday evening.[8]

By early 1966 the escalation of US involvement in Vietnam was the subject of a growing political debate. Many Americans were still in support of the US Cold War commitment to prevent the spread of communism by defending South Vietnam from communist aggression, but cracks were starting to show, particularly among more liberal college students and some civil rights groups. A movement was started in late 1965 on the campus of Emory University in Atlanta called Affirmation: Vietnam. This student-led movement of support for the US war effort in Vietnam reflected the views of more conservative college students across Georgia. In total, forty-seven of the fifty-two colleges and universities in Georgia had student groups join this movement. The goals were simple, to show support for US troops in Vietnam and help galvanize public opinion among Georgia youth toward supporting the conflict. The organization created to facilitate this movement planned a rally at the brand-new Atlanta–Fulton County Stadium for February 12, 1966. This event featured most of Georgia's political leaders and the US secretary of state, Georgia native Dean Rusk. Governor Carl Sanders asserted that the purpose of the rally was to "show to the thousands of American boys on the battlefields, to our allies, and our enemies, that our resolve in Vietnam is strong, and we will not back down."[9]

Students conducted a statewide poll of young people's support for the war in Georgia with the intention of presenting the results at the rally. The student leaders included future five-term Georgia Congressman George "Buddy" Darden. Secretary of State Rusk was the keynote speaker. Other speakers included Governor Sanders, Senators Russell and Talmadge, and retired General Lucius Clay, chief architect of the 1949 Berlin airlift. Clay was also a Georgia native. Press reports show an expected crowd of more than fifty thousand would attend, with special buses and motorcades from around the state. This rally was seen by many as an antidote to growing student protests, hippies, beatniks, and others the proponents deemed undesirables. An opinion column summed up a view of the organizers: "They are neither longhaired, bearded nor unbathed. They are well-mannered, disciplined and respectful."[10]

The entertainment for the rally was a patriotic who's who. The headliner was the conservative activist and entertainer Anita Bryant. She turned down the first request to attend, but an intrepid student flew to Florida and made a personal appeal for her participation, after which she agreed to attend. The second entertainer on the program was Graham Jackson. It would not be surprising that Jackson would be a supporter of the war effort. He was a veteran, and his generation was much more supportive of US involvement abroad. His friend Ralph McGill was a participant as well. The final entertainer was Staff Sergeant Barry Sadler, best known for his patriotic song "The Ballad of the Green Berets." He was a wounded Green Beret. His song was later used in the pro-war John Wayne film *The Green Berets*.

As the event approached, the civil rights community was divided over support for the rally. Some two hundred Atlanta University students planned to attend and participate in the rally. However, some civil rights

112 · The Life and Music of Graham Jackson

leaders took public positions in opposition to the war. Some fifty protesters planned to quietly picket the event. These protesters were an offshoot of SNCC called the Southern Coordinating Committee to End the War in Vietnam. Former SNCC leader Julian Bond was recently elected to the Georgia House of Representatives and refused a seat due to his opposition to the war. This group's position was that "we find the American Government committing atrocities there."[11]

The rally day came, a cold and wet February Saturday. The Atlanta police dispatched three hundred officers to handle the expected crowds. The extra police were not needed. One lone arrest was made when a man grabbed a picket sign from a protester. The expected crowd of 50,000 never materialized. The organizers put the crowd at 15,000, and others estimated as few as 8,000. Secretary Rusk gave a fifteen-minute oration on the administration's goals for Vietnam. Others made brief remarks. Anita Bryant, in a fur coat and standing in a puddle in alligator shoes, sang "The Battle Hymn of the Republic" and "America the Beautiful." Jackson received light applause for "Yankee Doodle Dandy" and thunderous applause when he played "Dixie." Sadler belted out his ballad. Many of the organizers were disappointed by the crowd but placed the blame squarely on the rain. An apologetic article put it this way: "Their purpose was to show the world that draft card burning Vietniks don't represent the majority of American youth."[12]

The Georgia gubernatorial race in 1966 made national headlines. Georgia politics were something of a mess. The legal structures supporting Jim Crow had tumbled. The 1964 Civil Rights Act and the 1965 Voting Rights Act brought the hammer of federal intervention and enforcement of civil rights. Massive resistance was on the wane. But White backlash, particularly among working-class and rural Whites, still seethed. Most progressive and liberal Whites, along with White business leaders, sought a slow and steady approach to integration and acceptance of federal mandates. One candidate in the 1966 race channeled that backlash and took advantage of a crowded primary field to become the most oddball governor Georgia ever had. That man was Lester Maddox.

In the early 1960s Graham Jackson was an aging Atlanta celebrity, and Lester Maddox was a cornpone businessman and nuisance candidate. Maddox owned a down-home restaurant called the Pickrick, near Georgia Tech. The catchy phrase "Picknick at the Pickrick" was inscribed over the door. To call Maddox an ardent segregationist was an understatement. Passage of the Civil Rights Act of 1964 meant that he was now forced to serve Black

"He Is an Honorable Man. Isn't That Enough?" · 113

customers. He refused, often brandishing a pistol or swinging a "Pickrick drumstick," an axe handle, at Blacks who sought service. The case *Willis v. Pickrick Restaurant*, 231 F. Supp. 396 (N.D. Ga. 1964), resulted in contempt charges against Maddox. He then closed the Pickrick and reopened it as the Lester Maddox Cafeteria, claiming his new establishment only served local customers and was exempt from federal intervention. After that failed, he closed his business rather than integrate it. The property was purchased by nearby Georgia Tech. After decades of use as a campus building, the Pickrick was demolished. A new park honoring the efforts of the civil rights movement in Atlanta was planned for the site. The incidents received national attention and made Maddox a hero to White resisters. Maddox announced his candidacy for the Democratic nomination for governor in 1966. Running a largely self-funded campaign, he traveled the state, often signing axe handles and hanging signs out of the back of his car.

Georgia was no stranger to odd and at times even illegal activities during gubernatorial campaigns. In 1946 the infamous "three governors" controversy arose in which the winner, Eugene Talmadge, died before taking office. The lieutenant governor, the incumbent lame-duck governor, and a write-in candidate, Herman Talmadge, the son of the dead winner, all claimed the governorship. In the end the legislature appointed Herman Talmadge. Since Reconstruction, Georgia had remained a solidly Democratic state, so the winner of the Democratic primary was usually the de facto governor. This changed in 1966 when a viable Republican candidate, Howard "Bo" Callaway, the son of Jackson's patron Cason Callaway, sought to flip the state to the Republican side. Five Democratic candidates sought the nomination in the primary. These candidates included former Governor Ellis Arnell, future governor and president Jimmy Carter, former Lieutenant Governor Garland Byrd, businessman James Grey, and Maddox. Arnell won almost 30 percent in the primary, with Maddox finishing a surprising second with 24 percent and Carter a close third.

Because no one received a majority, a runoff was required. Tim Boyd observes in his analysis of the 1966 race, "The idea that he [Maddox] might ultimately become governor remained preposterous to many. As the Democratic National Committee's analyst wrote to the White House, 'The feeling is that Arnell would clobber Maddox in the runoff.'"[13] Analysis of the vote in the runoff indicates that some Georgians viewed Arnell as too liberal and that since this was an open primary, many Republicans may have voted for Maddox, thinking he was the weaker candidate. Maddox won the runoff with 54 percent of the vote. In the general election in November Callaway garnered the most votes, barely surpassing Maddox. But due to the number of write-in votes for Arnell, Callaway only received 46 percent of the vote. Once again, the General Assembly had to decide, and the Democratic majority selected Maddox.

Writer Rex Reed interviewed Maddox in October 1967 for *Esquire* magazine. Reed's description of Maddox in the governor's office is fascinating:

> Dressed in an inexpensive, olive-drab suit with a Masonic pin in his lapel, he looks at fifty-two, like a fighting cock. Hairy hands hang from their coat sleeves in animated chunks. His round, balding head, too big for his stubby little body, rises above the rest of him with a few tiny strands of hair clinging for dear life to the crown, Dagwood Bumstead style. Horn-rimmed glasses sag heavily against a network of tiny varicose veins which threaten to fester and erupt on the tip of a nose supported by a red sunset of a face which continuously changes shades as his temper comes and goes.[14]

Maddox certainly knew of Graham Jackson before Jackson knew of Maddox. Jackson was never allowed into the Pickrick to eat. In the 1950s Maddox started running a regular series of comical newspaper ads for the Pickrick. In 1957 he made a failed run for mayor of Atlanta, losing to long-time mayor William Hartsfield. He lost again in 1961 to Ivan Allen Jr. In 1962 he lost the Democratic nomination for lieutenant governor. If Jackson was still unaware of Maddox, his antics in 1964 and 1965 certainly brought him to Jackson's attention. Jackson and Maddox would form a very unlikely friendship that resulted in Jackson's appointment in 1969 to the State Board of Corrections. This appointment made Jackson the first Black appointed to a constitutional state board in Georgia.[15]

Maddox and his family first met Jackson face to face in late 1966 at Johnny Reb's Dixieland restaurant, where Jackson was near the end of his long residency. It makes sense that Maddox and Jackson would hit it off, even in the face of Maddox's segregationist views. Both were larger-than-life figures, and both were showmen. They were relatively close in age, Jackson being twelve years the senior. Jackson had always been very comfortable around political figures, most all of those who held strong segregationist views. Maddox was a fan of Jackson's music, and the two sang together on several occasions. In many ways, Jackson's relationship with Maddox was like many relationships Jackson had formed over the previous four decades

Figure 18. Graham Jackson performing for Georgia Governor Lester Maddox outside the governor's mansion, 1969. Lester Maddox Photo Collection, VIS 105.02.05, James G. Kenan Research Center, Atlanta History Center.

with White patrons and politicians. But there seemed to be one key difference. Maddox's lack of formality, his unpretentiousness, and his self-deprecation made him and Jackson something of a comedy duo at times.

Their friendship resulted in Jackson becoming a regular at the governor's mansion, much as he had been during the 1940s and early 1950s during the Talmadge administrations. Maddox penned a letter to Jackson shortly after taking office in 1967: "My wife joins me in expressing our appreciation and gratitude to you for the many kindnesses you have shown us during our tenure in the Mansion. I hope that when you are in or near the Capitol, you will stop by and visit with me."[16] In November 1967, Jackson received a letter from Maddox's chief of staff, T. Malone Sharpe, announcing that Jackson was given the commission of admiral in the Georgia Navy.[17] This title is an honorary one given by Georgia governors. While Georgia had no active navy since the American Revolution, an inactive naval militia still existed. It is unclear how many of these titles Maddox doled out. In January 1968, likely responding to a New Year's telegram from Jackson, Maddox wrote, "Thanks for your thoughtful wire. We deeply appreciate your expression of support, confidence and friendship and wish for you and yours a year filled with an abundance of good health, happiness, and success. Don't forget where my office is located and do not hesitate to call upon me if I may be of assistance to you in any manner."[18]

Later that year, Maddox invited Jackson to perform at a watermelon and ice cream social for members of the General Assembly. A photo snapped at the event shows Jackson and Maddox, heads tilted side by side as they sang together while Jackson played his trademark accordion. They sang such old standards as "You Are My Sunshine," "Shine On Harvest Moon," and "Old Shanty Town." Jackson was quoted as saying to Maddox, "People in Atlanta would pay big money to hear singing like that." Maddox replied, "Lots of people in Atlanta don't like what I been singing!"[19] Maddox and Jackson were at it again. They performed together at the State Milk Producers Conference. Maddox posed for a photo grasping a cow's udder and squirting Lieutenant Governor George Smith in the face with milk. They performed "Someday You're Going to Want Me" and "Somebody Stole My Gal."[20]

Maddox was an unschooled politician. He was good with a quip or a joke but hapless when it came to wrangling bills through the General Assembly. One thing that surprised many observers was Maddox's unwavering dedication to righting wrongs of the "Little People," as he called them. These were the poor, the uneducated, and the working people whose roots he shared. Maddox grew up in the shadow of Atlantic Steel Mills, north of downtown. His was a working-class mill village, an integrated one at that. He dropped out of school to support his mother and siblings, largely because of an alcoholic father. His prudish and self-righteous indignation toward vices and communists and agitators likely grew out of his hardscrabble upbringing. Maddox used the standard arguments of White supremacists, including biblical and biological ones, to claim the inferiority of the Black race. But his chief argument was more nuanced and based largely on his libertarian notions of property rights and free association.

Maddox argued his case about his restaurant to a *New York Times* reporter in 1964, "I was shocked to hear . . . that I must as an American forgo my rights under the Constitution and become subservient to those who demand that I must surrender my rights as an American and my property. . . . It's involuntary servitude; it's slavery of the first order, it shows complete, utter disregard for the United States Constitution."[21] Once in office, Maddox was resolute in his determination to protect those like him who fell victim to government overreach, bureaucracy, graft, and incompetence. To accomplish this, he instituted "Little People's Day." Twice a month he would

"He Is an Honorable Man. Isn't That Enough?" · 117

open the doors to the governor's office to any Georgia citizen who wanted to speak to him. It was a huge success. For the first event, held in April 1967, more than four thousand people lined up. Maddox spoke with each one. It was through these open forums that Maddox got deeply involved in penal reform in Georgia.

Maddox had only been in office for a few months when he faced his first clemency request as governor. William Patrick Clark was convicted of rape and sentenced to die in the electric chair. Maddox stayed the execution with just twenty-two minutes to spare. Maddox said he spent a lot of time "soul searching" and was considering a blanket stay on all executions and the possibility of a statewide referendum on the death penalty.[22] Just days later, four young, Black males met Maddox during "Little People's Day" at the Capitol. They surrendered themselves to Maddox announcing that they were escapees from the Wilkerson County work camp. Their purpose in escaping was to plead with the governor to investigate the terrible conditions in prisons. Maddox took this in stride. He accepted their surrender and vowed to investigate their claims. "There is a lot of truth in their statements," Maddox said.[23] The county work camps often housed state prisoners. For years critics demanded more accountability for these camps. Standards varied, and many camps operated as fiefdoms for local officials who made money from the substandard conditions off the backs of mostly poor and often African American men confined in them for minor offenses. The *Atlanta Constitution* quickly praised Maddox for his position and pushed for a statewide investigation.[24]

The debate over prison reform in Georgia more than fifty years ago presaged many of the debates that sadly continue today concerning mass incarceration. Critics then viewed the work camps as veritable debtors' prisons, housing Blacks for misdemeanors who had no ability to pay fines and using them for cheap labor. Since sheriffs are constitutionally elected officers in Georgia, only the governor can suspend or remove them. The state prison system is part of the executive branch. This allowed Maddox to make changes without input from the General Assembly. Maddox saw prison conditions as an issue of basic fairness as well as an example of government hurting the little guy. He was convinced that those incarcerated needed more rehabilitation and less punishment.[25]

Maddox moved with alacrity. In May he ordered the Georgia Bureau of Investigation to investigate the State Board of Pardons. His order was largely based on stories that the board was not functioning well in making pardon decisions. Maddox stated that he was making plans to reorganize the board. His goal was to expand the board by adding more members.[26] Maddox showed up at facilities unannounced and conducted inspections. He found terrible conditions. Maddox was furious: "Deplorable conditions existing at both state and county camps result from failure on the part of the state government and State Department of Corrections to meet their responsibilities."[27] Critics of Maddox were surprised but happy that he was taking a serious interest in reform. An *Atlanta Constitution* editorial states, "In Lester Maddox we have a Governor who obviously is touched by human suffering produced by the system and understands the wasteful economics which make hardened criminals out of first-time offenders."[28]

The 1968 Georgia General Assembly largely ignored Maddox's wishes concerning prison reform. Maddox sought to expand the State Board of Corrections from five to fifteen members. The General Assembly did not agree and refused the change. Maddox's response was to create a statewide Citizens Corrections Panel to investigate and make recommendations. This nonpartisan, biracial, citizens group was charged with making recommendations by the end of the year. The twenty-member board included three Black members, two of whom were William Holmes Borders, pastor of the Wheat Street Baptist Church, and Howard H. Jordan Jr., president of Savannah State College.[29] In typical Maddox fashion, he announced his reform plan before the panel concluded its report. He proposed six wide-ranging reforms, among them the establishment of a research division, the phasing out of work camps, a public defender system, and the construction of six new, modern prisons. When asked how he would pay for this, his response was "If I can't get the money from the General Assembly for it I might just take it out of the emergency fund."[30] At this point Maddox's second year in office was near its end, and he had produced very little in the way of tangible prison reform. When challenged by the press about this, he gave one of his most quoted statements as governor: "We're doing the best we can. And before we can do much more we're going to have to get a better grade of prisoner!"[31]

Maddox entered year three of his governorship determined that prison reform was going to happen. His Citizens Corrections Panel delivered a report that was critical of the state prison system. The panel made seventy-eight reform recommendations. It blamed everyone for the terrible conditions in the system but most especially the public that allowed such a system to exist. They made two paramount recommendations for reform: moving day-to-day prison operations from the State Board of Corrections to a professional prison director to be hired by the governor, and ending the work camps across the state.[32] The General Assembly was again less amenable to these major changes. An editorial in the *Atlanta Constitution* showed the gap between these recommendations and the legislative outcome: "Twenty-five dollars and a suit of clothes (upon release) is considered a major reform. This joins a long list of things undone by the General Assembly."[33] As the year concluded, Maddox was still adamant that reform would happen. Two positions on the Board of Corrections would be vacant in the next few months, and Maddox would appoint people to those positions who, in his mind, cared about prison reform. Critics now showed more skepticism: "While Maddox has taken some baby steps in the area of prison reform, the giant steps are yet to be made."[34]

Graham Jackson was asleep when his telephone rang around midnight. On the line was a state patrolman calling from the governor's mansion. He called to notify Jackson that Governor Maddox planned to appoint him to the State Board of Corrections for a five-year term. Jackson was not anticipating such a call. He and Maddox had spoken several months before about possible appointments for Jackson, but there was nothing specific. Jackson accepted the post and planned to use it to "help and inspire people."[35] Why Jackson? Maddox insisted it was because Jackson was a "very honorable, dedicated man of integrity . . . a man of honesty and compassion . . . a man who loves his country."[36] But the reality was that Jackson was his second choice. Maddox originally sought the appointment of William Holmes Borders, but he turned the offer down. It is clear that Maddox intended to appoint an African American to the post, hence the late-night call to Jackson. Maddox noted that 60 percent of those incarcerated were Black and it was regrettable that no Black had ever been appointed to the board.[37]

Jackson admitted he had no special skills or knowledge about prisons. Furthermore, Jackson had suffered a massive heart attack and stroke in early 1969, making some question his fitness for the position. Jackson admitted that he was not expected to live, but said, "Can't you see I've fully recovered? That was a surprise to me. I was pronounced dead twice."[38] Jackson acknowledged that Maddox selected him because he was Black. "I see that Lester Maddox is anxious to make appointments of Black people in state government," Jackson said. However, he added, "I find him to be a very fine man, religious and straight forward. You don't find any tricks in him. He's sincere and wants to help the whole system and give it a new approach."[39] When asked directly how he could accept an appointment by a man opposed to civil rights, Jackson replied, "I'm a musician, not a politician. I never paid much attention to those axe handles. It was all an act. He has treated me very fine."[40]

Critics of Maddox, particularly in the Black press, quickly condemned the appointment. The *Chicago Daily Defender* was not impressed: "When Georgia's Governor Lester Maddox picked 77-year-old [incorrect age] Graham Jackson as the first Black man on a state appointive board in the state, he picked one of the 'safest' Negroes he could find. He has been quiet since Roosevelt (when people still regarded him as safe then) asked him to play his accordion."[41] A later article in a Texas newspaper went even further: "Maddox chose Negro Musician Graham Jackson for the State Board of Corrections. It did little to improve his racial image, however, or gain him favor among African Americans. Civil rights leaders dismissed the move as another mark for Uncle Tom."[42] The most disturbing of all editorials was penned by the *Atlanta Voice*'s "Auburn Avenue Sam," deliberately in dialect:

I know that bro jackson can play some good music but kin he take care of business. Will he be so grateful to lesser maddox fo gittin him that good job that he gon fergit why he is there: to help them po black folks who locked up in them goddam jails which aint worf noffing. Is he gon be so humble to the white folks that all he gon do is playing second fidder to the white man's beat.... but if he gits in there and jist gone be saying yassuh boss and nossuh boss then we gone give him hell even tho he is a black man jist like us. So, bro graham jackson, we hope you godspeed, but if you douber cross the people, the debbil better give you some speed.[43]

State Representative Bobby Hill, a Black member of the General Assembly from Savannah, was just as unimpressed with Jackson's credentials:

Graham Jackson is meaningless to me on the Board of Corrections as a piano player from Pittypat's porch. That wasn't significant at all. So that's the kind of people he's drawing in, so it's insignificant that they were Black to me. And it should have been intelligent Blacks. So, you know, I'm sure that they're some people.... He could count up his people and most of the people he brought in there were worthless in terms of being significant forces to help Black folks. Now, that does not take away from the fact that we have to recognize the percentage of people who think that was worthwhile and that're going to vote for him. I think that if the story is told clearly and cleanly then those people could be enlightened, and they would back off in the support that they might have for Lester. That's what I feel. Lester is still Lester. Lester is still ignorant. So Lester can't run state government.[44]

Maddox saw his appointment of Jackson and other Blacks as monumental and significant:

I put the first Black man on the State Constitutional Board in the history of this state, the first one. I put them [Blacks] in law enforcement, in white collar and executive positions—more than, not just one previous governor, but more than all of them combined, even on the Selective Service System that had been going on since World War II where there had been two Blacks appointed on the Selective Service draft boards; and I put some forty of them on there in a few months because Black people were drafted just like white people. They thought that was something that they had put two on there, but not one of them had put one in the GBI or Highway Patrol or on the State Board or in those top positions. But everybody belongs to the State—It is different from your home. It is different from your business. The State, the government, belongs to everybody, but they hadn't ever been represented.[45]

Maddox press secretary and biographer Bob Short notes simply, "Maddox kept his promise and did more for Blacks in Georgia than all previous governors combined."[46] Jackson served his term faithfully and took a very serious interest in doing his part to improve prisons. The board conducted a significant investigation of Cherokee County's work camp brutalities. The result of the investigation was the removal of state prisoners from the camp and the firing of the warden.[47]

Jackson was paid a modest per diem for his work on the board. His health struggles limited his ability to travel, hence most of his few job opportunities were local. Jackson's income in the 1970s seems to have come mostly from his continuing performances at Pittypat's Porch, with occasional other paid gigs. Helen Jackson's income as a teacher and school administrator provided most of their income. Jackson was now more and more a beloved relic. Stories in the press mostly focus on his past. In many ways he was a living symbol of Atlanta. In 1971 newly elected Governor Jimmy Carter named "The Honorable Graham Jackson the Official Musician of the State of Georgia." The proclamation went further, calling Jackson a man "of charitable heart towards the helpless and the underprivileged."[48]

Figure 19. Graham Jackson with fellow members of the State Board of Corrections and Governor Jimmy Carter in the governor's office, 1971. Graham W. Jackson Sr. and noted local and national individuals, Plaques and Photographs, box 8, folder 6, series 7, Graham W. Jackson Sr. Papers, Archives Division, Auburn Avenue Research Library on African-American Culture and History, Fulton County Library System, Atlanta.

A few months later he was awarded an honorary degree from West Georgia College and was honored by Washington High School during Negro History Week. July 1972 was the 125th anniversary of the founding of Atlanta. Jackson was the featured artist of the celebration. A letter from the Atlanta Chamber of Commerce said, "The whole event would not have been so successful had it not been for your help with the entertainment—you are to be congratulated!"[49] The event concluded with a duet by Jackson and Bert Parks singing "Happy Birthday" to Atlanta. One of the charities that Jackson supported in the period was the American Cancer Society. Jackson performed at fundraisers and events in 1972 and 1973. In March 1973 the American Cancer Society held a large volunteer training event in Atlanta, attended by four hundred volunteers. The highlight of the event was the entertainer and well-known accordionist Lawrence Welk, who was co-chair of the national campaign. He and Jackson performed at the event and swapped accordion stories and tips. Jackson also was honored by the

Figure 20. Graham Jackson accepting a proclamation from Governor Jimmy Carter naming him Official Musician of the State of Georgia, 1971. Graham W. Jackson Sr. and noted local and national individuals, Plaques and Photographs, box 8, folder 6, series 7, Graham W. Jackson Sr. Papers, Archives Division, Auburn Avenue Research Library on African-American Culture and History, Fulton County Library System, Atlanta.

Atlanta Falcons in 1973 by being selected to sing the National Anthem at a game.

Jackson found his opportunity to play for his sixth president in 1976. That was his fellow Georgian and admirer Jimmy Carter. As a candidate Carter broke with Democratic Party tradition. For decades, Democratic nominees opened their official campaigns in Detroit, in keeping with the powerful historical support of the union vote. Since Carter's Republican opponent, Gerald Ford, was a Michigander, his campaign decided on a kickoff at Warm Springs, in the shadow of FDR. Just as Kennedy had sixteen years earlier, Carter would begin his campaign in the shadow of FDR's cottage. And just as with Kennedy, Graham Jackson was on that stage again.

It was a warm, muggy Labor Day 1976 in Warm Springs. Thirty-one years had passed since FDR's death. In some ways Warm Springs remained frozen in time since April 12, 1945. The population was smaller, the buildings and homes more threadbare. The Warm Springs Institute no longer treated polio patients. Polio was defeated. In 1974 the state of Georgia took ownership of the facility and converted it into a general rehabilitation hospital. But the simple, white cottage still possessed meaning. A Carter campaign spokesperson explained, "Warm Springs is an extremely beautiful setting that holds significance for the country because of its relationship to Mr. Roosevelt."[50] Two of the Roosevelts' sons, Franklin Jr. and James, at-

Figure 21. Autographed photo of Graham Jackson with President Jimmy Carter and First Lady Roselyn Carter at the White House, 1977. Graham W. Jackson Sr. and noted local and national individuals, Plaques and Photographs, box 8, folder 6, series 7, Graham W. Jackson Sr. Papers, Archives Division, Auburn Avenue Research Library on African-American Culture and History, Fulton County Library System, Atlanta.

tended. Carter gave a strong speech that harkened both to FDR and to JFK, who visited in 1960. Jackson played "Happy Days Are Here Again," and Carter embraced him at the end. More than ten thousand people crowded into the hamlet to see and hear Carter.[51] A few weeks later Jackson performed at a fundraiser barbeque held for Carter at the farm of Senator Herman Talmadge.[52]

Figure 22. Graham Jackson with his sons, Gerald and Graham Jr., circa 1960s. Graham W. Jackson Sr. Family Photos, box 7, folder 5, series 7, Graham W. Jackson Sr. Papers, Archives Division, Auburn Avenue Research Library on African-American Culture and History, Fulton County Library System, Atlanta.

Carter's November 1976 victory over Ford made possible one last journey by Jackson to perform at the White House. His first performance was more than forty years earlier. Now his visit would be as much to honor Jackson himself as to celebrate Carter's inauguration. Jackson was picked up at his home by a Georgia state patrolman who transported him to the airport. Once he arrived in Washington, a White House military aide whisked him to the Hay-Adams hotel. That afternoon he arrived at the White House. He performed in the state dining room for a reception for Georgians from 4 to

126 · The Life and Music of Graham Jackson

5:30 p.m. Jackson described the joy he felt returning to the hallowed place: "Playing for six Presidents is something to remember, and everybody there seemed just happy about it. They had everything laid out for me. They had the piano, the accordion and the organ there for me."[53] It could not have been a more fitting moment for a Georgia icon.

Jackson's health continued to decline. The last few years of his life found him suffering more strokes and more heart issues. The Carters wrote to him in October 1978 wishing him a speedy recovery.[54] In the spring of 1979 Jackson returned to Warm Springs, this time as a patient. His most recent stroke had damaged his speech and his memory. Assisted by his adult sons, Graham Jr. and Gerald, he exited his car. He paused and looked over to the second column of Georgia Hall. His hand pointed and he said, "That's where it happened." Eager patients gathered, surprised that he was coming for treatment, not performing. His wife, Helen, as he was being wheeled into the building, said, "We are so proud of him and the way he has responded. Back home on Whitehouse Drive, he's been playing the piano and organ in his room. It is strange, a blessing really, that even though Graham has some difficulty with his speech and memory, he plays as well as he ever did." Jackson, overhearing his wife, said softly, "The music is still there." He spent a week at Warm Springs. James Roosevelt and his wife visited him, and they attended church services together.[55]

Epilogue

Jackson passed away "peacefully and without pain" on January 15, 1983. He suffered his final stroke in November 1982. After treatment at Crawford Long Hospital he was transferred to the Americana Health Care Center, where he died. Just weeks before his final stroke, he was still performing at Pittypat's Porch. Though his voice was gone and his playing was slower, he was still popular with crowds. He was interred in South View Cemetery in Atlanta. He was just a month short of his eightieth birthday.[1]

Helen Jackson shared this poignant description of his last days:

We had carried him to the hospital. And he had been in intensive care for a week, not speaking, not saying anything to anybody. And they moved him to his private room, and he lived in that for about two days. And he wouldn't open his eyes, he wasn't saying anything. We were exceedingly . . . [?]. And here comes Graham and Gerald. They went over to him, put their arms across him on the bed and kissed him. And he said: "Come over here and let me tell you something, both of you. You are two fine boys. Don't forget it." Those were the last words he ever said. "You are two fine boys,"—because they were young—"and don't forget it." And [he said] nothing else ever. We went every day. I remember putting him in the wheelchair with the assistance of others. We carried him to the piano, and I said, "Graham [Jr.], play something." And Graham [Jr.] started playing for him. And he raised up. He had never tried to sit up. When Graham [Jr.] started playing, he kept trying to push to get up. So I said, "Push him on over there to the piano." Which we did. Graham got up, and we pushed him over to the piano. And he put his hands on the keys and felt them. His eyes still closed. He felt the keys. He had long fingers, pretty hands. He reached over to the keys and tried something, but it didn't work. And he took his hand and banged on his head.[2]

Figure 23. Graham Jackson performing on WSB radio. Graham W. Jackson Sr. Playing the Accordion, box 7, folder 4, series 7, Graham W. Jackson Sr. Papers, Archives Division, Auburn Avenue Research Library on African-American Culture and History, Fulton County Library System, Atlanta.

Jackson's impact and influence are beyond dispute. He was a successful African American entertainer who performed for tens of thousands of people over his career. He broke color barriers by performing on radio and in White venues. He caught the ear of FDR and remained his musical solace and refuge. He volunteered to serve his nation in time of war and raised millions for that war effort. He became a living legend in Atlanta and was rightly called "the Ambassador of Goodwill."

Jackson was a musical prodigy, that much is clear. Consistently, over many decades, he was noted for the ability to play almost any song requested of him from memory. Jackson's musical career spanned many decades and many genres of music. His initial musical experience was in the traditional gospel music he experienced in church as a child. By his teenage years he was adept at ragtime and Dixieland styles but also in classical forms. In his twenties he was playing jazz with his bands and also playing the pipe organ and as an accompanist for silent films.

After the advent of talkies he made the quick transition to radio, where he performed both popular tunes of the American songbook and jazz and later swing as well as continuing his organ work. Jackson's musicality is reflective of the evolution of jazz and swing. Joachim-Ernst Berendt and Günther Huesmann observe how the music fits the times and the times fit the music: "The untroubled joy of Dixieland corresponds to the days just prior to World War I. The restlessness of the Roaring Twenties comes to life in the Chicago style. Swing embodies the massive standardization of life before World War II; perhaps, to quote Marshall Stearns, swing 'was the answer to the American—and very human—love of bigness.'"[3]

Jackson's musical style evolved over time. His extant recordings from the 1920s are jazz. His recordings in the 1950s are spirituals and organ. His recordings of the 1960s and 1970s are organ pieces, largely Civil War songs that reflected his residencies as house organist at Johnny Reb's Dixieland and Pittypat's Porch, both Confederate-themed restaurants. This may reflect his own interests but also what was marketable to Whites and popular at the time.

We know that Jackson was a gifted arranger of music, often adapting the same tunes on piano, organ, and accordion or for an orchestra. A search of copyrighted songs finds him credited as an arranger on about a half-dozen songs. The difficulty of composers receiving proper song attribution in those earlier times are many. Arrangers then had to work at a variety of jobs to generate income. John Wriggle notes, "An arranger's services were required at some step—or many steps—in just about every entertainment medium of the period, whether studio orchestras, night-club floor shows, radio broadcasts, song publications, theatrical productions, or films."[4] In generating steady income, Jackson also held positions as organist at different churches. He played for twenty-six years at the First Congregational Church of Atlanta and later at Saint Paul of the Cross Catholic Church.

Jackson was also a music teacher. He taught for twelve years at Booker T. Washington High School and later at Drexel Catholic High School. For most of his career he taught private lessons as well to students who ranged from noted White celebrities such as golfer Bobby Jones to hundreds of young African American students. One student of note was Roslyn Pope. As a teenager, Pope was selected as a guest soloist with the Atlanta Symphony Orchestra, the first African American to be selected.[5] Pope is best known for co-authoring "An Appeal to Human Rights" in 1960. This influential document was a product of the Atlanta student movement and instrumental in the success of desegregation efforts in Atlanta.[6]

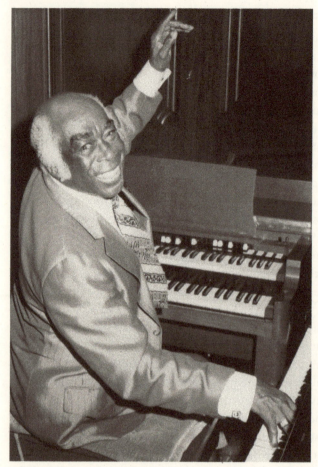

Figure 24. Graham Jackson performing on organ and piano, unknown location, 1978. Graham W. Jackson Sr. playing the organ or piano, box 8, folder 8, series 7, Graham W. Jackson Sr. Papers, Archives Division, Auburn Avenue Research Library on African-American Culture and History, Fulton County Library System, Atlanta.

It is fitting to end the story of this remarkable man by returning to April 13, 1945, that moment when Ed Clark stumbled over Jackson's foot and turned to capture that immortal moment in time. The photo shows the nation's collective grief and perhaps fear for the unknown. Jackson's uniform and regal bearing are in juxtaposition to the visceral tears flowing down his cheeks. Jackson was playing Dvorak's "Going Home." This is eminently appropriate both as a funeral dirge and as a symbol of the intersection of American culture through music. When Dvorak arrived in the United States, he quickly surmised that the future of American music was not European, but African. The power of Black musical forms and their influence on American music was clear to him. Graham Jackson's life and music are one of the best examples of this powerful new music.

Notes

Preface

1 Harold H. Martin, *Atlanta and Her Environs: A Chronicle of Its People and Events, 1940's-1970's* (Athens: University of Georgia Press, 1987), 111.

Chapter 1. We Didn't Have a Dime

1 Eric Arnesen, *Brotherhoods of Color: Black Railroad Workers and the Struggle for Equality* (Cambridge, MA: Harvard University Press, 2002), 1:26.

2 Lillian B. Garnett, *The Inimitable Life of Graham Jackson*, unpublished manuscript, Graham W. Jackson Papers, Atlanta History Center. This document is a short biography of Jackson that focuses mainly on Jackson's early life.

3 Ray Stannard Baker, *Following the Color Line: An Account of Negro Citizenship in the American Democracy* (1908; reprint, London: Forgotten Books, 2017), 158. Baker's classic work explores racism in the early twentieth century, particularly the impact of color and ancestry in the Black community.

4 Kwame Anthony Appiah and Henry Louis Gates Jr., eds., "M. Sissieretta Jones," in *Africana: The Encyclopedia of the African and African American Experience* (New York: Basic Civitas, 1999), 1065.

5 "Jackson Came to Play—Found His Promised Land," *Atlanta Journal*, November 19, 1969.

6 "Graham Jackson: The Man and His Music," *Atlanta Constitution*, February 24, 1976.

7 "Maestro Jackson's Music Thrilled Five Presidents," *Albany Sunday Herald*, n.d.

8 "Mother's Lullabies Left Music in the Heart of Graham Jackson," *New Journal and Guide*, October 4, 1941, 15.

9 Garnett, *Inimitable Life of Graham Jackson*. In an interview with the author, Graham Jackson Jr. confirmed that he was told this sad story.

10 Accession 41741, Records of Central State Hospital, 1874–1961, Virginia State Government Records Collection, Library of Virginia, Richmond.

11 Graham Washington Jackson birth certificate, Graham W. Jackson Papers, Atlanta History Center.

132 · Notes to Pages 4–11

12 M. Helen Bain v. Pauline Jackson, an insane person. Circuit Court of the City of Portsmouth, Virginia. May 1913.

13 "I. C. Norcom School Mid-Winter Finals," *New Journal and Guide*, February 10, 1923, 2.

14 In "Graham Jackson: The Man and His Music," *Atlanta Constitution*, February 24, 1976."

Chapter 2. Atlanta

1 Campbell Gibson, "Population of the 100 Largest Cities and Other Urban Places in the United States: 1790 TO 1990," Population Division, US Bureau of the Census, June 1998.

2 Harold E. Davis, *Henry Grady's New South: Atlanta, a Brave Beautiful City* (Tuscaloosa: University of Alabama Press, 1990).

3 Derrick P. Alridge, "Atlanta Compromise Speech," in *New Georgia Encyclopedia*, October 29, 2015.

4 Louis R. Harlan, *Booker T. Washington: The Making of a Black Leader, 1856–1901* (New York: Oxford University Press, 1972), 92.

5 W.E.B. Du Bois, *The Souls of Black Folk* (New York: Random House, 2003), 43, 45–46, 52.

6 Carole Merritt, "African-Americans in Atlanta: Community Building in a New South City," *Southern Spaces*, March 2004, https://southernspaces.org/2004/african-americans-atlanta-community-building-new-south-city/.

7 David Fort Godshalk, *Veiled Visions: The 1906 Atlanta Race Riot and the Reshaping of American Race Relations* (Chapel Hill: University of North Carolina Press, 2005), 13–14.

8 Russell Korobkin, "The Politics of Disfranchisement in Georgia," *Georgia Historical Quarterly* 74, no. 1 (1990): 20–58.

9 Gregory Mixon and Clifford Kuhn, "Atlanta Race Massacre of 1906," in *New Georgia Encyclopedia*, October 29, 2015, https://www.georgiaencyclopedia.org/articles/history-archaeology/atlanta-race-massacre-of-1906/.

10 Gregory Mixon, *The Atlanta Riot: Race, Class, and Violence in A New South City* (Gainesville: University Press of Florida, 2005).

11 "Lynching, White and Negroes, 1882–1968," Tuskegee University Archives Repository, Tuskegee, AL, available at http://hdl.handle.net/123456789/511.

12 Maurice J. Hobson, *The Legend of the Black Mecca: Politics and Class in the Making of Modern Atlanta* (Chapel Hill: University of North Carolina Press, 2017), 17.

13 "Jackson Came to Play—Found His Promised Land," *Atlanta Journal*, November 19, 1969.

14 "Jackson Came to Play."

15 Quoted in Lynn Abbott and Doug Serof, *The Original Blues: The Emergence of Blues in African American Vaudeville* (Jackson: University of Mississippi Press, 2017), 238.

16 Eric Smith, *African American Theatre Buildings: An Illustrated Historical Directory, 1900–1955* (Jefferson, NC: McFarland, 2003), 63.

17 "Midnight Frolic," *Atlanta Constitution*, February 5, 1924, 16.

Notes to Pages 11–15 · 133

18 Smith, *African American Theatre Buildings*, 33, 55.

19 Salem Tutt Whitney, "Timely Topics," *Chicago Defender*, March 3, 1928, 6.

20 Jackson, handwritten notes, n.d., box 5, folder 1, MSS 526, Graham W. Jackson Papers, Kenan Research Center, Atlanta History Center; "At 81 Theater," *Atlanta Constitution*, February 10, 1926, 16.

21 William Marks, "Atlanta's Graham Jackson: A Musician Who Performed for Four Presidents," *Atlanta Daily World*, October 29, 1976, 3.

22 William Barlow, *Looking Up at Down: The Emergence of Blues Culture* (Philadelphia: Temple University Press, 1990), 139.

23 Information comes from the author's interviews and conversations in 2022 with Celeste Simmons Shumake, Larry Shumake, and John Tanner of Chapel Music in Atlanta. Simmons's daughter, Celeste Simmons Shumake, is the author's aunt.

24 "Where the Etude Stands on Jazz," *The Etude* 42, no. 8 (August 1924): 515.

25 Maureen Anderson, "The White Reception of Jazz in America," *African American Review* 38, no. 1 (Spring 2004): 135.

26 Craig Martin Gibbs, *Black Recording Artists, 1877–1926: An Annotated Discography* (Jefferson, NC: McFarland, 2013), 206, 223.

27 Warren Vaché Sr., "Addison, Bernard (Sylvester)," in *The New Grove Dictionary of Jazz*, 2nd ed., ed. Barry Kernfeld (New York: Grove's Dictionaries, 2002), 1:16.

28 K. B. Rau, "The Recordings of Harry Cooper: An Annotated Tentative Personnel Discography," n.d., harlem-fuss.com.

29 David Flanagan and Barry Kernfeld, "Garland, Joe," in *The New Grove Dictionary of Jazz*, 2nd ed., ed. Barry Kernfeld, (New York: Grove's Dictionaries, 2002), 2:13–14.

30 Scott Yanow, "Biography of McKinney's Cotton Pickers," All Music, n.d., http://www.allmusic.com/artist/mckinneys-cotton-pickers-mn0000402451/biography.

31 Paul Oliver, *Songsters and Saints: Vocal Traditions on Race Records* (New York: Cambridge University Press, 1984), 8–9.

32 Ross Laird and Brian Rust, *Discography of OKeh Records, 1918–1934* (Westport, CT: Praeger, 2004), 119, 273.

33 Ronald C. Foreman Jr., "Jazz and Race Records, 1920–1932: Their Origins and Their Significance for the Record Industry and Society" (PhD diss., University of Illinois, 1968).

34 West Side Café ad, *Maroon Tiger*, April 1929, Morehouse College.

35 Mr. Duncan, Program Director at WSB to Graham Jackson, Director of the Seminole Syncopators, August 27, 1924, box 1, folder 1, MSS 526, Graham W. Jackson Papers, Kenan Research Center, Atlanta History Center; William Barlow, "Black Music on Radio during the Jazz Age," *African American Review* 29, no. 2, (Summer 1995): 325–328; William Randle, "Black Entertainers on Radio, 1920–1930," *Black Perspective in Music* 5, no. 1 (Spring 1977): 67–74.

36 "Steamboat Days Draws Applause from 81 Patrons," *Atlanta Constitution*, December 22, 1928, 17.

37 William "Count" Basie, *Good Morning Blues: The Autobiography of Count Basie, as told to Albert Murray* (New York: Random House, 1985), 94–95.

38 Peter Dana, "Graham Jackson's Fame Spreading," *Pittsburgh Courier*, July 26, 1941, 20.

39 In Jeffrey Green and Josephine Harreld Love, "Reminiscences of Times Past," *Black Perspective in Music* 18, no. 1/2 (1990): 194.

40 Dave Payton, "The Musical Bunch," *Chicago Defender*, December 17, 1927, 6.

41 WGST Radio Records, MS330, Archives, Library and Information Center, Georgia Institute of Technology, Atlanta.

42 J. W. Smith, "Writer Recalls Past Performances of That Master, Graham Jackson," *Atlanta Daily World*, October 9, 1932, 5A.

43 Bernard E. West, "Black Atlanta—Struggle for Development, 1915–1925" (1976), paper 542, Electronic Thesis and Dissertation Collection, Robert W. Woodruff Library, Atlanta University Center.

44 Millis Sutton to Graham Jackson, November 30, 1928; Principal of Booker T. Washington High School, January 29, 1929; both at box 1, folder 1, MSS 526, Graham W. Jackson Papers, Kenan Research Center, Atlanta History Center.

45 Hazel Reid, "Portsmouth News and Advertisements: Graham Jackson Scores as Musician in Georgia," *New Journal and Guide*, April 25, 1931, 11.

46 "Portsmouth Boy Recognized as a Musical Genius," *New Journal and Guide*, April 30, 1927, 10.

47 "Graham Jackson, Native Son, Heard in a Fine Recital," *New Journal and Guide*, September 8, 1928, 13.

48 Reid, "Portsmouth News."

49 First Congregational Church, United Congregational Church, Atlanta, Georgia, Collection, Archives Research Center, Robert W. Woodruff Library, Atlanta University Center.

50 "Annual Negro Charity Ball Draws Hundreds of Dancers," *Greenville News*, December 28, 1930, 20.

51 "S.R.O.," *Atlanta Constitution*, January 3, 1932, 8B.

52 "Graham Jackson and Glee Club to Appear in Concert on May 26," *Atlanta Constitution*, May 15, 1932.

53 Untitled article, *Atlanta Constitution*, May 29, 1932, 22.

54 John Clark McCall Jr., *A History of the Fox Theatre and Its Möller Organ* (American Theatre Organ Society, 2013). https://www.atos.org/sites/default/files/image/resources/fox_history_-_john_c_mccall.pdf.

55 Gordon DeLeighbor, "Graham Jackson, Noted Musician, Is Sued for $10,000," *Atlanta Daily World*, February 14, 1934, 1.

56 Eric Roberts, "Phototypes," *Atlanta Daily World*, September 23, 1934, 2.

57 "Rose Bowl Plane, Leaving Saturday, Can Take Two More," *Atlanta Constitution*, December 28, 1934, 2.

58 Jesse O. Thomas, "Musician Flies 3,000 Miles to Broadcast Once," *New Journal and Guide*, January 5, 1935, 1.

59 Marion Jacobson, *Squeeze This!: A Cultural History of the Accordion in America*. Champaign: University of Illinois Press, 2015.

60 Graham W. Jackson Jr., phone interview with the author.

61 Kenneth Bindas, *Swing, That Modern Sound* (Jackson: University Press of Mississippi, 2001).

62 Quoted in Grace Bradley, "Graham W. Jackson Lauded by White Newspapers," *Atlanta Daily World*, February 7, 1937, 3.

63 Quoted in Ralph McGill, "He Wants to Be a 'Toscanini,'" *Atlanta Constitution*, August 22, 1937, 62.

64 Peter Townsend, *Jazz in American Culture* (Edinburgh, Scotland: Edinburgh University Press, 2001), 76.

65 "Graham Jackson, Band to Pennsy," *Atlanta Daily World*, July 8, 1937, 3. For a photo see "Graham Jackson and His Orchestra Enroute to Greener Fields," *New Journal and Guide*, September 4, 1937, A16.

66 Mary Ware, "Washington High Evening Notes: BTW High Evening School Students Get High Rating," *Atlanta Daily World*, January 21, 1934, 2.

67 "Mrs. Jackson Wins First Verdict from Graham Jackson," *Atlanta Daily World*, December 26, 1938, 1.

68 Divorce order, March 8, 1939, box 1, folder 10, series 1, Graham W. Jackson Sr. Papers, Archives Division, Auburn Avenue Research Library on African American Culture and History, Fulton County Library System, Atlanta (hereinafter identified as Graham W. Jackson Sr. Papers, Auburn Avenue Research Library, Atlanta).

69 Untitled article, *Atlanta Constitution*, March 19, 1941, 5.

70 "Sunday Nuptials in City Attract National Attention," *Atlanta Daily World*, June 21, 1939, 3.

71 "Graham Jackson Released: Hearing Lasts Nearly Eight Hours Friday," *Atlanta Daily World*, June 8, 1940, 1.

72 "Jackson Charges Are Nolle Prossed," *Atlanta Constitution*, November 21, 1940, 5B; "Graham Jackson's Trial Underway," *Atlanta Daily World*, November 20, 1940, 6.

73 "Bobby Jones Appears as Character Witness for Popular Atlanta Musician," *Atlanta Daily World*, May 9, 1941, 5; "'30 Parade Memorable for Jones' Daughter," *Atlanta Constitution*, April 10, 1981, 54.

74 "Musician Again Wins Damage Suit: Jury Favors Graham Jackson Second Time in $25,000 Suit," *Atlanta Daily World*, May 10, 1941, 1.

75 "Jackson Ordered to Pay First Wife Alimony: Judge Rules He Must Pay Back and Current Fees," *Atlanta Daily World*, May 29, 1941, 2.

76 "Graham Jackson Acquitted in Criminal Case Monday: Jury Deliberates Ten Minutes to Reach Verdict," *Atlanta Daily World*, October 14, 1941, 1.

77 Helen Jackson, interview by Andrew Hill, June 20, 1995, author's collection.

78 Darlene Clark Hine, "Rape and the Inner Lives of Black Women in the Middle West," *Signs: Journal of Women in Culture and Society* 14, no. 4 (July 1989): 912.

79 David Ponton III, "Private Matters in Public Spaces: Intimate Partner Violence against Black Women in Jim Crow Houston," in "Mapping Gendered Violence," special issue, *Frontiers: A Journal of Women Studies* 39, no. 2 (2018): 58–96.

Chapter 3. The Ebony Echo of Cab Calloway

1 George Hatcher, "Roosevelt Gaining Ground in Georgia," *New York Times*, August 16, 1931, 5.

2 In "Big Barbecue for Roosevelt to Be Held in Warm Springs," *Atlanta Constitution*, September 3, 1931, 1.

3 Walter T. Brown, "Russell Assures Roosevelt He Can Count on Georgia Vote," *Atlanta Constitution*, October 5, 1931, 3.

4 Walter T. Brown, "More Than 2,000 to Attend 'Cue Honoring Gov. Roosevelt Today," *Atlanta Constitution*, October 13, 1931, 1.

5 Steve Neal, *Happy Days Are Here Again* (New York: Harper, 2005), 10.

6 Beulah M. Hill, "In the Realm of Music," *Atlanta Daily World*, October 30, 1932, 3A.

7 B. Hill, "In the Realm of Music."

8 For more on this see Patrick J. Maney, "They Sang for Roosevelt: Songs of the People in the Age of FDR," *Journal of American* and *Comparative Cultures* 23, no. 1 (Spring 2000): 85–89.

9 "50,000 Pupils Cheer Nominee on Visit to Atlanta Schools," *Atlanta Constitution*, October 25, 1932, 6.

10 B. Hill, "In the Realm of Music."

11 Quoted in Stan Windhorn, "Sarasota Scene: FDR's Musical Pal," *Sarasota Herald-Tribune*, October 20, 1960, 5.

12 "Graham Jackson's Band Back from Lengthy Tour," *Atlanta Daily World*, August 7, 1932, 5A.

13 Roosevelt started the Warm Springs Institute in 1926, and the Warm Springs Foundation was established shortly thereafter to support the institute.

14 L. A. Ferrell, "President Formally Accepts Georgia Hall And Lauds Donors of Gifts to Foundation," *Atlanta Constitution*, November 15, 1933, 1.

15 Paul Schubert, *Cason Callaway of Blue Springs* (Hamilton, GA, 1964), 69–71.

16 "Atlanta Negro Maestro Entertains President," *Atlanta Constitution*, December 8, 1935, 12.

17 "Graham Jackson Will Entertain at Local Presidents Ball," *Atlanta Daily World*, January 28, 1934, 6.

18 Andrew Hill, "Unforgettable Graham Jackson," *Readers Digest*, May 1996, 55–59.

19 "Robert Gives Dinner to Group in Capital," *Atlanta Constitution*, February 11, 1934, 14A.

20 A. Hill, "Unforgettable Graham Jackson," 56.

21 "Robert Gives Dinner to Group in Capital," *Atlanta Constitution*, February 11, 1934.

22 Mable Lee, interview, February 16, 2017, Jerome Robbins Dance Division, New York Public Library Digital Collections. https://digitalcollections.nypl.org/items/5ac7f56e-50ba-40d5-bdb9-b154a971688c.

23 John Edwin Mason, November 27, 2011, https://johnedwinmason.typepad.com/john_edwin_mason_photogra/2011/11/bourke-white-fdr-thanksgiving.html.

24 John B. Kirby, *Black Americans in the Roosevelt Era* (Knoxville: University of Tennessee Press, 1980), 12.

Notes to Pages 34–42 · 137

25 Kirby, *Black Americans*, 108.

26 Kirby, *Black Americans*, 92.

27 Kirby, *Black Americans*, 107.

28 Elizabeth McDuffie, "FDR Was My Boss," *Ebony*, April 1952, 65.

29 Nancy J. Weiss, *Farewell to the Party of Lincoln: Black Politics in the Age of FDR* (Princeton, NJ: Princeton University Press, 1983), 39.

30 Elise K. Kirk, *Music at the White House: A History of the American Spirit* (Urbana: University of Illinois Press, 1986), 229–232.

31 Weiss, *Farewell to the Party of Lincoln*, 41.

Chapter 4. Atlanta Goes Mad with the Wind

1 Thomas Cripps, *Slow Fade to Black* (New York: Oxford University Press, 1977).

2 "Red Paper Condemns 'Gone with the Wind,'" *New York Times*, December 24, 1939.

3 David Platt, "Fanning the Flames of War," *Daily Worker*, December 20, 1939.

4 James Tracy, "Revisiting a Polysemic Text: The African American Press's Reception of *Gone with the Wind*," *Mass Communication and Society* 4, no. 4 (2001): 426–427.

5 John Clarence Wright, "Gone with the Wind Review," *Atlanta Daily World*, December 16, 1939, 1.

6 Angelo Herndon, "Harlem Negro Leaders Slam 'Gone with the Wind,'" *Daily Worker*, December 27, 1939.

7 In Matthew Bernstein, "Selznick's March: *Gone with the Wind* Comes to White Atlanta," *Atlanta History* 43, no. 2 (Summer 1999): 10.

8 In Leonard J. Jeff, "'Gone with the Wind' and Hollywood's Racial Politics," *Atlantic Monthly*, December 1999, 108.

9 Jill Watts, *Hattie McDaniel: Black Ambition, White Hollywood* (New York: Amistad, 2007).

10 David Stephen Bennett, "Framing Atlanta: Local Newspapers' Search for a Nationally Appealing Racial Image (1920–1960)," PhD diss., Michigan State University, 2020, 131.

11 Bennett, "Framing Atlanta," 141.

12 Martin Luther King Sr., with Clayton Riley, *Daddy King: An Autobiography* (New York: William Morrow, 1980), 34.

13 "They Dedicated a New Pipe Organ at Ebenezer," *Atlanta Daily World*, November 3, 1940, 4.

14 Meyer Berger, "Atlanta Retaken by Glory of Past," *New York Times*, December 15, 1939.

15 In Herb Bridges, *Gone with the Wind: The Three-Day Premiere in Atlanta* (Macon, GA: Mercer University Press, 2011), 94.

16 "In the Evening (or the Morning) Darkies Sing," *Atlanta Constitution*, December 17, 1939, 10A.

17 Karen Kruse Thomas, *Deluxe Jim Crow: Civil Rights and American Health Policy, 1935–1954* (Athens: University of Georgia Press, 2011).

18 In Gary Pomerantz, *Where Peachtree Meets Sweet Auburn: The Saga of Two Families and the Making of Atlanta* (New York: Scribner, 1996), 134.

138 · Notes to Pages 42–48

19 In James Firth, "The Manger of the Movement: Atlanta and the Black Freedom Struggle" (PhD diss., Yale University, 1997), 200.

20 Firth, "Manger of the Movement," 159.

21 "Graham's Grin Is Wider—Gets New Accordion: Jackson a One-Man Parade of Praise to Benefactor," *Atlanta Constitution*, March 24, 1941.

22 W.E.B. Du Bois, *Black Reconstruction in America: An Essay toward a History of the Part Which Black Folk Played in the Attempt to Reconstruct Democracy in America, 1860–1880* (New York: Harcourt Brace, 1935).

Chapter 5. "A Good Chief Petty Officer"

1 James J. Cooke, *American Girls, Beer, and Glenn Miller: GI Morale in World War II* (Columbia: University of Missouri Press, 2012).

2 Donald Rugg, "American Morale When the War Began," in *Civilian Morale: Second Yearbook of the Society for the Psychological Study of Social Issues*, ed. G. Watson (Boston: Houghton Mifflin, 1942), 189–207.

3 Kenneth B. Clark, "Morale among Negroes," in *Civilian Morale: Second Yearbook of the Society for the Psychological Study of Social Issues*, ed. G. Watson (Boston: Houghton Mifflin, 1942), 228–248.

4 Kenneth B. Clark, "Morale of the Negro on the Home Front: World Wars I and II," in "The American Negro in World War I and World War II, special issue, *Journal of Negro Education* 12, no. 3 (Summer 1943): 417–428.

5 Roscoe E. Lewis, "The Role of Pressure Groups in Maintaining Morale among Negroes," in "The American Negro in World War I and World War II, special issue, *Journal of Negro Education* 12, no. 3 (Summer 1943): 464–473.

6 Clayton R. Koppes and Gregory D. Black, "Blacks, Loyalty, and Motion-Picture Propaganda in World War II," *Journal of American History* 73, no. 2 (September 1986): 383–406.

7 E. Franklin Frazier, "Ethnic and Minority Groups in Wartime with Special Reference to the Negro," 1942, paper 93, Faculty Reprints.

8 W. Y. Bell Jr., "The Negro Warrior's Home Front," *Phylon* 5, no. 3 (3rd quarter 1944), 271-278.

9 Gunnar Myrdal, *An American Dilemma: The Negro Problem and Modern Democracy* (New York: Harper and Brothers, 1944), 2:1017.

10 Harvard Sitkoff, "Racial Militancy and Interracial Violence in the Second World War," *Journal of American History* 58, no. 3 (December 1971): 661-681.

11 Sitkoff, "Racial Militancy."

12 Harold Orlansky, *The Harlem Riot: A Study in Mass Frustration*, Report No. 1 (New York: Social Analysis, 1943).

13 Earnest L. Perry Jr., "A Common Purpose: The Negro Newspaper Publishers Association's Fight for Equality during World War II," *American Journalism* 19, no. 2 (2002): 36.

14 *Negro Newspapers and Periodicals in the United States: Negro Statistical Bulletin No. 1*, August 26, 1946, Bureau of the Census, US Department of Commerce, Washington, DC.

Notes to Pages 48–52 · 139

15 Philleo Nash, oral history interview by Jerry N. Hess, August 17, 1966, Washington, DC, Harry S. Truman Library and Museum, Independence, MO. See also Charles W. Eagles, "Two 'Double V's': Jonathan Daniels, FDR, and Race Relations during World War II," *North Carolina Historical Review* 59, no. 3 (July 1982): 252–270.

16 "Report on Possible Pro-Axis Propaganda among Negros in Washington," n.d., memo/report, July 17, 1942; Mr. R. Kane from Division of Surveys, OWI, Subject: Spot Intelligence on Draft Evasion by Negroes, Meeting on Negro Problems, September 23, 1942, pp. 39-40, RG 83, series 207, box 4, National Archives and Records Administration, College Park, MD.

17 George Q. Flynn, "Selective Service and American Blacks during World War II," *Journal of Negro History* 69, no. 1 (Winter 1984): 14–25.

18 Lee Finkle, "The Conservative Aims of Militant Rhetoric: Black Protest during World War II," *Journal of American History* 60, no. 3 (December 1973), 692–713.

19 P. L. Prattis, "The Morale of the Negro in the Armed Services of the United States," in "The American Negro in World War I and World War II," special issue, *Journal of Negro Education* 12, no. 3 (Summer 1943): 355-363.

20 Prattis, "Morale of the Negro." On a personal note, this author's maternal grandfather, as a twenty-five-year-old married father of two, working in the textile industry in Georgia, an important war-related industry, was drafted in October 1944.

21 Phillip McGuire, "Desegregation of the Armed Forces: Black Leadership, Protest, and World War II," *Journal of Negro History* 68, no. 2 (Spring 1983): 147-158.

22 Gladyce H. Bradley, "A Review of Educational Problems Based on Military Selection and Classification Data in World War II," *Journal of Educational Research* 43, no. 3 (November 1949): 161.

23 L. D. Reddick, "The Negro in the United States Navy during World War II," *Journal of Negro History* 32, no. 2 (April 1947): 201-219.

24 Reddick, "Negro in the United States Navy," 210.

25 *The Negro in the Navy in World War II*, vol. 84 of *United States Naval Administration in World War II* (Washington, DC: Historical Section, Bureau of Naval Personnel), 4.

26 *Negro in the Navy*, 4.

27 *Negro in the Navy*, 4.

28 *Negro in the Navy*, 5.

29 *Negro in the Navy*, 5.

30 *Negro in the Navy*, 7.

31 Richard Miller, *The Messman Chronicles: African Americans in the U.S. Navy, 1932-1943* (Annapolis, MD: Naval Institute Press, 2004), 302.

32 "Graham Jackson's Trial Underway," *Atlanta Daily World*, November 20, 1940, 6; "Jackson Charges Are Nolle Prossed," *Atlanta Constitution*, November 21, 1940, 5B.

33 "Party Chiefs Gather," *Atlanta Constitution*, April 6, 1941, A5; Al Sharp, "Sharp Shootin': Wood Had Something to Celebrate," *Atlanta Constitution*, April 8, 1941, 19.

34 "Entertainment Plans Are Laid for Navy Relief," *News Journal*, May 4, 1942, 13. For more on the bravery of many of the players and coaches see Brian Curtis, *Fields*

of Battle: Pearl Harbor, the Rose Bowl, and the Boys Who Went to War (New York: Flatiron Books, 2016).

35 In "Maestro Jackson's Music Thrilled Five Presidents," *Albany Sunday Herald*, circa late 1960s.

36 Walter White, *A Man Called White: The Autobiography of Walter White* (New York: Viking, 1948), 190–191.

37 "South's Blues Master in Navy," *Atlanta Constitution*, May 17, 1942, 4A.

38 "Recruiting Personnel of Navy to Hold Parley," *Atlanta Constitution*, May 28, 1942, 19.

39 "Negro Musician Quits $200-a-Week Job, Joins Navy," *Washington Post*, June 11, 1942, 13.

40 Peter M. Bergman, *The Chronological History of the Negro in America* (New York: Harper and Row, 1969), 167-168.

41 Samuel A. Floyd Jr., "The Great Lakes Experience: 1942-45," *Black Perspective in Music* 3, no. 1 (Spring 1975): 17-24.

42 Morris J. MacGregor, *Integration of the Armed Forces, 1940-1965* (Washington, DC: Center of Military History, United States Army, 2001), 69.

43 In Howard Funderburg and Graham Jackson, "An Oral History: The Great Lakes Experience," interview by Samuel A. Floyd, *Black Perspective in Music* 11, no. 1 (Spring 1983): 43.

44 In Funderburg and Jackson, "Oral History."

45 "Packed House Expected to See Navy Induction: Grandmaster Dobbs Slated to Give Address Sunday," *Atlanta Daily World*, June 5, 1942, 1.

46 "Chief Petty Officer Graham Jackson Draws Praise of U.S. Navy Officers," *Atlanta Daily World*, June 8, 1942, 1.

47 "Recruit Station Opened in Decatur," *Atlanta Constitution*, June 28, 1942, 2A.

48 "Jackson Lists 12 Recruiters for U.S. Navy," *Atlanta Daily World*, July 16, 1942, 2.

49 "Graham Jackson on Bond Program," *Atlanta Daily World*, July 18, 1942, 3.

50 "Jackson Real Bond Salesman," *Pittsburgh Courier*, September 26, 1942, 21.

51 *Negro in the Navy*, 23.

52 *Negro in the Navy*, 11.

53 "Navy Issues Call for Negro Musicians, Ages 17 to 50," *New Journal and Guide*, November 21, 1942, 11.

54 President Roosevelt to Secretary of the Navy Knox, memorandum, February 1943, Franklin D. Roosevelt Library, Hyde Park, NY.

55 Lt. Comdr. S. A. Jones, USN, to William Good, International News Service, October 1, 1942, box 1, folder 5, MSS 526, Graham W. Jackson Papers, Kenan Research Center, Atlanta History Center.

56 Lamar Ball, "The Best Coffee in Atlanta Goes to the Service Men," *Atlanta Constitution*, November 15, 1942, 3D.

57 "State Department Lists Concert to Be Played on Day of Victory," *New York Times*, August 27, 1943, 8.

58 "Organ Concert Hailing Allies Set for Tonight; Songs of All Nations Will Comprise Program on Christmas," *Atlanta Constitution*, December 25, 1942, 3.

59 Sterling A. Brown, "Georgia Sketches," *Phylon*, Summer 1945, 225–231.

60 Joe Louis, quoted in *Yank Magazine*, August 3, 1945, 23.

61 In Isaac Gellis, "My Favorite American," *Facts*, March 1945 (reprint: *Negro Digest*, April 1945, 11).

62 Lucius Jones, "Sports Slants," *Atlanta Daily World*, April 5, 1942, 8.

63 "Hattie McDaniel Heads Army Camp Movie Group," *Pittsburgh Courier*, May 16, 1942, 21.

64 "Hattie McDaniel Wins Three Service Honors in One Week," *New Journal and Guide*, June 19, 1943, 16.

65 An excellent history of this program can be found in "A History of the United States Savings Bond Program" (Washington DC: US Savings Bond Division, US Department of the Treasury, 1991).

66 "History of the United States Savings Bond Program," 12.

67 Lawrence Samuel, *Pledging Allegiance: American Identity and the War Bond Drive of World War II* (Washington, DC: Smithsonian Institution Press, 1997), 173.

68 "Graham Jackson Wins Citation for Role in War Bond Programs," *Atlanta Constitution*, January 3, 1943, 16A.

69 "Navy Transfers Graham Jackson," *Atlanta Constitution*, January 10, 1943, 6A.

70 "Chief Specialist Graham Jackson, Transferred Here," *Afro-American*, February 6, 1943, 8; "Order Graham W. Jackson to Georgia Induction Post," *Afro-American*, March 27, 1943, 10.

71 Lt. (j.g.) W.P. Moore to Southern Bell Telephone Co., April 30 and May 7, 1943, box 1, folder 6, MSS 526, Graham W. Jackson papers, Kenan Research Center, Atlanta History Center.

72 "Jackson Recruits 56 for the Navy," *Atlanta Daily World*, April 18, 1943, 5.

73 "Graham Jackson Sets Record in Navy Enrollment," *Atlanta Daily World*, August 31, 1943, 1.

74 Malcom MacFarlane, "Bing's Entertainment and War Bond Sales Activities during World War II," in *Going My Way: Bing Crosby and American Culture*, ed. Ruth Prigozy (Rochester, NY: University of Rochester Press, 2007), 142-143.

75 Al Sharp, "More Than 10,000 See Crosby and Dudley Win: Largest Crowd in Golfing History," *Atlanta Constitution*, May 31, 1943, 16; "Bing and Graham Lock in Locker Room," *Afro-American*, June 12, 1943, 10; American Red Cross to Graham W. Jackson, June 6, 1943, box 1, folder 6, MSS 526, Graham W. Jackson Papers, Kenan Research Center, Atlanta History Center.

76 "Madame Chiang Visits Georgia," *Abilene Reporter-News*, June 27, 1943, 12.

77 Kathryn Brownell, "It Is Entertainment, and It Will Sell Bonds: 16mm Film and the World War II War Bond Campaign," *The Moving Image* 10, no. 2 (Fall 2010): 67.

78 James Sparrow, "'Buying Our Boys Back': The Mass Foundations of Fiscal Citizenship in World War II," *Journal of Policy History* 20, no. 2 (2008): 266.

79 Sparrow, "Buying Our Boys Back," 269.

80 "Appraisal of the Victory Loan Drive," *Program Surveys Report*, no. 41 (March 1946):

142 · Notes to Pages 61–65

11-12, tables 3 and 3a, box 22, Historical Files, 1941-69, Savings Bond Division, Office of the National Director, General Record of the Department of the Treasury, RG 56, National Archives and Records Administration, College Park, MD.

81 James Kimble, *Mobilizing the Home Front: War Bonds and Domestic Propaganda* (College Station: Texas A&M Press: 2006), 11.

82 "Atlanta's Graham Jackson Is Cited 2d Time for Bond Rally Services," *Atlanta Constitution*, December 26, 1943, 9C.

83 "Babcock Praises Graham Jackson for 'Influence on His Community,'" *Atlanta Constitution*, January 31, 1944, 10.

84 Regina Akers, "The Port Chicago Mutiny, 1944," in *Naval Mutinies of the Twentieth Century: An International Perspective*, ed. Christopher M. Bell and Bruce A. Elleman (Portland, OR: Frank Cass, 2003), 193-211.

85 For more see Townsend Hoopes and Douglas Brinkley, *Driven Patriot: The Life and Times of James Forrestal* (Annapolis, MD: Bluejacket, 1992).

86 Secretary of the Navy Forrestal to President Roosevelt, memorandum, May 20, 1944, Forrestal File, General Records of the Navy, Washington, DC.

87 Circular Letter No. 194-44, July 10, 1944, Bureau of Naval Personnel, Technical Library, Washington, DC.

88 ccxxxv *The Guide to Command of Negro Personnel*, NAVPERS-16092, February 12, 1945, Bureau of Naval Personnel, Washington, DC.

89 *The Guide to Command of Negro Personnel*, pamphlet, US Navy, 1944, p. 3.

90 Matthew Gunter, *The Capra Touch: A Study of the Director's Hollywood Classics and War Documentaries, 1934-1945*, (Jefferson, NC: McFarland, 2010), 105.

91 Gunter, *Capra Touch*, 133-134.

92 Thomas Cripps and David Culbert, "The Negro Soldier (1944): Film Propaganda in Black and White," in "Film and American Studies," special issue, *American Quarterly* 31, no. 5 (Winter 1979): 616-640.

93 "Negro Bond Show Tonight; $5 Buy Admits," *Atlanta Constitution*, July 1, 1944, 3.

94 "DuBois Honored at Atlanta, Ga. Testimonial," *Chicago Defender*, September 2, 1944, 11.

95 Lorraine Nelson, "Bette Davis in Atlanta; Denies Romance Report," *Atlanta Constitution*, September 23, 1944, 1A.

96 Quoted in Julia A. Stern, *Bette Davis in Black and White*. (Chicago: University of Chicago Press, 2021), 8.

97 Stern, *Bette Davis*, 8.

98 "3,000 at Ceremony at Booker T. Washington," *Atlanta Constitution*, October 28, 1944, 2.

99 Cecile David, "Circus Softens Troubles of Lawson Hospital GIs," *Atlanta Constitution*, November 10, 1944, 4.

100 "Infantry Show Sets 3-Day Run in Atlanta," *Atlanta Constitution*, November 20, 1944, 10.

101 "Women's Club, Debs Entertain Lawson Soldiers," *Atlanta Constitution*, December 21, 1944, 22.

102 Delacey Allen, American Legion State Chair, to Louis Summers, Commander,

American Legion of Georgia, January 15, 1945, box 1, folder 8, MSS 526, Graham W. Jackson Papers, Kenan Research Center, Atlanta History Center.

103 Geoffrey Ward, ed., *Closest Companion: The Unknown Story of the Intimate Friendship between Franklin Roosevelt and Margaret Suckley* (New York: Simon and Schuster, 1995), 348.

104 Grace May Carter, *Bette Davis* (New Word City, 2016), 220–222.

105 Carter, *Bette Davis*, 220–222.

106 Ed Sikov, *Dark Victory: The Life of Bette Davis* (New York: Macmillan, 2008), 245; William Hassett, *Off the Record with FDR* (New Brunswick, NJ: Rutgers University Press, 1958), 300-302.

107 David Rose, *Images of America: The March of Dimes* (Charleston, SC: Arcadia, 2003), 12.

108 Bentz Plagemann, "Poliomyelitis: A Case History," *Life*, August 15, 1949.

109 The following are the works consulted for this manuscript concerning this period: Jim Bishop, *FDR's Last Year: April 1944-April 1945* (New York: William Morrow, 1974); H. W. Brands, *Traitor to His Class: The Privileged Life and Radical Presidency of Franklin Delano Roosevelt* (New York: Anchor, 2008); Blanche Cook, *Eleanor Roosevelt*, vol. 3: *The War Years and After, 1939-1962* (New York: Viking, 2016); Doris Kearns Goodwin, *No Ordinary Time: Franklin and Eleanor Roosevelt; The Home Front in World War II* (New York: Simon and Schuster, 1994); Theo Lippman, *The Squire of Warm Springs: FDR in Georgia, 1924-1945* (New York: Simon and Schuster, 1977); Joseph Lelyveld, *His Final Battle: The Last Months of Franklin Roosevelt* (New York: Alfred A. Knopf, 2016); Joseph Persico, *Franklin and Lucy: President Roosevelt, Mrs. Rutherfurd, and the Other Remarkable Women in His Life* (New York: Random House, 2008); Grace Tully, *FDR My Boss* (New York: Charles Scribner's Sons, 1949); Ward, *Closest Companion*; David Woolner, *The Last 100 Days: FDR at War and at Peace* (New York: Basic, 2017).

110 Graham Jackson, recording by Ella May Thornton, AFC 1948/053, Archive of American Folk Culture, American Folklife Center, Library of Congress, Washington, DC. A copy of the transcript is in the Graham Jackson folder in the archives of Roosevelt's Little White House State Historic Site.

111 Eleanor Roosevelt, "My Day by Eleanor Roosevelt, December 20, 1945," United Press Syndicate.

112 William Rogers, "The Death of a President, April 12, 1945: An Account from Warm Springs," *Georgia Historical Quarterly* 75, no. 1 (Spring 1991): 106-120.

113 Rogers, "Death of a President," 114.

114 Jackson, recording by Thornton, 1.

115 Rogers, "Death of a President," 103.

116 Quoted in Rogers, "Death of a President," 103.

117 Quoted in Ward, *Closest Companion*, 404.

118 "'Life' Uses Page Picture of Atlanta Musician," *Atlanta Constitution*, April 21, 1945, 3.

119 Bishop, *FDR's Last Year*, 548.

120 Bishop, *FDR's Last Year*, 103, 116.

144 · Notes to Pages 71–78

121 Geoff Dyer, *The Ongoing Movement* (New York: Pantheon, 2005), 30-31.

122 Margarett Loke, "Ed Clark, 88, Eye behind Memorable Photos," *New York Times*, January 28, 2000, A21.

123 In Jodi Kanter, *Presidential Libraries as Performance: Curating American Character from Herbert Hoover to George W. Bush* (Carbondale: Southern Illinois University Press, 2016), 82-83.

Chapter 6. "A Negro Musician of Fine Character with an Excellent War Record"

1 Henry Morgenthau Jr., June 1-June 4, 1945, series 1, vol. 851, April 27, 1933-July 27, 1945, Morgenthau Diaries, Franklin D. Roosevelt Presidential Library and Museum, Hyde Park, NY (hereinafter cited as Morgenthau Diaries); Harry McAlpin, "Roosevelt's Favorite Entertainer Is First to Play for Truman," *Cleveland Call and Post*, June 23, 1945, 19.

2 In Morgenthau Diaries, June 5-June 7, 1945, p. 136.

3 "'Roger' Show and Graham Jackson Pull $400,000 into Bond Coffers," *New Journal and Guide*, July 14, 1945, B1.

4 Howard Woods, "Inter-Racial Crowd of 16,000 Thrilled at Music Festival," *Chicago Defender*, August 4, 1945, 9C.

5 Graham W. Jackson to Eleanor Roosevelt, n.d., box 1, folder 10, MSS 526, Graham W. Jackson Papers, Kenan Research Center, Atlanta History Center.

6 Robert W. Woodruff to Chestnut St. YMCA, March 26, 1947, box 1, folder 10, MSS 526, Graham W. Jackson Papers, Kenan Research Center, Atlanta History Center.

7 David J. Sullivan, "Don't Do This—If You Want to Sell Your Products to Negros!" *Sales Management* 52 (March 1, 1943): 48–50.

8 David J. Sullivan, "The American Negro—An Export Market at Home!" *Printers Ink* 208 (July 21, 1944): 46.

9 Copy of check from Coca-Cola to Graham W. Jackson, April 2, 1953, box 1, folder 16, MSS 526, Graham W. Jackson Papers, Kenan Research Center, Atlanta History Center.

10 Frederick Allen, *Secret Formula: How Brilliant Marketing and Relentless Salesmanship Made Coca-Cola the Best Known Product in the World* (New York: HarperCollins, 1994), 287. The Graham Jackson Coke sign is on display in the World of Coke Museum in Atlanta and included in a self-guided tour pamphlet available in the museum entitled *Highlights: African American History Month*.

11 "Kendrick Lauds WERD for Its Goodwill Here," *Atlanta Daily World*, August 13, 1950, 6.

12 "Graham Jackson Host to Coca-Cola Representatives," *Atlanta Daily World*, January 31, 1954, 5, 7.

13 Allen, *Secret Formula*, 287–290.

14 An excellent exploration of this criticism is found in Melissa Rubin's thoughtful essay "Advertising R Us," found online including at New River, https://www.newriver.edu/wp-content/uploads/2018/09/Jackson-all.pdf.

15 Brenna W. Greer, "Moss Kendrix, Coca-Cola, and the Identity of the Black American Consumer," blog post, February 18, 2015, Coca-Cola United, https://www

Notes to Pages 79–84 · 145

.cocacolaunited.com/blog/2015/02/18/moss-kendrix-coca-cola-identity-black-american-consumer.

16 The Ku Klux Klan Section II 1944–1958 (Washington, DC: Department of Justice, Federal Bureau of Investigation, May 1958), 11–12.

17 Ed Fain, "Klan Burns Cross at Swainsboro," *Atlanta Constitution*, February 4, 1948, 1.

18 Ralph McGill, "They Simply Do Not Trust Us," *Atlanta Constitution*, March 4, 1948, 8.

19 "The KKK Still Seeks Suckers," *Atlanta Constitution*, February 6, 1948, 8; "Into the Hands of Our Enemies," *Atlanta Constitution*, March 5, 1948, 10; "Ignoring the Hooded Hoodlums," *Atlanta Constitution*, March 24, 1948, 10; "The Klan—a Traitor to the South," *Atlanta Constitution*, March 7, 1948, 2D.

20 "FBI Investigates Klan Activity at Iron City," *Atlanta Constitution*, July 28, 1949, 14; "Ku Klux Flee Bullets in Iron City Clash: One Armed Mayor Nabs Florida Organizer after Wild Chase to Alabama," *Atlanta Constitution*, August 8, 1949, 5; "Klan-Battling Mayor Faces Six Warrants," *Atlanta Constitution*, August 12, 1949, 1; "Ex-Mayor Drake Is Fined in KKK's Iron City Row," *Atlanta Constitution*, January 15, 1950, 8B.

21 Ads in *Southern Israelite*, February 20, 1948, 7; February 11, 1949, 2.

22 "NAACP Spurs 1950 Membership Drive," *Atlanta Daily World*, February 5, 1950, 1.

23 Ralph McGill, "The Yellow Rats of Unadilla," *Atlanta Constitution*, April 11, 1950, 12.

24 "Senior Class to Present Graham Jackson Concert," *Donaldsonville News*, March 31, 1950.

25 "Protest Cards from 'Citizens Committee' Cancels Concert," *Donaldsonville News*, April 14, 1950, 1.

26 In "Protest Cards from 'Citizens Committee.'"

27 "Another Victory for Hate," *Atlanta Constitution*, April 13, 1950, 14.

28 "Klan Blamed for Canceling Graham Jackson's concert," *Atlanta Constitution*, April 12, 1950, 26; "Jackson's Concert Cancelled at Donaldsonville, Klan Blamed," *Atlanta Daily World*, April 12, 1950, 1; "Jackson Concert Cancellation Brings Check," *Atlanta Daily World*, April 14, 1950, 1; E. T. Smith, "How Long?," *Atlanta Constitution*, April 14, 1950, 22; "Georgia Editors Say: How Long? (Sylvania Telephone)," reprint, *Atlanta Constitution*, April 19, 1950, 15.

29 Untitled, *Donaldsonville News*, June 23, 1950, 1.

30 Bill Boring, "Atlanta Music Festival Lures Remarkable Artists," *Atlanta Constitution*, May 8, 1950, 3; William E. Fry, "The Greater Atlanta Music Festival: 1939–1950," *Georgia Music News*, Summer 2016, 25–29.

31 Celestine Sibley, "Screen Test to Sweet Music," *Atlanta Constitution*, June 9, 1950, 25.

32 Marjorie Smith, "Negro Police Suit," *Atlanta Constitution*, January 4, 1948, 6.

33 "Graham Jackson Is Second Negro Foreman of Jury," *Atlanta Daily World*, June 16, 1950, 1.

34 In Franklin Nix, "775 Special Officers Guard You While You Sleep," *Atlanta Constitution*, June 19, 1952, 1C.

146 · Notes to Pages 84–89

35 Quoted in Michael Harris, *Always on Sunday: An Inside View of Ed Sullivan, The Beatles, and Sinatra* (Word International, 2010).

36 Copy of check dated June 27, 1951, from Ed Sullivan Radio and Television Productions in the amount of $750 for performance, box 1, folder 14, MSS 526, Graham W. Jackson Papers, Kenan Research Center, Atlanta History Center.

37 Two clips are posted to *The Ed Sullivan Show* on YouTube: Graham W. Jackson Sr., "Home, Home on the Range," posted May 29, 2021; Graham W. Jackson Sr., "St. Louis Blues with the New York Yankees," posted June 16, 2021, at https://www.youtube.com/user/TheEdSullivanShow.

38 Quoted in Gerald Nachman, *Right Here on Our Stage Tonight!* (Berkeley: University of California Press, 2009), 317.

39 In Nachman, *Right Here*, 312.

40 "Talmadge Calls on TV to Stop Coracial Shows," *Atlanta Constitution*, January 6, 1952, 12A.

41 In "Georgia's Talmadge Assails Mixed TV Shows," *Jet*, January 17, 1952.

42 Ed Sullivan, "Did Talmadge Forget Jackson Day Plug?," column, *Atlanta Constitution*, January 16, 1952, 24.

43 "Ed Sullivan Hits Back," *Pittsburgh Courier*, January 19, 1952, 13.

44 "As Entertainer: Talmadge Gives Negro Honor Post," *Atlanta Constitution*, January 18, 1952, 11.

45 "Talmadge on 'Today' Show Here," *Atlanta Constitution*, May 15, 1956, 29.

46 "TV Offers Salute to Warm Springs," *Atlanta Constitution*, December 31, 1957, 6.

47 "Negro Buyer Plans to Run Radio Station WERD Here," *Atlanta Constitution*, September 18, 1949, 12B. For a detailed history of WERD see Gloria Blackwell, "Black-Controlled Media in Atlanta, 1960–1970: The Burden of the Message and the Struggle for Survival" (PhD diss., Emory University, 1973), 121–158.

48 Blackwell, "Black-Controlled Media," 122.

49 "Gladys Knight Gets Star's Welcome Today," *Atlanta Daily World*, May 18, 1952, 1; "Gets Royal Reception," *Atlanta Daily World*, May 20, 1952, 1; "Party at Little 'White House': Graham Jackson Fetes Gladys Knight with Studio Party Sunday Afternoon," *Atlanta Daily World*, May 21, 1952, 3.

50 "Graham Jackson Joins Cast of Cole-Vaughn Show," *Atlanta Daily World*, November 1, 1953, 2.

51 Will Friedwald, *Straighten Up and Fly Right: The Life and Music of Nat King Cole* (New York: Oxford University Press, 2020), 282–283.

52 Presidential Appointment Books, November 1953, Eisenhower Presidential Library; Resumes—Graham W. Jackson Sr., box 1, folder 2, series 1, Graham W. Jackson Sr. Papers, Auburn Avenue Research Library, Atlanta.

53 "Forecast," *Jet*, January 7, 1954, 11.

54 Rogers's notes from this 1957 interview with Jackson are archived in Ernest Rogers Papers, 1918–1967, Manuscript Collection no. 328, box 3, notebooks, Stuart A. Rose Manuscript, Archives, and Rare Book Library, Emory University, Atlanta.

55 "Report Graham Jackson Suit Is Slated for Hearing March 30," *Atlanta Daily World*, March 24, 1951, 1.

Notes to Pages 90–98 · 147

56 "Graham Jackson Suspended from Musicians Federation," *Atlanta Daily World*, July 21, 1951, 6; "Musicians Sustain Appeal of Graham Jackson," *Atlanta Daily World*, October 31, 1951, 5.

57 "Graham Jackson Cheat, Says Wife; Was FDR Pet," *Chicago Defender*, September 20, 1952, 1. The story also was covered in the *Atlanta Constitution, Atlanta Daily World, Jet*, and *Ebony*.

58 Leronne Bennet, "Judge Orders Graham W. Jackson to Pay Alimony," *Atlanta Daily World*, October 4, 1952, 1.

59 Marriage certificates, divorce decrees, and other legal paperwork are in box 1, folder 10, series 1, Graham W. Jackson Sr. Papers, Auburn Avenue Research Library, Atlanta.

60 "Graham Jackson Gets 30 Days to Pay Half of Alimony Debt," *Atlanta Daily World*, September 17, 1957, 1.

61 "Body of Women, 77, Found in Creek," *Atlanta Constitution*, November 29, 1990, 56.

62 Helen Jackson, interview by Andrew Hill, June 20, 1995, transcript.

63 Margaret Mitchell to Hughes Spalding, April 17, 1946, box 79, folder 3, Margaret Mitchell Family Papers, Hargrett Rare Book and Manuscript Library, University of Georgia Libraries, Athens.

64 "Graham Jackson Son Born; Calls Flood Hospital," *Atlanta Constitution*, October 27, 1954, 17.

65 "Junior Is the Ruler in the Graham Jackson's Home," *New Journal and Guide*, April 23, 1955, C4.

66 "Nick of Time," *Pittsburgh Courier*, March 22, 1958, 7.

67 Helen Jackson, interview by Hill.

68 Mac Murrill, "The Consoles Are up in Richmond," *Organ*, Winter 1960–1961, 8.

69 "Top of the Field," *Pittsburg Courier*, August 23, 1958, C3.

Chapter 7. "The Familiar Strains of Dixie, Played by Graham Jackson"

1 All of these legal and financial documents can be found in box 2, folders 2, 4, 7, MSS 526, Graham W. Jackson Papers, Kenan Research Center, Atlanta History Center.

2 Guy P. Land, "John F. Kennedy's Southern Strategy, 1956–1960," *North Carolina Historical Review* 56, no. 1 (January 1979): 50.

3 Ted Sorensen to Robert F. Kennedy, memo, November 4, 1959, box 26, Sorensen Papers, box 7, 1960 Campaign Series, Robert F. Kennedy Papers, Kennedy Presidential Library, Boston.

4 David K. Adams, "Bulletin," *British Association for American Studies*, new series, no. 7 (December 1963): 29–39.

5 Phillip Potter, "Kennedy Challenges Foe," *Baltimore Sun*, October 11, 1960, 6.

6 Detailed notes and agendas on the visit as well as other documents can be found in the Archival Collections of the Roosevelts' Little White House State Historic Site.

7 Lyndon B. Johnson, remarks in Atlanta at a breakfast of the Georgia Legislature, May 7, 1964, American Presidency Project, https://www.presidency.ucsb.edu/node/238754.

148 · Notes to Pages 98–104

8 "A Visitor from the White House Arrives; He'll Find Georgians Warm and Friendly," *Atlanta Constitution*, May 8, 1964, 4.

9 "Action on Rights," *New York Times*, May 10, 1964, E1.

10 Bill Wilson Photograph Collection, VIS 99.83.16, Kenan Research Center, Atlanta History Center; "They Get to Shake His Hand—the Lucky Ones, That Is," *Atlanta Constitution*, May 9, 1964, 10.

11 Michael Kammen, *Mystic Chords of Memory: The Transformation of Tradition in American Culture* (New York: Knopf, 1991), 10.

12 William Bradford Huie, *He Slew the Dreamer* (Jackson: University of Mississippi Press, 1998), 100.

13 "Aunt Fanny's Cabin," *Montgomery Advertiser*, July 14, 1955, 52.

14 Art Harris, "Old Times There Are Not Forgotten?," *Washington Post*, December 5, 1982.

15 Tommy H. Jones, "Aunt Fanny's Cabin," 1997, Tomitronics, http://tomitronics.com/old_buildings/aunt%20fanny/index.html.

16 For more on this see Neal Garber, *Walt Disney: The Triumph of the American Imagination* (New York: Knopf, 2006); Jason Sperb, *Disney's Most Notorious Film* (Austin: University of Texas Press, 2012).

17 "Atlanta's Uncle Remus," *Jet*, March 17, 1955.

18 Martin Luther King Jr. to Sylvester S. Robinson, September 27, 1956, box 64A, folders 22, 23, Martin Luther King Jr. Papers (1954–1968), Boston University.

19 J. Michael Martinez, "The Georgia Confederate Flag Dispute," *Georgia Historical Quarterly* 92, no. 2 (Summer 2008): 200–228.

20 Jamey Essex, "The Real South Starts Here: Whiteness, the Confederacy, and Commodification at Stone Mountain," *Southeastern Geographer* 42, no. 2 (November 2002): 211–227; Grace Elizabeth Hale, "Granite Stopped Time: The Stone Mountain Memorial and the Representation of White Southern Identity," *Georgia Historical Quarterly* 82, no. 1 (Spring 1998): 22–44.

21 Paul K. Atkinson, "Informality Reigns: Collard Greens with Candlelight," *Atlanta Constitution*, March 30, 1959, 23A.

22 Atkinson, "Informality Reigns."

23 John T. Edge, "How to Read a Menu," *Oxford American: A Magazine of the South*, Fall 2015, https://main.oxfordamerican.org/magazine/item/671-how-to-read-a-menu.

24 WSB-TV news film clip of delegates to the National Association of Colored People convention picketing Johnny Reb's restaurant in Atlanta, July 6, 1962, WSB-TV News Film Collection, Civil Rights Digital Library, http://crdl.usg.edu/do:ugabma_wsbn_32577.

25 William Schemmel, *Georgia Curiosities: Quirky Characters, Roadside Oddities, and Other Offbeat Stuff* (Lanham, MD: Rowman and Littlefield, 2011), 134–135; Amy Wenk, "Marietta's 'Big Chicken' restaurant getting $2 million renovation," *Atlanta Business Chronicle*, January 20, 2017.

26 Graham Jackson, liner note, *Johnny Reb's Presents: The Battle of Atlanta and Other Civil War Songs*, Johnny Reb's Records, LP-101, 1964.

Notes to Pages 104–114 · 149

27 S. R. Davis, president of Davis Brothers Enterprises Inc., to Graham W. Jackson, April 27, 1970, box 3, folder 1, MSS 526, Graham W. Jackson Papers, Kenan Research Center, Atlanta History Center.

28 John T. Edge, *The Potlikker Papers: A Food History of the Modern South* (New York: Penguin, 2017), 133–134.

29 George (Hoss) Parrish, "The Hoss' Mouth," *Atlanta Constitution*, October 28, 1967, 54. The quote is from an ad.

30 Advertisement, *Atlanta Constitution*, December 29, 1968, 102.

31 Phil Gailey, untitled, *Chicago Tribune*, February 18, 1973.

32 Patricia Moone to Graham W. Jackson, September 10, 1975, box 1, folder 5, series 1, Graham W. Jackson Sr. Papers, Auburn Avenue Research Library, Atlanta.

33 Walter Higbee, "Pittypat's Porch," *Rapid City Journal*, November 14, 2004.

34 Wesley Morris, "Music," in *The 1619 Project: A New Origin Story*, ed. Nikole Hannah-Jones (One World, 2021), 370.

35 In Rogers's notes, Ernest Rogers Papers, 1918–1967, box 3, manuscript collection no. 328, Stuart A. Rose Manuscript, Archives, and Rare Book Library, Emory University, Atlanta.

Chapter 8. "He Is an Honorable Man. Isn't That Enough?"

1 Eleanor Roosevelt to Graham Jackson, June 11, 1962, box 1, folder 4, series 1, Graham W. Jackson Sr. Papers, Auburn Avenue Research Library, Atlanta.

2 Andrew Hill, telephone interview by the author, May 13, 2019.

3 Helen Jackson, interview by Andrew Hill, Atlanta, 1987.

4 Helen Jackson, interview by Hill.

5 Ricard Conn, "The Evolution of a Song," *Washington Post*, February 21, 1988, 40.

6 In Sam Hopkins, "Recordings Are Hobby of History," *Atlanta Constitution*, February 18, 1969, 6.

7 Portia S. Brookins, "Frazier's Café, Oldest Black Owned Restaurant," *Atlanta Daily World*, August 13, 1978, 4B.

8 Student Nonviolent Coordinating Committee Executive Committee, minutes of meeting, March 5–6, 1965, Atlanta, SNCC digital archives, https://snccdigital.org/.

9 In Achsah Perry, "Students to Rally for Vietnam Support," *Atlanta Constitution*, January 5, 1966, 11.

10 Doris Lockerman, "Our Youth Is Abreast of the Future in Organizing Stadium Vietnam Meet," opinion, *Atlanta Constitution*, February 9, 1966, 18.

11 In Dick Herbert, "Viet Rally Splits Civil Rights Groups," *Atlanta Constitution*, February 11, 1966, 9.

12 Robert Coran, "Deluge Fails to Dampen Rally Spirits," *Atlanta Constitution*, February 13, 1966, 1.

13 Tim Boyd, "The 1966 Election in Georgia and the Ambiguity of the White Backlash," *Journal of Southern History* 75, no. 2 (May 2009): 323.

14 Rex Reed, "Well, Like He Says, It Was Better Back at the Pickrick," *Esquire*, October 1, 1967, 23.

150 · Notes to Pages 114–120

15 "Maddox Picks Jackson for Corrections Board," *Atlanta Constitution*, December 9, 1969, 1A.

16 Lester Maddox to Graham Jackson, February 22, 1967, box 2, folder 8, MSS 526, Graham W. Jackson Papers, Kenan Research Center, Atlanta History Center.

17 T. Malone Sharpe to Graham Jackson, November 1, 1967, box 2, folder 8, MSS 526, Graham W. Jackson Papers, Kenan Research Center, Atlanta History Center.

18 Lester Maddox to Graham Jackson, January 2, 1968, box 2, folder 9, MSS 526, Graham W. Jackson Papers, Kenan Research Center, Atlanta History Center.

19 Bob Short, *Everything Is Pickrick* (Macon, GA: Mercer University Press, 1999), 200.

20 "A Milking Maddox Squirts a Laughing Lt. Gov. Smith," *Atlanta Constitution*, January 17, 1968, 17.

21 "Restaurateur Defiant," *New York Times*, August 11, 1964, 24.

22 "Maddox Spares Rapist, Studies Execution Stays," *Washington Post*, April 11, 1967, A3.

23 In Duane Riner, "State to Investigate 4 Escapees Story," *Atlanta Constitution*, April 18, 1967, 1.

24 "Look at All of the Camps," *Atlanta Constitution*, April 18, 1967, 4.

25 Charles Pau, "Maddoxologists Fascinated by Governors Prison Stands," *Atlanta Constitution*, April 23, 1967, 7.

26 "GBI Investigates Board of Pardons," *Atlanta Constitution*, May 11, 1967, 9; "Maddox Considers Big Parole Board," *Atlanta Constitution*, May 25, 1967, 23.

27 In Duane Riner, "Governor Attacks Board over Prisons," *Atlanta Constitution*, July 10, 1967, 24.

28 "The Governor and the Prisons," *Atlanta Constitution*, August 13, 1967, 30A.

29 Duane Riner, "Corrections Panel to Be Named," *Atlanta Constitution*, March 13, 1968, 1; "20 Named to Biracial Panel to Probe Prison System," *Atlanta Constitution*, April 12, 1968, 1.

30 In Gene Stephens, "Governor Plans to Press for Several Prion Reforms," *Atlanta Constitution*, October 24, 1968, 1.

31 "Maddox: It's the Prisoners," *Atlanta Constitution*, November 22, 1968, 12.

32 "Once More a Challenge," *Atlanta Constitution*, January 9, 1969, 4.

33 "Prison Reform in Georgia," *Atlanta Constitution*, April 23, 1969, 4.

34 Gene Stephens, "Maddox Will Leave His Mark on Prison System," *Atlanta Constitution*, October 23, 1969, 4.

35 Stephens, "Maddox Will Leave His Mark."

36 In Stephens, "Maddox Will Leave His Mark."

37 Stephens, "Maddox Will Leave His Mark."

38 In Stephens, "Maddox Will Leave His Mark."

39 "Graham Jackson Named to Ga. Corrections Board," *Atlanta Voice*, December 14, 1969, 1.

40 "Graham Jackson Named to Ga. Corrections Board."

41 Diggs Datrooth, "National Hotline," *Chicago Daily Defender*, December 20, 1969, 2.

42 "Gubernatorial Humor Is Maddox Trait," *Corsicana Daily Sun*, July 12, 1970, 20.

43 "Auburn Avenue Sam Says," *Atlanta Voice*, December 28, 1969, 6.

44 Bobby Hill, oral history interview, May 3, 1974, location unknown, interview A-0071, Southern Oral History Program Collection, #4007, Southern Historical Collection, Wilson Library, University of North Carolina at Chapel Hill, published by Documenting the American South.

45 Lester Maddox, interview by John Allen, July 22, 1989, 158, P1988-22, series A, Georgia Governors, Georgia Government Documentation Projects, Special Collections and Archives, Georgia State University Library, Atlanta.

46 Bob Short, *Everything Is Pickrick*, 336.

47 "Jackson Shocked at Work Camp Brutality," *Atlanta Voice*, December 28, 1969, 14.

48 Harold Martin, "New Honor for Graham Jackson," *Atlanta Constitution*, March 15, 1972, 5A.

49 L. L. Gellerstedt Jr., president of the Atlanta Chamber of Commerce, to Graham Jackson, August 9, 1972, box 1, folder 8, series 1, Graham W. Jackson Sr. Papers, Auburn Avenue Research Library, Atlanta.

50 In James T. Wooten, "Carter to Stress Campaign in Areas of Ford Strength," *New York Times*, August 22, 1976, 1.

51 Charles Mohr, "Carter Opens Drive by Denouncing Ford as Timid President," *New York Times*, September 7, 1976, 69.

52 "A Carter Barbeque," *Atlanta Constitution*, September 29, 1976, 22.

53 George M. Coleman, "Graham Jackson; Playing for Six Presidents, Warm Memory," *Atlanta Daily World*, March 13, 1977, 10.

54 President Jimmy Carter to Graham Jackson, October 17, 1978, box 1, folder 8, series 1, Graham W. Jackson Sr. Papers, Auburn Avenue Research Library, Atlanta.

55 Bob Harvell, "FDR's Musician Returns to Warm Springs," *Atlanta Constitution*, April 5, 1979, 21.

Epilogue

1 Raleigh Bryan and Sam Hopkins, "Graham Jackson Is Dead; Often Performed for FDR," *Atlanta Constitution*, January 16, 1983, 1A; Hal Lamar, "Graham Jackson Cited as 'Inspirational' Man," *Atlanta Daily World*, January 20, 1983.

2 Helen Jackson, interview by Hill.

3 Joachim-Ernst Berendt and Günther Huesmann, *The Jazz Book: From Ragtime to the 21st Century* (Chicago: Lawrence Hill, 2009), 2.

4 John Wriggle, *Blue Rhythm Fantasy: Big Band Jazz Arranging in the Swing Era* (Urbana: University of Illinois Press, 2016), 3

5 Untitled article, *Jet*, September 3, 1953, 12.

6 Harry G. Lefever, *Undaunted by the Fight: Spelman College and the Civil Rights Movement, 1957–1967* (Macon, GA: Mercer University Press, 2005), 28.

Bibliography

Archives

Archive of Folk Culture, American Folklife Center, Library of Congress, Washington, DC.

Bureau of Naval Personnel, Technical Library, US Department of the Navy, Washington, DC.

First Congregational Church. United Congregational Church Atlanta Collection, Archives Research Center, Robert W. Woodruff Library, Atlanta University Center.

Forrestal File. General Records of the Navy, Washington, DC.

General Record of the Department of the Treasury, National Archives and Records Administration, College Park, MD.

Jackson, Graham W., Papers. Archives, Roosevelt's Little White House State Historic Site, Warm Springs, GA.

Jackson, Graham W., Papers. MSS 526, Kenan Research Center, Atlanta History Center.

Jackson, Graham W. Sr., Papers. Archives Division, Auburn Avenue Research Library on African American Culture and History, Fulton County Library System, Atlanta.

Kennedy, Robert F., Papers. Kennedy Presidential Library, Boston.

King, Martin Luther Jr., Papers. Boston University, Boston.

Mitchell, Margaret, Family Papers. Hargrett Rare Book and Manuscript Library, University of Georgia Libraries, Athens, GA.

Morgenthau, Henry Jr., Diaries. Franklin D. Roosevelt Presidential Library and Museum, Hyde Park, NY.

Presidential Appointment Books. Eisenhower Presidential Library.

Records of Central State Hospital, 1874–1961. Accession 41741, Virginia State Government Records Collection. Library of Virginia, Richmond.

Rogers, Ernest, Papers. Stuart A. Rose Manuscript, Archives, and Rare Book Library, Emory University, Atlanta.

Roosevelt, Franklin Delano, Presidential Library and Museum, Hyde Park, NY.

Tuskegee University Archives Repository, Tuskegee, AL.

WGST Radio Records. Archives, Library, and Information Center, Georgia Institute of Technology, Atlanta.

Wilson, Bill, Photograph Collection. Kenan Research Center, Atlanta History Center.

Discography

Graham Jackson Choir. *Spirituals.* WST-15029, Westminster Records, 1958.

Jackson, Graham. Recording by Ella May Thornton, AFC 1948/053, Archive of Folk Culture, American Folklife Center, Library of Congress, Washington, DC, 1948.

———. *In Concert at Pittypat's Porch.* No label listed. Circa 1970s.

———. *Johnny Reb's Presents: The Battle of Atlanta and Other Civil War Songs.* LP-101, Johnny Reb's Records, 1964.

———. *Solid Jackson.* WP-6084, Westminster Records, 1958.

Jackson, Graham, and T. M. Alexander Sr. *The Black Man's Revolt of Protest for Progress and Poems of Inspiration, Despair, and Courage.* NRCA 204, Nobel Recordings, 1969.

Seminole Syncopators. "Blue Grass Blues." OK-40228A, OKeh Records, 1924.

———. "Sailing on Lake Pontchartrain." OK-40228B, OKeh Records, 1924.

Interviews

Hill, Andrew. Telephone interview by the author, May 13, 2019.

Hill, Bobby. Oral history interview. May 3, 1974. Interview A-0071, Southern Oral History Program Collection, Southern Historical Collection, Wilson Library, University of North Carolina at Chapel Hill.

Jackson, Graham Jr. Telephone interviews by the author, 2020–2022.

Jackson, Helen. Interview by Andrew Hill, June 20, 1995.

Lee, Mable. Interview, February 16, 2017. Jerome Robbins Dance Division, New York Public Library Digital Collections. https://digitalcollections.nypl.org/items/5ac7f56e -50ba-40d5-bdb9-b154a971688c.

Maddox, Lester. Interviews by John Allen, November 22, 1988, and July 26, 1989. P1988-22, Series A, Georgia Governors. Georgia Government Documentation Projects, Special Collections and Archives, Georgia State University Library, Atlanta.

Nash, Philleo. Oral history interview by Jerry N. Hess, August 17, 1966, Washington, DC. Harry S. Truman Library and Museum, Independence, MO.

Shumake, Larry, and Celeste Shumake. Telephone interviews by the author, spring 2022.

Tanner, John. Telephone interview by the author, March 2022.

Secondary Sources

Abbott, Lynn, and Doug Serof. *The Original Blues: The Emergence of Blues in African American Vaudeville.* Jackson: University of Mississippi Press, 2017.

Adams, David K. "Bulletin." British Association for American Studies, New Series, no. 7 (December 1963): 29–39.

Akers, Regina. "The Port Chicago Mutiny, 1944." In *Naval Mutinies of the Twentieth Century: An International Perspective,* edited by Christopher M. Bell and Bruce A. Elleman, 193–211. Portland, OR: Frank Cass, 2003.

Albertson, Robert. *Portsmouth Virginia (Images of America).* Charleston, SC: Arcadia, 2002.

Allen, Frederick. *Secret Formula: How Brilliant Marketing and Relentless Salesmanship*

Made Coca-Cola the Best Known Product in the World. New York: HarperCollins, 1994.

Alridge, Derrick P. "Atlanta Compromise Speech." In *New Georgia Encyclopedia*, January 23, 2004, updated October 1, 2020, https://www.georgiaencyclopedia.org/articles/history-archaeology/atlanta-compromise-speech/.

Anderson, Maureen. "The White Reception of Jazz in America." *African American Review* 38, no. 1 (Spring 2004): 135–145.

Appiah, Kwame Anthony, and Henry Louis Gates Jr., eds. "M. Sissieretta Jones." In *Africana: The Encyclopedia of the African and African American Experience*, 1065. New York: Basic Civitas, 1999.

Arnesen, Eric. *Brotherhoods of Color: Black Railroad Workers and the Struggle for Equality.* Cambridge, MA: Harvard University Press, 2002.

Baker, Ray Stannard. *Following the Color Line: An Account of Negro Citizenship in the American Democracy* (1908; reprint, London: Forgotten Books, 2017.

Barlow, William. "Black Music on Radio during the Jazz Age." *African American Review* 29, no. 2 (Summer 1995): 325–328.

———. *Looking Up at Down: The Emergence of Blues Culture.* Philadelphia: Temple University Press, 1990.

Basie, William "Count." *Good Morning Blues: The Autobiography of Count Basie, as told to Albert Murray.* New York: William Heinemann, 1985.

Bell, W. Y. Jr. "The Negro Warrior's Home Front." *Phylon* 5, no. 3 (3rd quarter 1944): 271–278.

Bennett, David Stephen. "Framing Atlanta: Local Newspapers' Search for a Nationally Appealing Racial Image (1920–1960)." PhD diss., Michigan State University, 2020.

Berger, Mark L. "Franklin D. Roosevelt and Cason J. Callaway: An Enduring Friendship." *Georgia Historical Quarterly* 79, no. 4 (Winter 1995): 904–919.

Bergman, Peter M. *The Chronological History of the Negro in America.* New York: Harper and Row, 1969.

Bernstein, Matthew. "Selznick's March: *Gone with the Wind* Comes to White Atlanta." *Atlanta History* 43, no. 2 (Summer 1999): 8–16.

Bindas, Kenneth. *Swing, That Modern Sound.* Jackson: University Press of Mississippi, 2001.

Bishop, Jim. *FDR's Last Year: April 1944–April 1945.* New York: William Morrow, 1974.

Blackwell, Gloria. "Black-Controlled Media in Atlanta, 1960–1970: The Burden of the Message and the Struggle for Survival." PhD diss., Emory University, 1973.

Boyd, Tim. "The 1966 Election in Georgia and the Ambiguity of the White Backlash." *Journal of Southern History* 75, no. 2 (May 2009): 305–340.

Bradley, Gladyce H. "A Review of Educational Problems Based on Military Selection and Classification Data in World War II." *Journal of Educational Research* 43, no. 3 (November 1949): 161–174.

Branch, Taylor. *Parting the Waters: America in the King Years 1954–63.* New York: Simon and Schuster, 1989.

156 · Bibliography

Brands, H. W. *Traitor to His Class: The Privileged Life and Radical Presidency of Franklin Delano Roosevelt*. New York: Anchor, 2008.

Berendt, Joachim-Ernest, and Günther Huesmann. *The Jazz Book: From Ragtime to the 21st Century*. Chicago: Lawrence Hill, 2009.

Bridges, Herb. *Gone with the Wind: The Three-Day Premiere in Atlanta*. Macon, GA: Mercer University Press, 2011.

Brown, Sterling A. "Georgia Sketches." *Phylon* 6 (Summer 1945): 225–231.

Brownell, Kathryn. "It Is Entertainment, and It Will Sell Bonds: 16mm Film and the World War II War Bond Campaign." *The Moving Image* 10, no. 2 (Fall 2010): 60–82.

Callaway, Howard H. "Bo." *The Story of a Man and a Garden: Cason Callaway and Callaway Gardens*. New York: Newcom Society of North America, 1965.

Carter, Grace May. *Bette Davis*. New Word City, 2016.

Clark, Kenneth B. "Morale among Negroes." In *Civilian Morale: Second Yearbook of the Society for the Psychological Study of Social Issues*, ed. G. Watson, 228–248. New York: Houghton Mifflin, 1942.

———. "Morale of the Negro on the Home Front: World Wars I and II." In "The American Negro in World War I and World War II," special issue, *Journal of Negro Education* 12, no. 3 (Summer 1943): 417–428.

Cook, Blanche. *Eleanor Roosevelt*, vol. 3: *The War Years and After, 1939–1962*. New York: Viking, 2016.

Cooke, James J. *American Girls, Beer, and Glenn Miller: GI Morale in World War II*. Columbia: University of Missouri Press, 2012.

Cripps, Thomas W. "The Reaction of the Negro to Motion Picture Birth of a Nation." *The Historian* 26 (November 1963): 344–362.

———. *Slow Fade to Black*. New York: Oxford University Press, 1977.

Cripps, Thomas, and David Culbert. "The Negro Soldier (1944): Film Propaganda in Black and White." In "Film and American Studies," special issue, *American Quarterly* 31, no. 5 (Winter, 1979): 616–640.

Cronin, Jan. "'The Book Belongs to All of Us': *Gone with the Wind* as Post Cultural Product." *Literature Film Quarterly* 35 (1) (2007): 396–403.

Curtis, Brian. *Fields of Battle: Pearl Harbor, the Rose Bowl, and the Boys Who Went to War*. New York: Flatiron, 2016.

Dalfiume, Richard M. "The 'Forgotten Years' of the Negro Revolution." *Journal of American History* 55, no. 1 (June 1968): 90–106.

Davis, Anita Price. *The Margaret Mitchell Encyclopedia*. Jefferson, NC: McFarland, 2013.

Davis, Harold E. *Henry Grady's New South: Atlanta, a Brave Beautiful City*. Tuscaloosa: University of Alabama Press, 1990.

Drane, Gregory. "The Role of African-American Musicians in the Integration of the United States Navy." *Music Educators Journal* (March 2015): 63–67.

Du Bois, W.E.B. *Black Reconstruction in America: An Essay toward a History of the Part Which Black Folk Played in the Attempt to Reconstruct Democracy in America, 1860–1880*. New York: Harcourt Brace, 1935.

———. *The Souls of Black Folk*. New York: Random House, 2003.

Dyer, Geoff. *The Ongoing Movement*. New York: Pantheon, 2005.

Eagles, Charles W. "Two 'Double V's': Jonathan Daniels, FDR, and Race Relations during World War II." *North Carolina Historical Review* 59, no. 3 (July 1982): 252–270.

Edge, John T. "How to Read a Menu." *Oxford American: A Magazine of the South* 90 (Fall 2015). https://main.oxfordamerican.org/magazine/item/671-how-to-read-a-menu.

———. *The Potlikker Papers: A Food History of the Modern South*. New York: Penguin, 2017.

Essex, Jamey. "The Real South Starts Here: Whiteness, the Confederacy, and Commodification at Stone Mountain." *Southeastern Geographer* 42, no. 2 (November 2002): 211–227.

Ferguson, Karen J. "The Politics of Inclusion: Black Activism in Atlanta during the Roosevelt Era, 1932–1946." PhD diss., Duke University, 1996.

Finkle, Lee. "The Conservative Aims of Militant Rhetoric: Black Protest during World War II." *Journal of American History* 60, no. 3 (December 1973): 692–713.

Firth, James. "The Manger of the Movement: Atlanta and the Black Freedom Struggle." PhD diss., Yale University, 1997.

Flanagan, David, and Barry Kernfeld. "Garland, Joe." In *The New Grove Dictionary of Jazz*, 2nd ed., edited by Barry Kernfeld, 2:13–14. New York: Grove's Dictionaries, 2002.

Floyd, Samuel A. Jr. "Alton Augustus Adams: The First Black Bandmaster in the U.S. Navy." *Black Perspective in Music* 5, no. 2 (Autumn 1977): 173–187.

———. "The Great Lakes Experience: 1942–45." *Black Perspective in Music* 3, no. 1 (Spring 1975): 17–24.

Flynn, George Q. "Selective Service and American Blacks during World War II." *Journal of Negro History* 69, no. 1 (Winter 1984): 14–25.

Foreman, Ronald C. Jr. "Jazz and Race Records, 1920–1932: Their Origins and Their Significance for the Record Industry and Society." PhD diss., University of Illinois, 1968.

Frazier, E. Franklin. "Ethnic and Minority Groups in Wartime with Special Reference to the Negro." 1942. Paper 93, Faculty Reprints, Howard University. http://dh.howard.edu/reprints/93.

Friedwald, Will. *Straighten Up and Fly Right: The Life and Music of Nat King Cole*. New York: Oxford University Press, 2020.

Fry, William E. "The Greater Atlanta Music Festival: 1939–1950." *Georgia Music News* (Summer 2016): 25–29.

Funderburg, Howard, and Graham Jackson, "An Oral History: The Great Lakes Experience." Interview by Samuel A. Floyd. *Black Perspective in Music* 11, no. 1 (Spring 1983): 41–61.

Garnett, Lillian B. *The Inimitable Life of Graham Jackson*. Unpublished manuscript, Graham W. Jackson Papers, Atlanta History Center.

Gellis, Isaac. "My Favorite American." *Facts*, March 1945. Reprint, *Negro Digest*, April 1945, 11.

Gibbs, Craig Martin. *Black Recording Artists, 1877–1926: An Annotated Discography*. Jefferson, NC: McFarland, 2013.

Garber, Neal. *Walt Disney: The Triumph of the American Imagination*. New York: Knopf, 2006.

158 · Bibliography

Gibson, Campbell. "Population of the 100 Largest Cities and Other Urban Places in the United States: 1790 TO 1990." Washington, DC: Population Division, US Bureau of the Census, June 1998.

Glickman, Lawrence B. *Buying Power: A History of Consumer Activism in America*. Chicago: University of Chicago Press, 2009.

Godshalk, David Fort. *Veiled Visions: The 1906 Atlanta Race Riot and the Reshaping of American Race Relations*. Chapel Hill: University of North Carolina Press, 2005.

Goodwin, Doris Kearns. *No Ordinary Time: Franklin and Eleanor Roosevelt; The Home Front in World War II*. New York: Simon and Schuster, 1994.

Green, Jeffrey, and Josephine Harreld Love. "Reminiscences of Times Past." *Black Perspective in Music* 18, no. 1/2 (1990): 179–213.

Greer, Brenna W. "Moss Kendrix, Coca-Cola, and the Identity of the Black American Consumer." Blog post, February 18, 2015. Coca-Cola United. https://www.cocacolaunited.com/blog/2015/02/18/moss-kendrix-coca-cola-identity-black-american-consumer.

Gunter, Matthew. *The Capra Touch: A Study of the Director's Hollywood Classics and War Documentaries, 1934–1945*. Jefferson, NC: McFarland, 2010.

Hale, Grace Elizabeth. "Granite Stopped Time: The Stone Mountain Memorial and the Representation of White Southern Identity." *Georgia Historical Quarterly* 82, no. 1 (Spring 1998): 22–44.

Hall, Ben M. *The Best Remaining Seats: The Story of the Golden Age of the Movie Palace*. New York: Bramhall House, 1961.

Harlan, Louis R. *Booker T. Washington: The Making of a Black Leader, 1856-1901*. New York: Oxford University Press, 1972.

Harris, Michael. *Always on Sunday: An Inside View of Ed Sullivan, The Beatles, and Sinatra*. Word International, 2010.

Hassett, William. *Off the Record with FDR*. New Brunswick, NJ: Rutgers University Press, 1958.

Hine, Darlene Clark. "Rape and the Inner Lives of Black Women in the Middle West," *Signs: Journal of Women in Culture and Society* 14, no. 4 (July 1989): 912–920.

Hobson, Maurice J. *The Legend of the Black Mecca: Politics and Class in the Making of Modern Atlanta*. Chapel Hill: University of North Carolina Press, 2017.

Hoopes, Townsend, and Douglas Brinkley. *Driven Patriot: The Life and Times of James Forrestal*. Annapolis, MD: Bluejacket, 1992.

Huck, Karen F. "White Minds and Black Bodies in the War for Democracy: Race, Representation, and the Reader in Life Magazine, 1938–1946." PhD diss., University of Utah, 1993.

Huie, William Bradford. *He Slew the Dreamer*. Jackson: University of Mississippi Press, 1998.

Jacobson, Marion. *Squeeze This!: A Cultural History of the Accordion in America*. Champaign: University of Illinois Press, 2015.

Kammen, Michael. *Mystic Chords of Memory: The Transformation of Tradition in American Culture*. New York: Knopf, 1991.

Kanter, Jodi. *Presidential Libraries as Performance*. Carbondale: Southern Illinois University Press, 2016.

Kemp, Kathryn W. "Notes and Documents: Warm Springs Recollections from the Graham Jackson Papers." *Atlanta Historical Journal* 29, no. 1 (1985): 63–71.

Kimble, James J. *Mobilizing the Home Front: War Bonds and Domestic Propaganda*. College Station: Texas A&M University Press, 2006.

King Martin Luther Sr. With Clayton Riley. *Daddy King: An Autobiography*. New York: William Morrow, 1980.

Kirby, John B. *Black Americans in the Roosevelt Era*, Knoxville: University of Tennessee Press, 1980.

Kirk, Elise K. *Music at the White House: A History of the American Spirit*. Urbana: University of Illinois Press, 1986.

Koppes, Clayton R., and Gregory D. Black. "Blacks, Loyalty, and Motion-Picture Propaganda in World War II." *Journal of American History* 73, no. 2 (September 1986): 383–406.

Korobkin, Russell. "The Politics of Disfranchisement in Georgia." *Georgia Historical Quarterly* 74, no. 1 (1990): 20–58. http://www.jstor.org/stable/40582099.

Kuhn, Clifford M., Harlon E. Joye, and E. Bernard West. *Living Atlanta: An Oral History of the City 1914–1948*. Athens: University of Georgia Press, 2005.

Laird, Ross, and Brian Rust. *Discography of OKeh Records, 1918–1934*. Westport, CT: Praeger, 2004.

Land, Guy P. "John F. Kennedy's Southern Strategy, 1956–1960." *North Carolina Historical Review* 56, no. 1 (January 1979): 41–63.

Lawson, R. A. *Jim Crow's Counterculture: The Blues and Black Southerners, 1890–1945*. Baton Rouge: Louisiana State University Press, 2010.

Lee, Ulysses. *The Employment of Negro Troops*. Washington, DC: Center of Military History, United States Army, 2001.

LeFever, Harry G. *Undaunted by the Fight: Spelman College and the Civil Rights Movement, 1957–1967*. Macon, GA: Mercer University Press, 2005.

Lewis, Roscoe E. "The Role of Pressure Groups in Maintaining Morale among Negroes." In "The American Negro in World War I and World War II," special issue, *Journal of Negro Education* 12, no. 3 (Summer 1943): 464–473.

Lippman, Theo. *The Squire of Warm Springs: FDR in Georgia, 1924–1945*. New York: Simon and Schuster, 1977.

Lelyveld, Joseph. *His Final Battle: The Last Months of Franklin Roosevelt*. New York: Alfred A. Knopf, 2016.

MacFarlane, Malcom. "Bing's Entertainment and War Bond Sales Activities during World War II." *In Going My Way: Bing Crosby and American Culture*, edited by Ruth Prigozy, 142-143. Rochester, NY: University of Rochester Press, 2007.

MacGregor, Morris J. *Integration of the Armed Forces, 1940–1965*. Washington, DC: Center of Military History, United States Army, 2001.

Martin, Harold H. *Atlanta and Her Environs: A Chronicle of Its People and Events, 1940's–1970's*. Athens: University of Georgia Press, 1987.

Martinez, J. Michael. "The Georgia Confederate Flag Dispute." *Georgia Historical Quarterly* 92, no. 2 (Summer 2008): 200–228.

Maney, Patrick J. "They Sang for Roosevelt: Songs of the People in the Age of FDR." *Journal of American* and *Comparative Cultures* 23, no. 1 (Spring 2000): 85–89.

Mason, Herman Jr. *Black Atlanta in the Roaring Twenties*. Charleston, SC: Arcadia, 1997.

McCall, John Clark Jr. *A History of the Fox Theatre and Its Möller Organ*. American Theatre Organ Society, 2013. https://www.atos.org/sites/default/files/image/resources/fox_history_-_john_c_mccall.pdf.

McDonald, Janice. *Fox Theatre*. Charleston, SC: Arcadia, 2012.

McGuire, Phillip. "Desegregation of the Armed Forces: Black Leadership, Protest, and World War II." *Journal of Negro History* 68, no. 2 (Spring 1983): 147–158.

Merritt, Carole. "African-Americans in Atlanta: Community Building in a New South City." *Southern Spaces*, March 2004. https://southernspaces.org/2004/african-americans-atlanta-community-building-new-south-city/.

Miller, Richard. *The Messman Chronicles: African Americans in the U.S. Navy, 1932–1943*. Annapolis, MD: Naval Institute Press, 2004.

Mixon, Gregory. *The Atlanta Riot: Race, Class, and Violence in a New South City*. Gainesville: University Press of Florida, 2005.

Mixon, Gregory, and Clifford Kuhn. "Atlanta Race Massacre of 1906." *New Georgia Encyclopedia*, October 29, 2015. https://www.georgiaencyclopedia.org/articles/history-archaeology/atlanta-race-massacre-of-1906/.

Morris, Wesley. "Music." In *The 1619 Project: A New Origin Story*, edited by Nikole Hannah-Jones. One World, 2021.

Murrill, Mac. "The Consoles Are up in Richmond." *Organ*, Winter 1960–1961, 8–11.

Musto, R. J. "Struggle, Strife, and Sacrifice on the Home Front." *History Magazine*, August–September 2009, 12–15.

Myrdal, Gunnar. *An American Dilemma: The Negro Problem and Modern Democracy*. 2 vols. New York: Harper and Brothers, 1944.

Nachman, Gerald. *Right Here on Our Stage Tonight!* Berkeley: University of California Press, 2009.

Neal, Steve. *Happy Days Are Here Again*. New York: Harper, 2005.

Newby-Alexander, Cassandra. *Portsmouth, Virginia*. Black America Series. Charleston, SC: Arcadia, 2003.

Oliver, Paul. *Songsters and Saints: Vocal Traditions on Race Records*. New York: Cambridge University Press, 1984.

Orlansky, Harold. *The Harlem Riot: A Study in Mass Frustration*. Report No. 1. New York: Social Analysis, 1943.

Perry, Earnest L. Jr. "A Common Purpose: The Negro Newspaper Publishers Association's Fight for Equality during World War II." *American Journalism* 19, no. 2 (2002): 31–43.

Persico, Joseph. *Franklin and Lucy: President Roosevelt, Mrs. Rutherfurd, and the Other Remarkable Women in His Life*. New York: Random House, 2008.

Pomerantz, Gary. *Where Peachtree Meets Sweet Auburn: The Saga of Two Families and the Making of Atlanta*. New York: Scribner, 1996.

Ponton, David III. "Private Matters in Public Spaces: Intimate Partner Violence against Black Women in Jim Crow Houston." In "Mapping Gendered Violence," special issue, *Frontiers: A Journal of Women Studies* 39, no. 2 (2018): 58–96.

Prattis, P. L. "The Morale of the Negro in the Armed Services of the United States." In "The American Negro in World War I and World War II," special issue, *Journal of Negro Education* 12, no. 3 (Summer 1943): 355–363.

Randle, William. "Black Entertainers on Radio, 1920–1930." *Black Perspective in Music* 5, no. 1 (Spring 1977): 67–74.

Reddick, L. D. "The Negro in the United States Navy during World War II." *Journal of Negro History* 32, no. 2 (April 1947): 201–219.

Rogers, William Warren Jr. "The Death of a President, April 12, 1945: An Account from Warm Springs." *Georgia Historical Quarterly* 75, no. 1 (Spring 1991): 106–120.

Rose, David. *Images of America: The March of Dimes*. Charleston, SC: Arcadia, 2003.

Rugg, Donald. "American Morale When the War Began." In *Civilian Morale: Second Yearbook of the Society for the Psychological Study of Social Issues*, edited by G. Watson, 189–207. Boston: Houghton Mifflin, 1942.

Rust, Brian A. L., and Malcolm Shaw. *Jazz and Ragtime Records: 1897–1942*. Denver: Mainspring, 2002.

Ryan, Kathleen M. "'Don't Miss Your Great Opportunity': Patriotism and Propaganda in Second World War Recruitment." *Visual Studies* 27, no. 3 (November 2012): 248–261.

Samuel, Lawrence. *Pledging Allegiance: American Identity and the War Bond Drive of World War II*. Washington, DC: Smithsonian Institution Press, 1997.

Schemmel, William. *Georgia Curiosities: Quirky Characters, Roadside Oddities, and Other Offbeat Stuff*. Lanham, MD: Rowman and Littlefield, 2011.

Schofield, Mary Anne. "Marketing Iron Pigs, Patriotism, and Peace: Bing Crosby and World War II—A Discourse." *Journal of Popular Culture* 40, no. 5 (2007): 867–881.

Schubert, Paul. *Cason Callaway of Blue Springs*. Hamilton, GA: privately printed, 1964.

Short, Bob. *Everything Is Pickrick*. Macon, GA: Mercer University Press, 1999.

Sikov, Ed. *Dark Victory: The Life of Bette Davis*. New York: Macmillan, 2008.

Silver, Murray. *Daddy King and Me*. Savannah, GA: Continental Shelf, 2009.

Sitkoff, Harvard. "Racial Militancy and Interracial Violence in the Second World War." *Journal of American History* 58, no. 3 (December 1971): 661–681.

Sklaroff, Lauren Rebecca. *Black Culture and the New Deal: The Quest for Civil Rights in the Roosevelt Era*. Chapel Hill: University of North Carolina Press, 2009.

Smith, Eric. *African American Theatre Buildings: An Illustrated Historical Directory, 1900–1955*. Jefferson, NC: McFarland, 2003.

Southern, Eileen. *Biographical Dictionary of Afro-American and African Musicians*. Westport, CT: Greenwood, 1982.

Sowers, Alexandra. "The Different Faces of Scarlett: Media Coverage of Differing Views Concerning the Atlanta Premiere of 'Gone with the Wind' and the Gone with the Wind Phenomenon." *Atlanta Review of Journalism History* 8 (Fall 2009): 114–143.

162 · Bibliography

Sparrow, James T. "'Buying Our Boys Back': The Mass Foundations of Fiscal Citizenship in World War II." *Journal of Policy History* 20, no. 2, (2008): 263–286.

Sperb, Jason. *Disney's Most Notorious Film*. Austin: University of Texas Press, 2012.

Stern, Julia A. *Bette Davis in Black and White*. Chicago: University of Chicago Press, 2021.

Stole, Inger L. *Advertising at War: Business, Consumers, and Government in the 1940s*. Urbana: University of Illinois Press, 2012.

Sullivan, David J. "The American Negro—An Export Market at Home!" *Printers Ink* 208 (July 21, 1944): 46–50.

———. "Don't Do This—If You Want to Sell Your Products to Negros!" *Sales Management* 52 (March 1, 1943): 48–50.

Thomas, Karen Kruse. *Deluxe Jim Crow: Civil Rights and American Health Policy, 1935–1954*. Athens: University of Georgia Press, 2011.

Townsend, Peter. *Jazz in American Culture*. Edinburgh, Scotland: Edinburgh University Press, 2001.

Tracy, James. "Revisiting a Polysemic Text: The African American Press's Reception of 'Gone with the Wind.'" *Mass Communication and Society* 4, no. 4 (2001): 426–427.

Tuck, Stephen. *Beyond Atlanta: The Struggle for Racial Equality in Georgia, 1940–1980*. Athens: University of Georgia Press, 2003.

———. "Black Protest during the 1940s: The NAACP in Georgia." In *The Civil Rights Movement Revisited: Critical Perspectives on the Struggle for Racial Equality in the United States*, edited by Patrick B. Miller, 61–82. Hamburg, Germany: LIT Verlag, 2001.

Tully, Grace. *FDR My Boss*. New York: Charles Scribner's Sons, 1949.

Vaché, Warren Sr. "Addison, Bernard (Sylvester)." In *The New Grove Dictionary of Jazz*. 2nd ed., edited by Barry Kernfeld, 1:16. New York: Grove's Dictionaries, 2002.

van Rijn, Guido. *Roosevelt's Blues: African-American Blues and Gospel Songs on FDR*. Jackson: University Press of Mississippi, 1997.

Ward, Geoffrey, ed. *Closest Companion: The Unknown Story of the Intimate Friendship between Franklin Roosevelt and Margaret Suckley*. New York: Simon and Schuster, 1995.

Watts, Jill. *Hattie McDaniel: Black Ambition, White Hollywood*, New York: Amistad, 2007.

Weiss, Nancy J. *Farewell to the Party of Lincoln: Black Politics in the Age of FDR*. Princeton, NJ: Princeton University Press, 1983.

Wenk, Amy. "Marietta's 'Big Chicken' Restaurant Getting $2 Million Renovation." *Atlanta Business Chronicle*, January 20, 2017. https://www.bizjournals.com/atlanta/news/2017/01/20/mariettas-big-chicken-restaurant-getting-2-million.html.

West, E. Bernard. "Black Atlanta—Struggle for Development, 1915–1925." 1976. Paper 542, Electronic Thesis and Dissertation Collection, Robert W. Woodruff Library, Atlanta University Center.

White, Walter. *A Man Called White: The Autobiography of Walter White*. New York: Viking Press, 1948.

Woolner, David. *The Last 100 Days: FDR at War and at Peace*. New York: Basic, 2017.

Wriggle, John. *Blue Rhythm Fantasy: Big Band Jazz Arranging in the Swing Era*. Urbana: University of Illinois Press. 2016.

Yanow, Scott. "Biography of McKinney's Cotton Pickers." All Music, n.d. http://www.allmusic.com/artist/mckinneys-cotton-pickers-mn0000402451/biography.

———. *Swing*. San Francisco: Miller Freeman, 2000.

Zarafonetis, Michael James. "The 'Fabulous' Fox Theatre and Atlanta, 1929–1975." PhD diss., Auburn University, 2010.

Index

Photographs are indicated by page numbers in *italics*.

ABC radio, 74

accordion: Dobbs's gift, 42; history of, 20–21; Hohner L'Organla, 21

Addison, Bernard, 14

advertising to Blacks, 76–77, *77*, 78, 144n10

Affirmation: Vietnam, student group, 110–12

Alexander, T. M., Sr., 109–10

Allen, Allie Mae, 17, 23

Allen, Dorothy, *61*

Allen, Ivan, Jr., 103, 114

Allen, Steve, 85

American Cancer Society, 122

American Federation of Musicians Local 416, 89–90

American Negro Musical Festival, 64

American Women's Volunteer Service, 58

"An Appeal to Human Rights," 129

Anthony, Anton (A. J.), 104

antilynching legislation, 34

Armstrong, Daniel, 53

Armstrong, Louis, 14, 22, 56, 57, 106

Army: draft and manpower shortages, 49; general classification test, 49

Arnell, Ellis, 113

Atlanta: Black Catholics, 108–9; Black population, 10, 18; Black upper class, 18; colleges and universities, 10; economic success, 6, 8–9; evolution of, 6; FDR in, 35; *Gone with the Wind*, 36–43; Jackson's navy service, 54; Johnson in, 98, *99*; mixed-race jury, 83; police officers, 83–84; postwar, 63; postwar racial policies, 83–84; pro-FDR crowds, 27–28, 29; race issue, 6, 8–9, 83–84, 103; race riots (1906), 9–10; sports teams, 103; Techwood Homes project, 35

Atlanta Compromise, 6, 7, 10

Atlanta Women's Club Christmas dinner for servicemen, 65

Auburn Avenue, 54; Odd Fellows Building, 12; segregation and, 10; significance of, 10

"Auburn Avenue Sam," 120

Augusta National Golf Course, 88–89

"Auld Lang Syne," 64

Aunt Fanny's Cabin, 100, 105

Babcock, J. V., 61–62

Bailey, Charles, 11

Bailey's 81 Theater, 11–12

Bailey's Royal Theatre, 64

Bain, Helen (aunt), 4

Baker, Lurlene, 23, 90

Baker, Ray Stannard, 131n3

Balton, Helen Catherine, 91–92

Balton, William and Gertrude, 91

Bartholomew, Dave, 54

Basie, Count, 15, 77

Basket, James, 101

Bates, Peg Leg, 85

Battle of Atlanta, 104

Bell, Y. W., 46

Bennet, Constance, 59

Benny, Jack, 58

Berger, Meyer, 41

Berlin, Irving, 29

Big Chicken, 104

166 · Index

Birth of a Nation premiere, 37
Black-on-Black rape accusations, 26
Blayton, Jesse B., Sr., 87–88
"Blue Grass Blues," 14
"Blue Ridge Mountains," 89
Blue Springs, 31, 32
blues, 11, 12, 14
Bond, Julian, 112
Bonner, Daisy, 33, 70
Borders, William Holmes, 118, 119
Borglum, Gutzon, 102
Bourke-White, Margaret, 33
Boy, Long, 12
Boyd, William, 88
Brotherhood of Sleeping Car Porters, 45
Brown, Betty, 69, 70
Bruenn, Howard, 68, 70
Bryant, Anita, 111, 112
Burroughs, Baldwin, 88
Byrd, Garland, 113

Callaway, Cason J., 31, 32, 33, 89, 95
Callaway, Howard "Bo," 113
Calloway, Cab, 88
Camp Smalls, 53–54
Cannon, Alma, 4
Capra, Frank, 63
"Caravan," 93
Carter campaign fundraiser, 124
Carter, Jimmy, 113, 121, *122, 123, 124*
Carter, Rosalynn, *124*
Catholic Church, 108–9
Cermak, Anton, 27
Chandler, H. G., 59
Chicago conventions (1932), 28
children: view of their father, x. *See also*
    Jackson, Gerald Wayne; Jackson, Graham
    Washington, Jr.
Chitlin Circuit, 16
Christmas concert (1942), 56–57
church and spiritual music, 3, 14; organist,
    3–4, 13, 17, 40, 108, 109, 129
Citizens Corrections Panel, 118
civil rights: Jackson on younger generation,
    108; Jackson's connection to, 109–10; John-
    son on, 97, 98; Kennedy on, 96; songs, 109;
    television and, 85

Civil Rights Act of 1964, 97, 103, 112
Civil War: Black hero of, 53; hundredth an-
    niversary, 102; period songs, 104. *See also*
    Lost Cause mythology
Clark, Ed, ix, 60, 71, 130
Clark, William Patrick, 117
Clay, Lucius, 111
Clay, Ryburn, 29
Coca-Cola: advertising to Blacks, x, 76–77, *77,*
    78, 144n10; fiftieth anniversary celebration,
    77; patrons, 75–77; Rose Bowl (1935), 20
Coke v. City of Atlanta et al, 101
Colbert, Claudette, 58
Cold War, 110
Cole, Nat King, 88, 106
collective memory, 99
Coltrane, John, 54
community health screening, 83
Congress of Industrial Organizations, 109
Cooper, Gary, 58
Cooper, Harry, 14
Copeland, Derrick D., 4
Copeland, Dorothy, *61*
Cox, Ida, 11
"Crazy Love," 14
Crompton, Nanci, 84
Crosby, Bing, 60
crossover artists, 22
CSS *Virginia,* 1

Dall, Anna Roosevelt, 28, 29, 68, 107
Daniels, Jonathan, 48
Darden, George "Buddy," 111
Davis, Ben, Jr., 37
Davis, Bette, 58, 64; at Warm Springs, 66–67,
    67
Davis Brothers Enterprises, 104
Davis, Sammy, Jr., 106
Davis, Stanley "Tubby," 102, 104
Decatur Street, 11
defense industry discrimination, 45–46
defense spending, 59
Delano, Laura, 68, 70
Democratic National Convention (1932), 28,
    32
Derby Day fete, 23
desegregation: Black Catholic schools, 109;

Johnny Reb's restaurant chain, 103; Navy, 62–63

Detroit wartime riots, 47

Dietrich, Marlene, 64

divorce and alimony: first marriage, 23, 24–25, 93; second marriage, 90–91, 93

"Dixie," 20, 60, 105

Dobbs, Henri T., Sr., 42

Dobbs House restaurant, 101

Dobbs, John Wesley, 18, 24, 41–42

Donaldson, Lou, 54

Donaldsonville, Georgia, 80–82

Dorsey, Thomas, 11

Dorsey, Tommy, 22

"Double V" campaign, 44, 47

draft, 48–49, 55; Navy switch, 59–60; personal note, 139n30

Drake, Mayor, 80

Drexel Catholic High School Glee Club, 108

Driver, Francis Hinton (aunt), 4

Du Bois, W. E. B., 2; "A Litany of Atlanta," 10; on cultural denial, 43; testimonial dinner for, 64; as Washington critic, 6–8

Duke Ellington Orchestra, 88

DuPont family, 23

Dvorak, Antonin, 130

Early, Stephen, 63

Ebenezer Baptist Church, 39, 40

Ebenezer Choir, 41

Edgewater Beach Hotel in Chicago, 23

81 Theatre, 11–12

Eisenhower, Dwight, 88–89

Eisenhower, Mamie, 89

elites, Black: "Deluxe Jim Crow," 41; gains reversed, 10; Jackson in, 17–18; racial uplift concept, 18; social class status, 18; status quo and, 8

Ellington, Duke, 22, 77, 88

Emory University Glee Club, 31

Esperancilla, Joe, 60

Excelsior Laundry, 2

Executive Order 8802, 45

Executive Order 9279, 55

Fabulous Fox Theatre, 19

Farley, James, 32

FDR (Franklin Delano Roosevelt): Black service in the Navy, 50–51; Black voters and, 35; Cason Calloway, 31; death, ix, 65, 68–71, 71; favorite entertainer, x; Georgia support for, 27–28, 29; homemade musical lyrics and songs, 29; Jackson allegations, 30–31; as Jackson fan, 32; Jackson performance, 67–68, 67; Jackson relationship, 27, 32–33, 34; Jackson's memories of death of, 69–70; Lucy Mercer Rutherford, 66, 107; memorial services, xi, 95, 107; musical tastes, 28, 33; nomination, 27–28; polio treatments, 27; race issue, 34, 47–48; triumphal return to Georgia, 29. See also Roosevelt administration; Warm Springs, Georgia

Filipino sailors, 49

films, military morale and, 63–64

First Congregational Church of Atlanta, 17

Fitzgerald, Ella, 29

Flick, Pat C. "Patsy," 84

Ford, Captain, 60

Ford, Gerald, 123

Forrest, Nathan Bedford, 102

Forrestal, James, 62

Foster, Stephen, 105

Frazier, E. Franklin, 46

Frazier's Café Society, Graham Jackson Room, 110

Freeman, Von, 54

Funderburg, Howard, 54

Gable, Clark, 39, 58

Gaither, A. S., 77

Garland, Joe, 14, 57

Garland, Judy, 29

Garland, Lurlene, 91

Garroway, Dave, 8, 6–87, 86

Garson, Greer, 64

genres, 14; changes in taste, 12; Depression era changes, 15–16; expanded, 18; FDR's tastes, 33; overview, 128–29; swing, 21–22

Georgia county commissioners' convention, 83

Georgia Hall, ix, 31, 32, 66, 69, 71

Georgia Tech football fans, 20

Godfrey, Arthur, 84, 85–86

168 · Index

"Going Home," ix, x, 69, 74, 81, 87, 130; Jackson account, 62
Gone with the Wind imagery, 104–5
Gone with the Wind premiere, 36–43; Jackson participation, 40–41, 42; picketing and boycotts, 38; place in Atlanta history, 42–43; press coverage, 37–38
Goodman, Benny, 22
Grady, Henry W., 6
Graham Jackson and His Modernistics, 19
Graham Jackson and His Orchestra, 18
Graham Jackson Choir, 93, *93*
Great Depression, 15, 19, 39
Green, Victor Hugo, 22
Grey, James, 113
gubernatorial races, 9, 112, 113

Hampton, Lionel, 22, 74, 77
"Happy Days Are Here Again," 89, 98, 124
Hardwick, Thomas, 9
Harlem Globetrotters, 77, 85
Harreld, Kemper, 15
Harris, Joel Chandler, 101
Harrison, De Sales, 24
Hartsfield, William B., 36, 39, 74, 78, 114
Heisler, Stuart, 63
Hemingway, James, 12
Hendrix, Bill, 80
"Here's Your Infantry," 65
Herndon, Alonzo, 11, 17
Herzig, John, 21
Heywood, Eddie, 11
Higbee, Walter, 105
Highlander Folk School, 109
"High Noon" 89
Hill, Andrew, 32, 91, 108
Hill, Bobby, 120–21
Hinton, Pauline (mother), 2–3, 4–5
Hinton, William (grandfather), 2
Holbrook, Carrie, 92
Hollowell, Donald L., 101
Hollywood Canteen, 64
"Home on the Range," 89
Hope, Bob, 60
Horton, Zilphia, 109
Houston, 26, 34
Howell, Clark, 9, 24, 41, 51

"How Sweet Is the Air," 69
Hubert, James, 38
Humphreys, John D., 24

Ickes, Harold, 34
"I'm Going up to Washington," 96
immigration, accordion related, 20
Ingram, Rex, 64
integration, 112
Iron City shootout, 80
Irwin, Charles, 70

Jackson, David (great-grandfather), 2
Jackson, Edmond (great-great-grandfather), 2
Jackson, Gerald Wayne (son), 21, 92, *125*, 126, 127
Jackson, Graham Washington: as astute businessman, 27; birth, 3; cars, 90, 92; characterized, ix–x, 14, 52, 69–70, 106; choir, *93*; civil rights connection, 109–10; Coca-Cola advertising, 77, *77*; commission of admiral in Georgia Navy, 115; Confederate nostalgia and, 104–6; death of, 127; early life, 3–4; education, 5, 15; as elder statesman entertainer, 107; FDR association, 69–70, 95; financial struggles, 95, 108; goal of fame, 84; health issues, 119, 121, 126; King Sr. compared, 40; lineage, 1–2; memories of FDR's death, 69–70; navigating Jim Crow, 78; in Navy, 52–53, 55–56, *56*; as Official Musician of the State of Georgia, 86, 121, *123*; portrayals of, ix; postwar activism, 80; postwar change, 73; on race, 106; recruitment efforts, 54–56, 59–60, 61–62; siblings, 4; as South's Cab Calloway, 53; as "special" police officer, 83–84; State Board of Corrections appointment, 113, 119–21, *122*; Talmadge and, 82, *83*, 84; in uniform, *75*; war bond campaigns, 55, 59, 61–62, *61*, 64, 65, 73–74; wartime era issues, 51. *See also* divorce and alimony; marriages; *specific musical entries*
Jackson, Graham Washington, Jr. (son), *125*, 126, 127; accordion, 21; birth, 91–92; conversations with, xii, 131n9; father's advice, 18, 127; views of father, x
Jackson, Graham Wilson (father), 1, 2, 4

Jackson, Harriet Huggins (grandmother), 1
Jackson, Helen (third wife), 32, 91–92, 109, 121, 126
Jackson, Lurlene (second wife), 23, 90
Jackson, Mahalia (singer), 94
Jackson, Maynard (mayor), 24, 42
Jackson, Oscar (grandfather), 1–2
Japanese American internment, 46, 51
jazz: Atlanta scene, 12, 13; elite view, 13; Jackson on, 13; swing music related, 22–23
Jazz Singer, 15
Jim Crow: Bourke-White photos, 33–34; "Deluxe Jim Crow," 41; gubernatorial race in, 1966, 112; Hattie McDaniel, 58; Jackson and, 78; King Sr. challenges, 40; wartime critiques, 46
Johnny Reb's Chick, Chuck, and Shake, 104
Johnny Reb's Dixieland, 102, *103*, 105; Jackson meets Maddox, 114
Johnny Reb's restaurant chain, 101–4, *103*, 107
Johnson, Lyndon, 97–98, *99*
Jolson, Al, 15
Jones, Bobby, 24, 51, 88, 89, 129
Jones, Matilda Sissieretta ("Black Patti"), 3
Jordan, Howard H., Jr., 118
Junior League of Atlanta ball, 41
"Just a Closer Walk with Thee," 89

Kai-shek, Chiang, Madame, 60
Kefauver, Estes, 96
Kendrick, Moss, 76–77, 78
Kennedy, John F., 95–97, *97*
Kimbell 2/4 organ, 12
King, Martin Luther, Jr.: birthplace, 10; Dobbs House restaurant, 101; *Gone with the Wind* premiere, 40–41; Ray and, 100; Selma march, 110; spiritual music, 94
King, Martin Luther, Sr. ("Daddy" King): *Gone with the Wind* premiere, 39–42; Jackson compared, 40; as Mason, 18
Knight, Gladys, 88
Knox, Henry, 49–50, 51, 62
Ku Klux Klan (KKK), 37, 78–82, 102; Gestapo compared to, 82

Leaf, Ann, 93
Lee, Lark, 12

Lee, Mabel, 33
Lee, Pinky, 84
legal issues: ads for gigs using his name, 89; breach of contract suit, 19–20; financial challenges, 95; sexual assault, 24, 25–26, 51, 89; union rules violation, 90. *See also* divorce and alimony; patrons, White
Leibert, Dick, 93
Lester Maddox Cafeteria, 113
literacy and draft, 49, 54
Little White House: Jackson replica, 74–75, *76*; Kennedy at, 96–97, *97*; in Warm Springs, xi, 33, 65, 66, 69
Little White House State Historic Site, xi, 31
Loew's Grand Theatre, 36
Longworth, Alice Roosevelt, 30
Lord, Cissie, 33
Lost Cause mythology, 32, 36, 42, 99, 102, 106
Louis, Joe, 57–58, 88
lynchings, 10, 26; antilynching legislation, 34
Lytell, Bert, 59

McDaniel, Hattie, 36, 39, 58
McDuffie, Irvin, 34
McDuffie, Lizzie, 33, 34
McGill, Ralph, 65, 79, 80, 86, 111
McIntire, Ross, 70
McIntyre, Marvin, 32
MacKenna, Isoline Campbell, 100
Mack, Ted, 85, 88
Maddox, Lester, 112–21; background, 116; on Black appointments, 121; friendship with Jackson, 114–15, *115*; "Little People's Day," 116–17
Mamie's Cabin, 89
Mammy's Shanty, 100
manhood protocols, 18
"Marching Song" (Norcom High School), 5
March of Dimes, 31, 87, *87*
Mariners, 85–86
Mario (canary), 88
Markham, Pigmeat, 85
marriages: first, 17, 23; second, 23; third, 32, 91–92, 109, 121, 126
Masons/Freemasonry, 17–18
mentors, 3
Mercer Rutherford, Lucy, 68, 107

170 · Index

middle class, Black: ancestors in, 1–2; Atlanta as beacon, 10; Booker T. Washington and, 7

migration: to Atlanta, 8, 10, 40; to northern cities, 12, 46; urban to rural, 2, 8–9; World War II, 46, 76

Miller, Doris, 50–51

Miller, Glenn, 14, 29

Mills Brothers, 14, 29

Minidoka War Location Center, 51

minstrel imagery, x, 13, 42, 89, 106

minstrel show for FDR, 69

misogyny, 25

"Missouri Waltz," 89

Mitchell, Margaret, 39, 42, 93

Möller organ (the "Mighty Mo"), 19

Montgomery, T. Neal, 12

Moore, Tim, 85

Moore, Will, 33

morale issue, wartime, 44–50, 53, 58, 62–64; draft restrictions, 49; key issues, 45; OWI role, 48

Morehouse College, 15, 17, 30

Morehouse Glee Club, 14

Morgenthau, Henry, Jr., 58, 73, *74*

Morris Brown College event, 83

Morton, Jelly Roll, 14

Moss, Carleton, 64

movies: military films, 63–64; silent, 128; *Song of the South*, 101; sound films, 15

mulatto, 2

Muni, Paul, 74, *75*

musical career: as arranger, 129; beginnings, 3–4; evolution of his style, 129; fame, 19–20; high school days, 13; later recognition, 122–23; later stages, 95, 99

musical talents: praise for, 15, 16–17, 18–19, 53, 94; prodigy status, 3, 128; superior memory, 13; versatility with instruments, 21

music education, 15

music teaching career, ix, 129; New York Yankees baseball players, 84; private lessons, 129; Saint Paul of the Cross Catholic Church, 108; Washington High School, 16–17, 33, 129

Myrdal, Gunnar, 46

NAACP (National Association for the Advancement of Colored People), 7, 10, 17, 46, 50, 80, 103, 110

Nash, Phileo, 48

Navy: bands in, 53, 54; Black officer training, 62–63; Black sailors in, 49–50, 62; Civil War era, 1; desegregation, 62–63; discrimination and Jackson, 59; discrimination as wasteful, 63; films to educate, 64; honorable discharge, 74; instructions to White officers, 63; Jackson in, 52–53, 55–56, *56*; paternalism in, 53

Navy Day, 64–65

NBC's *Today Show*, 86–87, *86*

Negro Newspaper Publishers Association, 47–48

neo-Confederate religion, 104

New Deal, 34; imagery, 96

"New Frontier," 96

New South, 6, 8, 9, 39, 42

newspapers, 9, 11; "Double V" campaign, 44, 47; *Gone with the Wind*, 37–38, 41; Negro Newspaper Publishers Association, 47–48; readership, 47–48; wartime discrimination, 45; white, 19, 41

New York University incident, 84

Norcom High School, 5

N-word, 38–39, 82

O'Conner, Basil, 66, 87

Odd Fellows Building, 12

Office of War Information (OWI), 47–48, 60; Black morale and film, 63–64

Official Musician of the State of Georgia, x, 86, 121, *123*

OKeh Records, 13, 14

"Old Shanty Town," 116

"Old South" performance style, 27, 40; FDR and Jackson performances, 32; recording, 93–94. *See also* Plantation Revue

"Old South" themes: Aunt Fanny's Cabin, 100; cultural denial, 43; Dobbs House restaurant, 101; *Gone with the Wind* premiere, 36, 37–38, 39; Johnny Reb's restaurant chain, 101–4, *103*; later restaurant venues, 99; Mammy's Shanty, 100; Pittypat's Porch, 104–5; recordings, 104; Woodruff on, 78

Open Door Canteen, 56
organ music, *130*: Atlanta White high society, 16; childhood experience, 3, 4; church organist, 3–4, 13, 17, 40, 108, 109, 129; Kimbell 2/4 organ, 12; Möller organ (the "Mighty Mo"), 19; recordings, 93; silent films, 128; Wurlitzer pipe organ, 40
Osmena, Sergio, 68
Owens, Jesse, 77

Pappy's Plantation Lounge, 100
Parks, Bert, 122
patrons, White, 20, 23, 27, 78; Callaway, 31–32; Coca-Cola, 75–77, 78; funerals of, 95; Hartsfield, 36; legal issues and, 24, 25, 26, 51, 89; McGill, 65; overview, ix–x, 115–16
Patterson, Eleanor "Cissy," 30
Patterson, William L., 38
Pearl Harbor, 44
Perryman, Rufus "Speckled Red," 12
Philippine independence, 68
photos: differences in depictions, 33–34; with FDR (November, 1944), 21; *Gone with the Wind* premiere, 41; iconic, of Jackson on FDR's death, ix, x, xi, 21, 65, 70, 71, 75, 130; Thanksgiving (1938), 33
piano: 81 Theatre, 11; jazz scene, 12; marathon, 5; Southern Piano Championship, 17
Pickaninny coffee shop, 100
Pickrick restaurant, 112–13
Piedmont Driving Club benefit for wounded, 65
pipe organ, 18
Pittypat's Porch, 42, 104–5, 107, 120, 121, 127, 129
Plantation Revue, 31–32, 40, 42
Platt, David, 37
politics, Black elites and, 18
Ponce de Leon Ball Park, 65
Pope, Roslyn, 129
Port Chicago explosion, 62
Portsmouth, Virginia, 1, 2, 3, 4, 5, 17, 92; ceremony at, 75
Prattis, P. L., 49
presidents, performing for: Carter, 123, 125–26; Eisenhower, 88–89; Johnson, 98,

99; Kennedy, 95–97, *97*; Truman, 73. *See also* FDR (Franklin Delano Roosevelt)
press. *See* newspapers
Prettyman, Arthur, 70
Prince, Al, 57
prison reform, 117–21

Quiggs, Harvey, 12

race riots: Atlanta, 9–10; northern, 10; wartime, 46–47, 48, 62
racial uplift, 17, 18, 42, 110
racism, jazz and, 13
radio: career, 87–88; regular show live from the Fox, 19; success, 84. *See also specific radio stations*
Rainey, "Ma," 11, 12
Randolph, A. Phillip, 45
Ray, James Earl, 100
"Rebel" flag, 101–2
recordings: as arranger, 129; *Every Time I Hear the Spirit*, 94; evolution/overview, 129; "Going Home," 69, 70; jazz, 13; *Johnny Reb's Presents: The Battle of Atlanta and Other Civil War Songs; By Graham Jackson*, 104; organ music, 93; performances at Pittypat's Porch, 105–6; "race records," 14; *Solid Jackson*, 93; spirituals, 93; spoken-word album, 110; Syncopators, 13–14; *The Black Man's Revolt of Protest and Progress and Poems of Inspiration, Despair, and Courage*, 109; Westminster Records, 93
Red Cross fundraiser, 60
Reed, Rex, 114
restaurant venues, 99–106
Riddick, W. E., 17
Riley, Lewis A., 64, 66
Rivers, E. D., 41
Robbins, Nicholas, 68
Robert, Lawrence "Chip," 32, 89
Robeson, Paul, 81–82
Robinson, Jackie, 57
Robinson, Prince, 14
Rogers, Ernest, 89
Roosevelt administration: allocation of wartime resources, 58–59; Executive Order 8802, 45; Executive Order 9279, 55;

172 · Index

Roosevelt administration—*continued*
  Knox on Black recruits, 50; Selective Service Act of, 1940, 48–49; war preparations, 48–49; wartime morale issue, 44–50, 53, 58, 62–64
Roosevelt Clubs, 27
Roosevelt, Eleanor, 35, 69, 74, 87, *87*, 96, 107–8
Roosevelt, Franklin Delano. *See* FDR (Franklin Delano Roosevelt)
Roosevelt, Franklin, Jr., 123–24
Roosevelt, James, 123–24, 126
Roosevelt, Theodore, 17
Rose Bowl (1935), 20
Rose Bowl (1941), 51
Rose Bowl (1942), 52, *52*
Rosenwald Fund, 107
Ross, Donald, 23, 31
Rosser, Luther Z., 24
Rosser, Luther Z., Sr., 24
Ross, Lanny, 59
rural to urban migration, 2, 8–9
Rusk, Dean, 111, 112
Russell, Louis, 57
Russell, Richard B., 2, 27, 89, 111

Sadler, Barry, 111, 112
"Sailing on Lake Pontchartrain," 14
Saint Paul of the Cross Catholic Church, 108
Sanders, Carl, 111
savings bonds, 58–59
Sawyer, Frank, 89
segregation: Atlanta, 10; Bette Davis on, 64; entertainment for troops, 58; FDR on, 34; *Gone with the Wind* premiere and, 36; King Sr. challenges, 40; in the Navy, 49–51; Talmadge and, 82; Truman ending, 62; wartime morale, 62
Selective Service Act of, 1940, 48–49, 121
Selznick, David O., 38–39
Selznick International Pictures, 38
Seminole County High School benefit concert, 80–82
Seminole Syncopators, 13–14, 15, 16, 57; name change, 18
Sharpe, T. Malone, 115
Sheraton-Mount Royal Hotel, Montreal, 92

"Shine on Harvest Moon," 116
Short, Bob, 121
"Shortnin' Bread Stomp," 93
Shoumatoff, Elizabeth, 68, 70, 95
Simmons, Edd, 12
slave trade, 42
Sledge, E. Deloney, 76
Smalls, Robert, 53
Smith, Alfonso, 101
Smith, Bessie, 11, 14, 15
Smith, Hoke, 9
Smith, Mamie, 14
Smith, Merriman, 30
Smith v. Allwright, 78
Smyrna, Georgia, 100
Snapp, Troy, 12
SNCC (Student Nonviolent Coordinating Committee), 110, 112
Snyder, Monty, 70
"Somebody Stole My Gal," 116
"Someday You're Going to Want Me," 116
Southern Bell Telephone Company, 59–60
Southern Broadcasting Company (SBC), 16
Southern Christian Leadership Conference, 110
Southern Coordinating Committee to End the War in Vietnam, 112
southern strategy, Kennedy, 96
Spand, Charlie, 12
Spaulding, Hughes, 91
spiritual music: Clark photo and, 71; as constant, 3; exposure to, 12; history of, 94; influence on swing, 22; love of, 106; other genres and, 94; recordings, 93
Standard Oil president, 32
State Board of Corrections, 118–19, *122*
State Board of Corrections appointment, 113, 119–21, *122*
State Milk Producers Conference, 116
Statler Hotel, Washington, DC, 73
Stephens, Hazel, 69
Stevenson, Adlai, 95
Stimson, Henry, 49, 63
Stone Mountain, 102, 106
Suckley, Margaret, 68, 70
Sullivan, Ed, 84–85, *85*, 86

Index · 173

Sutton, Mills, 17
Swainsboro rally, 79
"Sweet Georgia Brown," 93
swing music, 21–23, 129; jazz related, 22–23

Talmadge, Eugene, 84, 113
Talmadge, Herman, 51, 80, 85–87, 111, 113, 115, 124; Godfrey's TV show, 85–86; Jackson and, 82, 83, 84, 89; Klan endorsement, 79
Tatum, Reese "Goose," 77
television appearances, 84–87, 85, 86
"That Thing Called Love," 14
theaters, 11. See also individual theaters
Thebom, Blanche, 84
Thomas, Norman, 34
Thornton, Ella May, 69, 70
Thurmond, Strom, 83
Truman, Harry, 62, 73, 78, 89
Tully, Grace, 69
Tuskegee Airmen bond show, 73–74

Unadilla, Georgia, Klan activity, 80, 81
Uncle Remus character, 101
Uncle Tomism, 106, 120
"Until," 5
Urban League, 38, 46, 62, 78

venues: Atlanta theaters, 11–12; Depression years, 22; Fox Theatre, 19; Plantation Revue, 42; racial transitions, 15; restaurant, 99–106. See also specific venues
victory loan drives. See war bonds
Vietnam War debates, 110–12
voter registration, 40
Voting Rights Act of, 1965, 112

Wade, Wallace, 51
Wallace, Henry, 48
war bond rally, 59
war bonds, 55, 58–59, 60–61, 64, 65, 73–74
War Manpower Commission, 55
Warm Springs Foundation, 31, 136n13; fundraising, 32; presidential balls, 32
Warm Springs, Georgia, 27; Bette Davis at, 66–67, 67; Carter campaign, 123–24;

Eleanor Roosevelt at, 107; FDR's death, ix; FDR's trips, 27–28, 29, 30, 65–68, 67; fundraising, 32; Georgia Hall, 31, 32; Jackson as patient, 126; later significance, 123–24; penultimate trip to, 66–68; significance for author, xi–xii; Thanksgiving celebrations, 30–31, 33, 66. See also FDR (Franklin Delano Roosevelt)
Warm Springs Institute, ix, 66, 123, 136n13
Washington, Booker T.: Atlanta Compromise, 5–6; church opening, 17; critics of, 7; Jackson as disciple, 3, 106, 108; Odd Fellows Building, 12; racial uplift, 18
Booker T. Washington High School: Allie Jackson at, 23; fundraiser, 19; Jackson dismissed, 24, 25, 51; music director/teacher, 16–17, 33; Navy Day at, 64–65; opening of, 16
watermelon and ice cream social, Georgia General Assembly, 116
Watson, Tom, 9
Webb, Edgar, 12
Welk, Lawrence, 20, 122
WERD radio station, 87–88
"We Shall Overcome," 109
West Side Café, 14
WGST radio station, 16
White backlash, 112
White House, Jackson and FDR, 32–33
White patrons. See patrons, White
White primary system outlawed, 78
White resistance, 78, 97–98, 112; illusion of happy Black, 106; Jonson and, 97–98; Klan resurgence, 79; Maddox as hero, 113; postwar, 73; "Rebel" flag, 102; Smith v. Allwright, 78; Stone Mountain, 102. See also Ku Klux Klan (KKK)
White supremacy, 9, 116
White, Walter, 17, 38, 53
Whitehouse Drive, 74, 88
Williams, Happy, 14
Willis v. Pickrick Restaurant, 113
Withers, Jane, 61
women, rape accusations, 25–26
Woodruff, R. W., 23, 75, 78, 88, 89
World War I, 44, 45

174 · Index

World War II, 44; Hollywood Victory Committee, 58; impact on the nation, 51; Jackson's enlistment, 52–53; morale issue, 44, 62; musicians in, 53–54, 55, 56, 57; postwar change, 73; racial strife, 46–47, 48, 62; USO shows, 56, 58
Wright, John C., 24
Wrightsville cross burning, 79
WSB radio station, 14–15

"Xerxes Largo," 108

Yankovic, Frankie, 20
Yankovic, Weird Al, 20
"The Yellow Rose of Texas," 98
Yoshihara, Jack, 51
"You Are My Sunshine," 116
"You Can't Keep a Good Man Down," 14
"You Tell Me Your Dream," 89
Young, Donald, 64

zoot-suit riots, 46

David Cason is associate professor in the Honors Program at the University of North Dakota. A Georgia native, he holds a PhD from Georgia State University. David spent a decade volunteering and mentoring students who worked at Roosevelt's Little White House State Historic Site. His areas of expertise include southern American history, civil rights, leadership in history, and political socialization. He is married and the father of three children. This is his first book.